Why PowerBuilder Objects? Why The Instant Guide?

PowerBuilder 5.0 is the latest version of Powersoft's best-selling client/server development tool. The new version includes many new features which enhance its object-oriented capabilities and make it much easier to reuse code in your applications. Some of the new features include better support for OLE and OCX/ActiveX controls, true function overloading and a brand new foundation class library (the PFC) which ships with the Enterprise edition of the product. All of these features promote the effective reuse of code and ease the design of application frameworks and class libraries.

The Instant Guide to PowerBuilder Objects is written by PowerBuilder and Sybase certified developers with many years experience in the fields of database design, distributed systems and object-oriented design and development. Aimed at developers who are already familiar with the PowerBuilder environment and PowerScript syntax, the book concentrates fully on the object-oriented capabilities of the product so that by the time you reach the last chapter you'll already be thinking in terms of classes, frameworks and objects.

What is Wrox Press?

Wrox Press is a computer book publisher which promotes a brand new concept - clear, jargon-free programming and database titles that fulfill your real demands. We publish for everyone, from the novice through to the experienced programmer. To ensure our books meet your needs, we carry out continuous research on all our titles. Through our dialog with you we can craft the book you really need.

We welcome suggestions and take all of them to heart - your input is paramount in creating the next great Wrox title. Use the reply card inside this book or contact us at:

feedback@wrox.com	**Wrox Press Ltd.**	**Tel: +1 (312) 465 3559**
	2710 W. Touhy	
Compuserve 100063, 2152	**Chicago**	**Fax:+1 (312) 465 4063**
	IL 60645	
http://www.wrox.com/	**USA**	

Instant
PowerBuilder Objects

Basant Nanda
Prasad Bodepudi
Bruce Hartwell

Wrox Press Ltd.®

Instant
PowerBuilder Objects

© 1996 Wrox Press

Published by Wrox Press Ltd. 30 Lincoln Road, Olton, Birmingham, B27 6PA.
Printed in Canada
Library of Congress Catalog no. 96-60556

ISBN 1-861000-06-5

Trademark Acknowledgements

Wrox has endeavored to provide trademark information about all the companies and products mentioned in this book by the appropriate use of capitals. However, Wrox cannot guarantee the accuracy of this information.

Credits

Authors
Basant Nanda
Prasad Bodepudi
Bruce Hartwell

Contributing Authors
Ramesh Chandak
Jack Frosch
Arvind Walia

Technical Reviewers
Jack Frosch
Bruce Hartwell
Craig Wagner
Bob Davis
Jay Madore
Andy Kramek

Additional Material
Charles Radi
Tom Finegan
David R. Miller
Roger P. Brock

Development Editor
Graham McLaughlin

Technical Editors
Gina Mance
Graham McLaughlin

Production Manager
Joanne Sawyer

Design/Layout
Neil Gallagher
Andrew Guillaume
Hetendra Parekh

Proof Readers
Pam Brand
Melanie Orgee

Indexer
Simon Gilks

Cover Design
Third Wave

For more information on Third Wave, contact Ross Alderson on 44-121 236 6616
Cover photo supplied by The Image Bank

Author Bios

Basant Nanda
Basant Nanda is a Vice President of Information Technology at a major investment bank in New York. He is an experienced Client/Server and object-oriented architect and has designed and developed numerous PowerBuilder applications since version 2.0. Basant has also co-authored an introductory level book on PowerBuilder 4.0.

Prasad Bodepudi
Prasad Bodepudi is a certified Sybase DBA and PowerBuilder developer with over six years of extensive software development experience in Enterprise Client/Server environments. His areas of specialization include network/database administration, database design and performance tuning and object-oriented applications design and development. You can reach him at prasad@applied-software.com.

Bruce Hartwell
Bruce Hartwell has eight years of experience in the design, development and implementation of distributed systems. He has been working with PowerBuilder since its initial release, and has seen it grow from a rudimentary programming tool, to an enterprise development environment.

Dedications

Basant Nanda
To Abita for her love,
To my parents for their blessings,
        and
To my family for their encouragement.

Prasad Bodepudi
To my father Nageswara Rao and my mother Nagaratnam.

Bruce Hartwell
To my father, who taught me to always finish what I had started.

Acknowledgements

Prasad Bodepudi
I would like to thank Susan Donahue and Cecile Roux at Powersoft for their invaluable and timely assistance. I would also like to thank Atul Sharma and Sampath Rangaswamy for their constant encouragement and incisive recommendations.

Basant Nanda
Thanks to Graham McLaughlin for arranging this book with limited time and working with my erratic schedule! To the entire team at Wrox for refining the book. Also, I would like to extend my gratitude to Arvind Walia and ObjectTech for writing the chapter on Component-based Design and Design Patterns.

Table of Contents

Chapter 11: PowerBuilder Foundation Class Library 227

Chapter 12: Distributed Computing 239

PowerBuilder Objects

Introduction

Who is this Book For?

This book isn't a beginner's guide. It's designed to teach object-oriented programming software development skills in PowerBuilder and give direction for the application of those skills. The book assumes a basic knowledge of PowerBuilder. We will, however, be discussing all of the concepts and terminology needed for object-oriented programming.

Instant PowerBuilder Objects is written for:

 PowerBuilder developers who already understand most of the product's basic features but wish to add object-oriented programming knowledge to their skill set.

 Experienced programmers who are coming to PowerBuilder from an environment such as Visual Basic or Delphi.

What's Covered in this Book?

The goal of Instant PowerBuilder Objects is to teach the object-oriented programming skills required to create applications with PowerBuilder 5.0 and to point you in the right direction for further development with the product.

The book starts off with an introduction to object-oriented concepts and how they're applied in PowerBuilder. We then look at user objects and C++ class objects to show how you can use these concepts to design your own reusable objects. In this section, you'll design some useful objects that you can use in your own applications.

In the next chapter, we'll look at how menus fit into the object-oriented design of an application and then examine in detail at PowerBuilder's enhanced support for OLE. These chapters go into detail on how you can use OLE in windows and DataWindows and how to take advantage of OCX/ActiveX custom controls. They finish off with several examples of OLE Automation.

The final section of the book concentrates on object-oriented analysis and design. We start off by looking at the ideas behind component-based design and the use of design patterns in PowerBuilder. We then discuss creating application frameworks and class libraries and finish off the section with a look at the new PowerBuilder Foundation Class library (PFC) that ships with PowerBuilder Enterprise.

In the final chapter, we describe how distributed computing has become a reality with PowerBuilder 5.0 and show you an example of how you ca use this new feature.

What's Not in this Book?

The book doesn't attempt to cover every feature of PowerBuilder. To do so would be well beyond the scope of a single volume. Instead, we're focusing on one particular facet—object-oriented programming—and looking at how this particular feature can be used to efficiently develop applications that are robust, easy to use, maintain and reuse.

We're going to assume that you already have a knowledge of PowerScript. There are already far too many books that claim to offer the developer something new, while taking up half of the book explaining elementary concepts which the average developer knows inside out. You won't find an introduction to the basics of PowerBuilder, the PowerScript language or painters. Instead, we'll begin our discussions at a more technical level.

System Requirements and Installation Overview

To run the examples on the disk, you must have the following minimum system configuration:

 Windows 3.1 or later

 Approximately 1.5 MB disk space

All of the screenshots in the book were taken on Windows 95, so these may differ slightly if you're not running this operating system. Some of the examples in the OLE chapters use third-party products, such as Microsoft Excel and OCXs, so you'll need access to these to run the examples.

Installing the software is straight forward. Insert the disk (we'll assume that this drive is drive A) and then:

For Windows, Windows for Workgroups, and Windows NT:

 Choose Run from the Program Manager's File menu

 Type in **A:\SETUP**

 Click OK

For Windows 95:

- Go to Explorer
- Select the **A:** drive
- Double click on **SETUP**

In both cases, follow the instructions on the screen.

Conventions

We've used a number of different font and layout styles to indicate different types of information in the book. Here are examples of them and what they mean.

> Comments in boxes like these are bits of interesting information that you should take a look at.

```
Program code is in this font.
There are two styles
This is new code.
This is code that you've already seen.
Don't worry, it makes sense when you see it.
```

When we're talking about **bits of code** in the main text, they'll be in a **chunky font** as well.

Text that appears on your screen, for example on a menu or dialog box, also has its own font.

Tell Us What You Think

We've worked hard on this book to make it useful. We've tried to understand what you are willing to exchange your hard earned money for and tried to make the book live up to your expectations.

Please let us know what you think about this book. Tell us what we did wrong and what we did right. This isn't just marketing flannel—we really do all huddle around the e-mail to find out what you think. If you don't believe it, send us a note. We'll answer and we'll take whatever you say on board for future editions. The easiest way is to use e-mail:

feedback@wrox.com
Compuserve 100063,2152

You can also find more details about Wrox Press on our web site. Here you'll find the code form our latest books, sneak previews of forthcoming titles and information about the authors and editors. You can order Wrox titles directly from the site or find out where your nearest local bookstore with Wrox titles is located. Look at the advert in the back of this book for more information. The address of our site is:

http://www.wrox.com

An Introduction to PowerBuilder and OOP

This chapter introduces the terms and concepts you'll need to understand to get the most from PowerBuilder 5.0's improved object-oriented features. We'll look at the basics of object-oriented programming, such as what classes and objects are and how they are created, and then discuss how you can implement other object-oriented techniques, such as inheritance, encapsulation and polymorphism in PowerBuilder.

The Benefits of Object Orientation

Much has been written on the potential benefits (and drawbacks) of object orientation, but, for the moment, we're going to highlight just two benefits: **reusability** and **extensibility**.

Reusability

Reusability has always been something of a holy grail to programmers. How many times have you written code, only to realize when you finish that it's actually the same as the code you wrote in another part of the application? Until now, the only solution to this problem has been to use 'library code' which is either called as a procedure or else explicitly cut and pasted into each new situation.

However, if you use library code and call it as a procedure, you can't modify it without affecting all the applications that use it. Alternatively, if you copy and paste and *then* modify the code, you end up with multiple copies to maintain. One of the most important benefits of object orientation is that it makes maintenance *much* easier.

Extensibility

The principle of extensibility is easily demonstrated but is much harder to explain. Consider how many times you have had to almost, but not quite, duplicate an existing function to account for a special set of conditions or circumstances. Sometimes, you can adopt the library code approach with all of its attendant maintenance problems, but more often you'll either rewrite the existing function to account for the special conditions or simply accept that you need to duplicate code.

Neither approach is very efficient and both mean that you have to rewrite existing code with all the implicit possibilities of introducing error. As we shall see, the same technology that confers reusability also provides you with the means of extending functionality, without having to touch existing, proven code.

Classes and Objects

For now, I'm going to intentionally discuss classes and objects in distinctly non-PowerBuilder terms. I want you to begin thinking in general object terms.

Classes and objects are very closely related in any object-oriented environment. Fundamentally, a **class** is a template or blueprint for an **object**.

Classes

There's no more important concept in object-oriented programming than the idea of a class. It's the fundamental building block with which we can model the physical world around us.

Those familiar with C++ or Smalltalk should be comfortable with the notion of a class. By the end of this chapter, you should be as comfortable as the pointer-heads who do C++. (I'm one of those pointer-heads, so I say that with affection!)

So what is a class? A class defines the characteristics of an object—what it will look like and behave like—at least initially. A class is *not* an object; it's the template or blueprint for that object. Classes don't perform functions or do any work—they don't even take up memory. They exist only as a tool for modeling your business and the world around you.

Objects

Once you're comfortable with the notion of a class, objects are a breeze. Objects are said to be **instances** of a class. You can't fly on Boeing 757 (a class), but you *can* fly on Boeing 757 Serial Number #4321 (if a Boeing 757 with that serial number existed). In short, in the physical world, objects are those things which occupy space. In the software world, objects occupy memory.

You create an object by **instantiating** a class. In the following examples, the classes are said to be **autoinstantiated**, which means that, to allocate memory for the object, you need do no more than declare the variable reference:

```
airbus_300      ab300_4321
boeing757       b757_1996
```

A good analogy of the relationship between objects and classes is the relationship between a fruit pie (object) and the recipe (class) that was used to make it. If you're hungry now, having the recipe alone isn't much use to you—all it tells you is how to make the pie; you need the actual pie to satisfy your hunger.

Class Hierarchies

New classes are created as subclasses of existing classes—either PowerBuilder classes or user-defined ones. A class is, therefore, always related to at least one other class. These parent-child relationships constitute a **class hierarchy**.

Objects instantiated from a subclass will have all the characteristics of that subclass. They will also inherit characteristics from the subclass's parent class and from any class in the hierarchy which is above the parent and from which the parent itself has inherited characteristics. The content of levels below that from which the object is created will, of course, have no effect on the object.

The process of defining a class hierarchy or **application framework** can be very time consuming. You need to put a lot of time and thought into analyzing, identifying, defining and designing the classes that you'll use in your application. So, although OOP can pay off, it's not necessarily in terms of speedy development. Of course, the payoff that OOP brings is two-fold—not only are you creating reusable code that you can use to speed development in subsequent projects, but you also save time in the coding and maintenance, since many of the properties and behaviors of a subclass are already provided for by the previously defined ancestor.

> Note that the terms ancestor-descendant and parent-child are interchangeable.

When you're changing the attributes or behavior, you need only do so once at the appropriate level in the application framework and voila! the change is propagated to all descendant objects at recompile. Another benefit is that classes are developed independently of the application, so they can be tested separately from the application build.

However, many managers forego proper object-oriented analysis and design because it's just so tempting to jump in and start coding, to prove progress is being made. Later, they inevitably find that inserting new subclasses in the middle of the hierarchy is a real pain in the class!

Abstraction

Abstraction is the process of being able to recognize a class or object from a few distinguishing characteristics. This is advantageous because it avoids the need to evaluate the whole set of information about the class or object.

This concept is best illustrated by looking at an example from the real world. Let's consider a familiar object—a Boeing 757—in terms of classes.

The term Aircraft covers a rather wide range of flying machines. At the top of the hierarchy we can define the properties of this class as including empty weight, maximum weight, number of crew required, number of passengers, takeoff distance, landing distance and maximum altitude. This is a purely abstract definition, since all aircraft have many more properties than these. However, it is sufficient for this level as it comprises our abstraction of an aircraft.

What about the number and characteristics of the engines? Well, gliders have no engines, so if we made these properties of the Aircraft class, the Glider objects would unnecessarily have all the overhead associated with engine information. Likewise, wing information is superfluous to hot air balloons, autorotation characteristics only apply to helicopters, etc. If we include all of these properties and behaviors in our Aircraft class, the class definition will become quite thick, even though most of the information doesn't apply to a particular type of aircraft.

The way round this is to create subclasses. In this case, it's useful to break the Aircraft class into the following subclasses: Fixed Wing, Rotary and Lighter-than-air. All of these subclasses inherit the properties of the Aircraft class, but also have properties of their own.

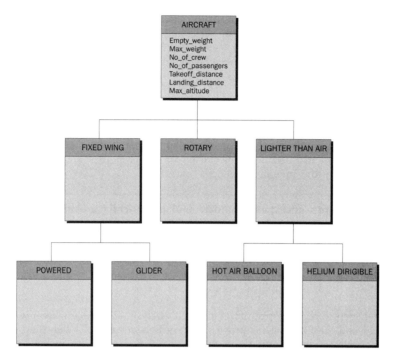

That's great, but as we start defining characteristics of the subclasses, we soon discover that they are also too general. Sure, all fixed wing aircraft have characteristics associated with wings, but only powered aircraft have engine characteristics, not gliders. Likewise, only hot air balloons have propane burners; helium dirigibles do not. We soon find that we need another level of subclasses. And perhaps another after that, and so on, until all objects that we'll need in our project can be fully described by a class definition.

To define a specific object, we must supply more detailed information—the **instance properties**—which will differentiate the specific instance from the generic class. So we can create an actual Boeing 757 from the Boeing 757 definition.

> Perhaps the first and most serious mistake that a new object-oriented developer often makes is to create fat ancestors. They load up the top level classes with every conceivable attribute and method and then, just to make it an OOP application, they create descendants which override much of the ancestor definition with their own class definition. This is *not* the way to do OOP.
>
> I'm not saying that ancestors shouldn't contain more code and variables than descendants—they often will. What I'm saying is, descendants should be using most of what the ancestor has to offer. This means that you should spend time designing your classes so that when you start coding, you don't find yourself having to override a lot of the ancestor definition.
>
> However, fat ancestors were not always the fault of novice OOP developers. In earlier versions of PowerBuilder, performance suffered significantly if the number of levels of subclasses grew too great. Often, the only practical recourse was to load up the ancestors.

Properties and Functions

A class definition includes properties and functions which define the state of an object of that class. An object's properties are stored as data variables and its behavior is represented by functions and events in the class.

You won't come across **methods** in PowerBuilder as it uses the term **function**. You may also hear the terms **data** and **services** being used to describe the contents of a class. I have no doubt there are probably a dozen other terms which represent the same concepts—popular technologies always attract a wealth of terms to communicate the concepts involved.

PowerBuilder's Class Hierarchy

PowerBuilder is an object-oriented tool internally as well as externally. The product provides the developer with base objects, such as windows, user objects and DataWindows for developing applications, each of which is derived from an internal PowerBuilder class. These classes make up PowerBuilder's internal class hierarchy.

> Classes and objects can be a confusing issue in PowerBuilder as it refers to most things as *objects*. This is because, in most cases, PowerBuilder handles instantiating a class into an object for you. As such, when you create a window, it is created within a running version of PowerBuilder which has already instantiated the window object from an internal window class. Also, most people recognize the term *object* more readily than *class*.
>
> In C++ or other language-based environments, it's much easier to conceptualize the difference between an object and a class. A *class* is what you code and an *object* is what becomes of that code when you run your program. In 4GL languages, this difference gets blurred as the environment does most of this internally. However, classes are fundamental to the concept of object-oriented programming and you should make sure that you're comfortable with the term.

In PowerBuilder, all classes are ultimately derived from the PowerBuilder super class, **PowerObject**. This forms the top level of the class hierarchy, along with the **SystemFunctions** class. PowerObject is an internal abstract class that encapsulates the standard functions available in any PowerBuilder object. As an abstract class, it can't be instantiated—you can't create a PowerObject.

The PowerObject class has a number of descendant classes from which the standard PowerBuilder objects made available to the developer are derived. Let's take a look at the PowerBuilder class hierarchy.

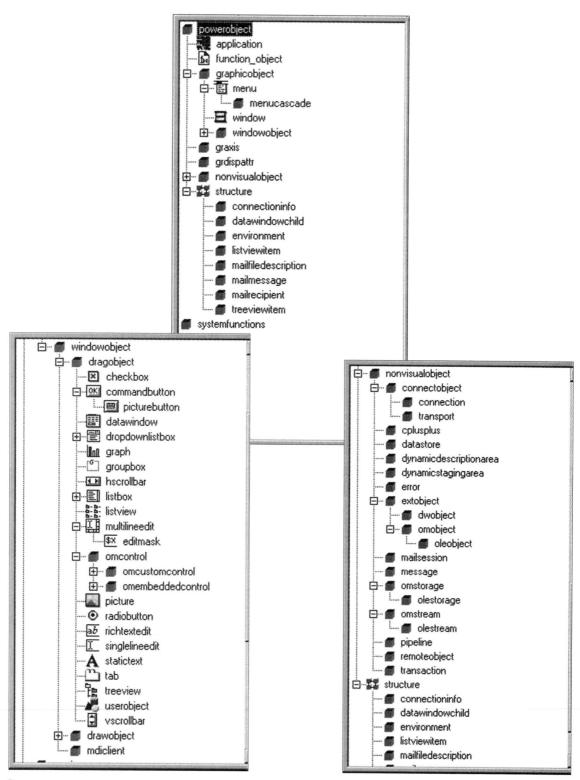

The PowerObject class has seven direct descendants, each further defining the base functionality for the standard objects that are provided to the developer. These direct descendants are as follows:

- **Application** is used to instantiate the application object, which is the starting point for all PowerBuilder applications.

- **Function_object** is used to instantiate a global function object. A global function object is a special purpose object that encapsulates a single method. Global functions are used by developers to create globally accessible logic.

- **GraphicObject** is the ancestor of all of PowerBuilder's visual objects. Menu and window classes are inherited from this class, as is the WindowObject class. The WindowObject class is the ancestor of all visual object classes. It, in turn, has three descendants, each with further refined attributes. PowerBuilder's class hierarchy breaks down visual objects into three categories: objects that can be dragged, objects that can't be dragged and a special class for MDI client objects.

- **GrAxis** provides the base functionality for PowerBuilder's graph object. The GrAxis class has three descendant classes: Category, Series and Values.

- **GrDispAttr** is the base class used to specify the appearance of text objects on a graph. PowerBuilder provides descendant classes from the GrDispAttr class for graph titles, legends, pie graph text and two descendant classes (DispAttr and LabelDispAttr) for each of the three axes (category, series and value) in a graph.

- **NonVisualObject** is the base class for non-visual PowerBuilder objects, such as the error object and the message object.

- **Structure** is the base class for a special object that encapsulates a number of properties, but doesn't have methods. In PowerBuilder, a structure provides a mechanism to store related data elements.

Each of the seven descendants is further refined as we move down PowerBuilder's class hierarchy until a specific object type is made available to the developer. The developer creates instances of these objects using the PowerBuilder painters.

The Object Browser

PowerBuilder's Object browser is really a class and object browser as it has two uses. It allows you to view the class hierarchy in both PowerBuilder itself and your own application and also lets you view the properties, events and functions that are available in any object that you have created. The System tab is where you can view PowerBuilder's internal class hierarchy. The other tabs allow you to view objects that you have created in your application.

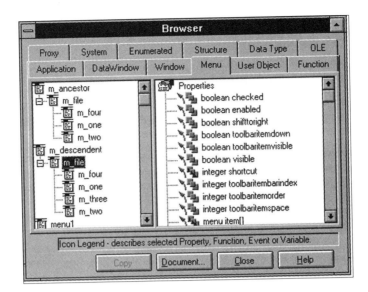

Objects are displayed in the left panel and the right panel displays the various properties, events, functions, variables and structures associated with any object that you select.

Clicking the right mouse button in the left panel allows you to expand each object. For example, expanding a window object will display all the objects that are painted in that window. You can display object hierarchies wherever inheritance is supported by PowerBuilder, i.e. in the **Window**, **User Object** and **Menu** tab folders.

The icons in the right panel indicate several things about the property, event, function, variable or structure under scrutiny:

 An anti-clockwise arrow shows that the property/variable/event/function/structure is inherited.

 The number of squares shows whether the property/variable/event/function/ structure is public (three squares), protected (two squares) or private (one square).

 Other restrictions, such as being read-only, are shown by half-colored squares.

The **Document...** button allows you to display the information in rich text format, which you can then print or copy to the clipboard for pasting into a Windows word processor. The **Copy** button allows you to copy and paste properties, variables, functions, events and structures into your code. The browser is also useful for reviewing OLE objects and controls.

Support for Objects

PowerBuilder is a tool that depends on objects for almost all of its capabilities. It enables the developer to define objects based on a series of predefined classes. As well as the development painters, there are several system painters that allow the developer to interact with the development environment.

In addition to these tools, the PowerBuilder language, PowerScript, provides the developer with the capability to programmatically manipulate objects. PowerScript enables you to access objects, create and destroy instances of objects and manipulate the data encapsulated within objects. The focus of this book is object orientation in PowerBuilder, so we won't go into the details of PowerScript syntax here. However, we *will* take a moment to explain the calling conventions and keywords that you'll need when you're writing PowerScript to manipulate PowerBuilder objects.

Accessing Object Attributes

The **dot convention** is used for accessing object properties. For example, to change the title of a window, you use:

```
w_main_window.Title = "New Title"
```

In this case, **w_main_window** is the name of the window object and **Title** is the property of the window that you want to change. Similarly, if you have an object that contains another object, (i.e. a window with controls) you can access the 'nested' objects using:

```
w_main_window.cb_ok.Enabled = True
w_main_window.uo_user_object1.cb_sort.visible = false
```

> Note that this code actually breaks one of the concepts of object orientation, namely encapsulation. We won't go into the details of why right now because we'll cover encapsulation later in the chapter.

You can also call object level functions with the dot convention:

```
w_main_window.cb_ok.Hide()
```

PowerBuilder 5.0 offers a new keyword that makes accessing object attributes of DataWindow and OLE objects a little easier: **Object**. For example, to set the DataWindow row 1, column 1 value to 10, you could use:

```
dw_DataWindowControl1.Object.Data[1,1] = 10
```

The following example calls the **About** function for the OLE object inside the OLE control:

```
ole_Ole_Control1.Object.About()
```

This is an important addition to PowerBuilder as it solves the problem associated with having container type controls which contain existing objects.

Referring to Objects within an Object Hierarchy

There are three keywords available for referring to objects: **This**, **Parent** and **ParentWindow**. **This** refers to the object for which you're writing the code:

```
//For a CommandButton in a window
This.enabled = true              // Enables the current object
```

```
//For a Window
this.windowstate = maximized!    // Maximizes the window
close (this)                     // Closes the window
```

Parent refers to the object in which the current object is placed. For example, if you had a command button in a window, you could use:

```
//For the CommandButton's clicked event
close (Parent)                   // Closes the window
```

```
//For the CommandButton's clicked event
Parent.WindowState = Maximized!  // Maximizes the parent window
```

ParentWindow can only be used in scripts for menus and refers to the window with which the menu is associated:

```
// For the clicked event of a 'Close' option on a menu.
Close (ParentWindow)             // Closes the window
```

Creating an Instance

An object is an instantiated class. This means that an object is created at run time from a class, which acts as the definition of the object. You can use two commands to create an instance of a class, depending on whether you want to display the created object on screen. These are **Open** and **Create**.

Using Open

You only need to write one line of code to create and display an instance of an object on the screen. We'll have a look here at how you can create an instance of a window, a window in an MDI frame (a sheet) and a user object, both with and without parameters.

Open

The first formats we'll look at create an instance of a specified window in memory and display it on the screen:

```
Open( WindowVariable {, ParentWindowVariable} )
```

```
Open( WindowVariable, WindowType {,ParentWindowVariable} )
```

A window can be opened as a **child window**, which means that it exists within the boundaries of a parent window, or it can be opened as a **main window**, which can exist outside of other windows. To open a child window, you specify the name of the parent window as the second parameter.

PowerBuilder allows you to supply the data type of the window to be opened at run time. This can be useful in cases when the window that is opened depends on a selection made by the user, in which case, you can't know in advance which one it will be.

OpenWithParm

The next format is similar, but allows you to send a parameter to the opening window:

```
OpenWithParm( WindowVariable, Parameter {,ParentWindowVariable})

OpenWithParm( WindowVariable, Parameter, WindowType
              (,ParentWindowVariable})
```

The parameter is stored in the **message object**, which is a special object maintained by PowerBuilder that can be used to pass data between objects. We'll look in detail at the message object in the next chapter.

OpenSheet/OpenSheetWithParm

The next format opens a window as a sheet in either an MDI frame or MDI frame with MicroHelp window. MDI windows are special in that they are designed to have child windows that can only exist within the boundaries of a parent frame window. The advantage of this is that we can logically organize a number of presentation sheets within a single application frame. Applications such as Microsoft Excel take advantage of this technique. The syntax is as follows:

```
OpenSheet( Windowvar {,WindowNameString}, MDIWindowName
           {,Position {, WindowArrangeStyle}} )

OpenSheetWithParm(Windowvar, Parameter {, WindowNameString},
           MDIWindowName {, Position{, WindowArrangeStyle}} )
```

For example, the following line opens **w_sheet** in the **w_frame** window and cascades the windows:

```
OpenSheet (w_sheet, w_frame, 2, Cascaded!)
```

OpenUserObject/OpenUserObjectWithParm

Finally, to open a user object and place it in the specified window at the chosen x and y coordinates, use the following formats:

```
WindowName.OpenUserObject( UserObject{, x, y} )

WindowName.OpenUserObject(UserObject, ObjectType{, x, y })


WindowName.OpenUserObjectWithParm ( UserObject, Parameter {, x, y })

WindowName.OpenUserObjectWithParm (UserObject, Parameter, ObjectType
           {, x, y })
```

Creating Multiple Instances of an Object

In the previous section, we looked at a number of ways to open a single window. However, one of the advantages of object-oriented systems is that you can instantiate a class multiple times so that you have many instances of the same object. This has a number of benefits. For example, in our MDI sheet example, we may have three sheets open within a frame. Each provides the same services, but is used differently by the user. In this case, each sheet is an instance of the custom window class designed by the developer.

When we use the **Open** function, we have two options. The first is to provide the actual name of the window class to be opened:

```
/* Method 1: Specifying the window name directly */
Open (w_item_master)
```

The second is to supply a variable of the same type as the window class you want to open:

```
/* Method 2: Using a variable */
w_item_master lWindow1
Open (lWindow1)
```

In PowerBuilder, once you've defined a class, you can define variables to reference instances of that class, just as you can define variables to reference standard data types. In essence, a PowerBuilder class is a data type within the development environment.

Because of the way PowerBuilder allocates memory to the objects that you create, using the first method means you can only define one instance of the object. When you create an instance by passing the window name to the **Open** function, PowerBuilder allocates memory and links it to the name you provided (in this case, the name of the window). If you try and call the **Open** function again, using the same name, PowerBuilder simply returns you to the current instance.

This happens because any object you define through a painter is declared as global (you can check this for yourself by creating a window, exporting it from the Library painter and looking at the **.srw** file), so any reference to it is recognized throughout the application and can't be duplicated.

With the second method, you can open more than one instance of the window, because it's basing the instance of the object on a variable that can be given a scope. Imagine that you're opening this window from a menu option. To open more than one instance of the window, you can declare the window variable as local in the menu script. The local variable is created when the script starts executing and will be destroyed when it completes. This means that each time the script executes, a new variable is created and memory will be allocated to it. Note that if you declared the window variable as an instance, you would only be able to open one instance of the window; the variable would be created when the menu was created and destroyed when the menu was destroyed. So, as long as the menu exists, the memory allocated for the menu would be the same.

Unfortunately, there's a problem associated with using local variables to create multiple instances of an object—you lose the external reference to all windows except the active one. Suppose you open four instances of a window, the third window is active and you want to disable a command button in the first instance. With the above method, you can't specifically reference instance 1, so you can't disable the command button.

> The same applies to interactive debugging—you can't see or access other
> instances other than the active sheet. In this situation, you might need to
> include debug statements, like **MessageBox**, to allow you to debug.

To solve the problem of referencing the instances, you can declare an array of instance window
variables like this:

```
// Declare these 2 variables as instance variables for the menu
w_item_master i_item_master[]
Int InstanceNo = 1

// Script for the menu item
OpenSheet(i_item_master[i], ParentWindow, 1, Cascaded!)
InstanceNo++
```

The functions in this code create an instance in memory for each instance that's displayed on the
screen.

If you want to create an instance without having to display it on the screen, you can either set the
Visible attribute after creating the instance, or use the **Create** statement to create an object that
exists only in memory.

Using Create

So far, we've been discussing how an object is instantiated and displayed. The **Create** command
allows us to instantiate an object that has no visual component.

Transaction objects don't have a visual component, so we don't want to instantiate them using the
Open command. For these objects, all we need do is allocate a place for them in memory and set
a reference to them that the application can use to access the new object.

Let's look at an example of how objects are created, using the transaction object. Let's say that
your application requires a connection to two different databases at the same time. In this case,
you'll need two transaction objects. One of the transaction objects, SQLCA, is available by default,
but you'll need to create the second one for the second connection. Here's the code that creates a
new transaction object instance:

```
Transaction g_TranForSybase
g_TranForSybase = Create Transaction
```

g_TranForSybase is now available for use in your code—just set the right values and connect to
the database.

If you look at the exported definition of the application **inheritance** in the **Ch01.pbl** library,
you can follow the **Create** statements that PowerBuilder uses to create all the global objects
internally:

```
on inheritance.create
appname = "inheritance"
message = create message
```

```
sqlca = create transaction
sqlda = create dynamicdescriptionarea
sqlsa = create dynamicstagingarea
error = create error
end on
```

Creating Instances from a String Variable

In the previous section, we saw how you can instantiate a non-visual object using the **Create** keyword. Often, however, the name of the object that you would like to create isn't known until the application is running. With PowerBuilder 4.0, if the user selected an item from a screen that resulted in an object being created, we needed to supply a **Case** statement and a series of all the possible objects.

With PowerBuilder 5.0, we have the option of supplying a string variable that contains the name of the object to be created, instead of the **Case** statement. This makes our code a lot simpler.

Let's look at an example of this technique. In this example, we'll list all the menu names from a specified library on a DataWindow. The user can then select a library, which we'll create in memory.

Our first step is to list all of the menus in the library. This is done by importing the names using the **ImportString** function and supplying a **DirMenu!** filter to the **LibraryDirectory** function.

```
// Read all menu entries in the library and populate DataWindow
dw_menus.ReSet()
dw_menus.ImportString ( Librarydirectory( "userlib.pbl", DirMenu! ) )
```

We then define a variable of type **Menu**, that we'll use to point to the menu that we create. Along with this is a string variable that contains the name of the menu class to instantiate:

```
// variables
Menu      Menu
String l_user_menu_name
```

Now we simply get the name of the selected item, assign the name to our string variable and use the **Create Using** syntax to create a menu of the class name supplied.

```
// Get user selected menu into l_user_menu_name
l_user_menu_name = dw_menus.GetItemString( dw_menus.GetRow(), dw_menus.GetColumn() )

//Create the menu
Menu = Create Using l_user_Menu_name
```

Creating User Objects

A user object is a custom object that PowerBuilder provides to allow the developer to define objects that have attributes not available in the standard classes. You can define user objects based on an existing PowerBuilder class, or independently.

The **Create** keyword is used to instantiate user objects much like any other object. For example:

```
nc_string_functions    l_str_cls
l_str_cls = create nc_string_functions
```

The **l_str_cls** variable would then be used to reference the instantiated user object. With the advent of PowerBuilder 5.0, a new option is available that simplifies this process. Version 5.0 provides a special property in the base user object class, called **AutoInstantiate**. When this is set to true, you don't need to go through the process of defining a variable and then creating an instantiated object using that variable. PowerBuilder handles these details and you're left to simply supply the variable that will be used to access the object.

```
// If autoinstantiate is set, use the following
nc_string_functions    l_str_cls
```

Destroying an Instance

Just as PowerBuilder provides a mechanism to create objects, it must also provide a means to destroy them and release the memory allocated. There are two ways of destroying an instance of an object and which one you choose depends on how you created the object in the first place. If you created the instance using one of the **Open** functions, you should destroy it with the **Close** function, which clears the instance from the screen and from memory, for example:

```
// Clears instance of window w_item_master
Close (w_item_master)
```

In the case of a visual user object, the same approach applies:

```
// Clears instance of user object uo_commandButton
CloseUserObject (uo_commandButton)
```

If you created the instance using the **Create** statement (a transaction object, for example), you must remove it from memory with the **Destroy** statement:

```
// Clears the instance l_str_cls and removes it from memory
Destroy l_str_cls
```

You can only create and destroy one object at a time and you must always destroy any objects that you have created. Repeatedly creating objects and not destroying them causes memory leaks in applications. Also, I find that the code is much easier to follow when a **Create** is followed by a **Destroy** in all cases.

Inheritance

Inheritance is one of the most beneficial attributes of object orientation. It allows you to reuse code by taking elements of existing classes and using them over and over again in other applications. The real benefit, however, is that not only can these prebuilt classes be plugged into an application, but the recipient program can add to the functionality of a class by including additional features in the descendant class. An inherited class gets all the features of its ancestor, plus whatever you add.

PowerBuilder supports inheritance from three objects types:

- Menus
- Windows
- User objects

You can inherit from an existing class in two ways:

- By selecting Inherit from the Select dialog box, which is displayed when you invoke one of these object painters.
- By selecting File/Inherit... when you're in the relevant object painter.

When an object is inherited, everything in the ancestor class is passed to the descendant. If another object is derived from the descendant, that new object will inherit everything from the first ancestor, as well as anything new that is defined in subsequent ancestors.

Inheritance works in approximately the same way for all three types of objects, but, to show you how it's used, we'll concentrate on windows.

Inherited Windows

In a descendant window you can override, overload or extend ancestor scripts, access protected and public functions, read or modify public or protected instance variables and modify the properties of inherited controls. What you *can't* do is delete or change the name of any controls that were painted in the ancestor.

You can change the position of controls in the descendant window, but you should note that if you do this, further changes to the position of the control in the ancestor window won't be reflected in the descendant window. The same is true of any changes you make to any other properties in the descendant window—what you're doing, in effect, is overriding the ancestor's property values.

> **Although you can't delete controls from an ancestor window in a descendant, you can simply hide the control if you don't need it.**

Scripts

When you select a control in the Window painter, the script icon will change to display script lines if there's any script for any events associated with that control:

However, this is only the case if there's a script for an event associated with that particular window—the icon won't change to show scripts in the ancestor window. This can become a bit tedious when you're debugging an application, because you have to go into the Script painter to determine whether there are any scripts that have been inherited from an ancestor window.

The appearance of the icon next to the event name tells you where the script is written:

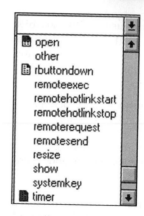

Icon	Description
Full color	The script only exists for the event in the ancestor window.
Black and white	The script only exists for the event in the descendant window.
Half color/half black and white	The script exists for the event in both the ancestor and descendant windows.

You can view the ancestor script by selecting Design/Display Ancestor Script....You can't edit an ancestor script from the descendant script, but you can, if you need to, copy and paste the script to and from the clipboard.

Manipulating Ancestor Scripts

If both the ancestor and descendant windows have scripts, the script for the ancestor window will be the first to execute. This is PowerBuilder's default behavior and can be specified by selecting Design/Extend Ancestor Script from the menu in the Script painter.

If you don't want the ancestor script to execute, you can select Design/Override Ancestor Script. However, this only works if a descendant level script exists. If you want to prevent an ancestor level script from executing but have no script that you want to execute in the descendant window, you can simply add a comment in the descendant script.

The other thing you might want to do is to make your object initialize some data or perform some action before the ancestor script runs. If you override the script, the ancestor code will never run automatically. What you can do, though, is to override the ancestor script, write the script for the descendant window and then call the ancestor script, using the following syntax:

Call Super::<Event Name>

The pronoun **Super** refers to the immediate ancestor of the object. The double colon is referred to as a **scope resolution operator** in C++, but Powersoft seems to avoid calling it anything except the **::** operator. If you do the above, the local script gets first crack at handling the event, and then the ancestor script is executed.

> When it is used with variables, as in `::lRowCount`, Powersoft calls the `::` operator a global scope operator. It means 'Use the global variable instead of the local variable with the same name which is effectively masking the global.'

This calling mechanism is what actually occurs in inherited classes. You can see this if you print out a descendant window's definition.

If you inherit from an inherited object, you end up with a grandparent-parent-child hierarchy. The same rules apply for extending and overriding ancestor scripts—you just have an extra level (or levels) to think about.

One caution is warranted here: you're going to need a good understanding of what the class' ancestors are doing. If one of the descendants in the hierarchy overrides an event script without later calling the ancestor's script, that effectively puts a roadblock in the way of handling the event in higher ancestors in the hierarchy. Suppose you have three windows, **Window_A**, **Window_B** (inherited from **A**) and **Window_C** (inherited from **B**). If you want a **Window_C** event to be handled by **Window_A** code, but **Window_B** has overridden the event script, you'll have to call **Window_A**'s script directly.

In this case, you won't be able to use the **Super** pronoun as above, because the **Super** for **Window_C** will refer to **Window_B**. Instead, you'll have to specify the ancestor class directly:

```
Call Window_A::<event name>
```

Because this call occurs in **Window_C**, the execution will not then fall through to **Window_B** after **Window_A** is done, but will return to **Window_C** from where it was called.

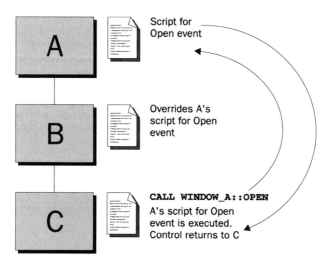

You can see this working in the **inheritance** application in the **Ch01.pbl** library.

Multiple Inheritance

Up to this point we have looked at single inheritance, which means that a descendant is created from a single ancestor. With single inheritance, you can create multiple descendants from the same ancestor, but you can't create a single descendant from multiple ancestors.

Multiple inheritance, on the other hand, does allow you to create a single descendant from multiple ancestors. In this case, the descendant class has all the attributes of both ancestors, plus whatever you add to it.

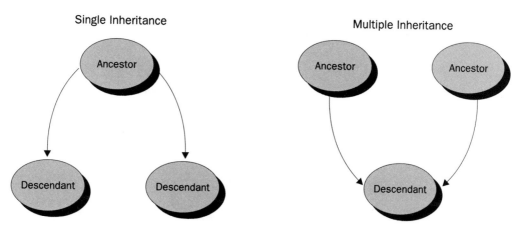

However, the trade-off for this flexibility is often increased complication, confusion and error. Many OOP gurus are coming to believe that a better way to get the benefits of multiple classes is through using **composition**. Composition is the inclusion in one class definition of another class definition. You should immediately notice this is different to inheritance because we can't extend the functionality of the included class, but we can fully exploit its attributes and behaviors.

This is what we do in PowerBuilder. PowerBuilder doesn't directly support multiple inheritance, so you can't derive a descendant class from multiple ancestors. However, user objects can be used to achieve the same effect.

For example, suppose your application requires a dialog box that presents a number of edits and controls to the user. Your shop has set up a library of standard objects that can be used for this purpose, but your application requires a dialog that combines the attributes of two of the standard objects your shop has made available. What to do?

Simple really, you have two options. The first is to inherit your application window from one of your shop's standard windows and then provide the additional functionality required through a standard user object. A visual user object can be placed on the descendant window to provide additional edits, drop-downs or other visual controls. If functionality is what you're looking for, you can use a non-visual user object to provide the additional functions and properties that you need.

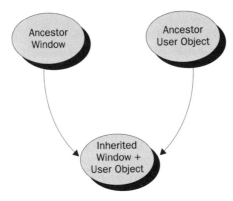

The second option doesn't really involve inheritance, but produces the same net effect. If your shop has developed a class library of standard dialogs using custom visual user objects, you can drop one of these user objects on a window and then drop another standard user object on the surface of the first user object. The window really does nothing more than provide a frame in which to display the user objects.

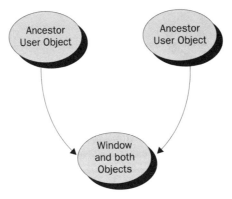

You can see examples of both these solutions in the **multiple_inheritance** application in **Ch01.pbl**:

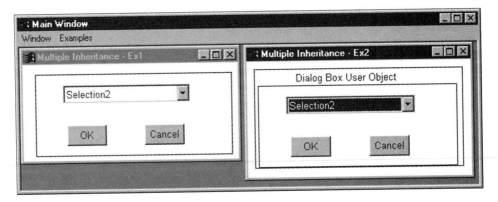

PowerBuilder, Delphi and Java have all adopted the single-inheritance model.

Encapsulation

Encapsulation is another central principle in object-oriented programming which can be implemented in different ways. It refers to the packaging of properties and methods into a self-contained package, the idea being that the object knows *how* to do its job—all you need to do is tell it what you want. This idea is what really differentiates object-oriented programming from traditional procedural programming, where data and functions which operate on that data are spread throughout the application.

You can think of a software object as a black box. You just need to know three things about it:

- What it's supposed to do
- What information (if any) it requires to do its job
- How it will communicate the results of its actions to its environment

An object must be able to protect itself from interference by its environment. The object is the capsule and its properties and methods are the things that are enclosed or hidden. Encapsulation is the process whereby the object's data and internal structures are hidden and protected by an external shell. The external shell acts as the interface through which all access to the object must pass.

The benefits of encapsulation should be clear. Once you've created a well-encapsulated object, you can use that object in different applications, saving yourself further development time and effort. Also, if the object's properties and methods (functions) are protected, that object can't be changed unexpectedly.

You can protect methods and properties in your objects by specifying access rights, using the keywords **public**, **private** or **protected**. We'll look at this in more detail in the next chapter.

Polymorphism

Polymorphism is one of those OOP buzzwords that sounds a lot more complicated than it actually is. Polymorphism is the ability of related classes to define methods with the same name but different content and it really comes into its own when you call functions within objects. It's a mechanism by which the actual process executed is dependent on where a function is called; the function will process differently depending on where in the class hierarchy it is called.

If you look at the PowerBuilder system class hierarchy, you'll see that the picture button control is inherited from the command button control, which makes sense because both of these perform the same function.

Whenever you click on a command button, the script for the **Clicked** event is executed. The same applies to a picture button. Since these two controls are inherited from the same class, there's no need to call different event names for them. They can have the same event, but execute different scripts. This is polymorphism in practice—the same event is called in both cases, but the script that is executed is passed like a parameter to the executing function, depending on which control is clicked.

As another example, say we have a function called **Save**, and for the purposes of standards and consistency, we want to have the **Save** function save data at any level of the class hierarchy (i.e. the ancestor has a **Save** function, as do its descendants). In this case, we can define a **Save** function in the base window and then define the same function, but write a completely different script for it in a descendant master window or a descendant transaction window.

PowerBuilder starts looking for a function from the current object level upwards, so calling the function in the master window will execute the logic you wrote in the master window **Save** function. This method of using the same function name and arguments in derived classes is called **inheriting an interface**. If the **Save** function is called from one of the descendants, it might process completely differently, but the end result is still saved data.

Using this technique, you can create a standard **Save** function that can be used from any class in your hierarchy to save data. To the user, it's is the same function call, although internally it may be running very different code. This allows you to provide a clean, consistent interface to the developer by hiding the internal complexities of the object's processing.

Function Overloading

PowerBuilder 5.0 allows you to use true function overloading. This is closely related to polymorphism, but instead of having different objects with functions of the same name, overloading allows you to have one object with different versions of the same function. It enables you to use the same function name to get various results or behaviors from your script. PowerBuilder achieves this flexibility by using the parameters that are sent with the function call to distinguish the actual function scripts to execute.

Previous versions of PowerBuilder only allowed function overloading to occur when a function was defined in an ancestor and a descendant, with the parameter list supplied to the function differentiating the two calls. PowerBuilder 5.0 allows the developer to define function calls that are differentiated by parameter list within a single object. To get a feel for this, let's first take a look at function overloading using inheritance.

Function Overloading Using Inheritance

In **Ch01.pbl**, there's a window, called **w_browse**, which allows you to browse a file in your application. The window has a MultiLineEdit control that is used to display the information and a **Read** function, called by an Open button, that reads the file data into the display.

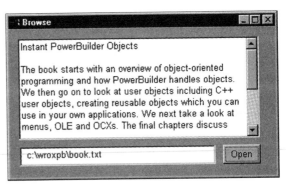

26

The **Read** function is a window level function which is declared as protected. It accepts a string parameter representing the file name to read:

```
Function Read ( sFileName String ) Access is Protected Returns Boolean
```

The script for the Open button includes:

```
if ( Read( sle_filename.text) = false ) then
    MessageBox ("Message","Unable to Read File")
end if
```

Run the window and type in a file name to see how it works.

We've also expanded the system to browse files in hex as well as ASCII. To accomplish this, we inherited a new window from the browse window for our hex browse display. This is **w_enhbrowse**:

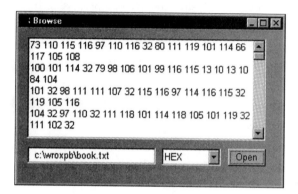

The new window has all the features of its ancestor, plus a drop-down list box that we can use to select the browse mode desired. Just as in the parent window, a window level function is provided to actually read the data into the descendant's MultiLineEdit. The new **Read** function is declared as a protected function that accepts two string parameters, one representing the file name and the other representing the browse mode:

```
Function Read ( sFileName String, sBrowseMode String ) Access is Protected &
                    Returns Boolean
```

The processing for this new function includes logic to read the file and display its contents in hex. The usefulness of function overloading comes to light when we look at how the **Read** function is called in the descendant window's Open button:

```
if ( ddlb_Type.text = "HEX" ) then
    if (  read( sle_FileName.text, "HEX" ) = FALSE ) then
          MessageBox ( "Message", "Unable to Read File" )
    end if
else
    if (  read( sle_FileName.text ) = FALSE ) then
          MessageBox ( "Message", "Unable to Read File" )
    end if
end if
```

As you can see in this example, we simply call a **Read** function with the parameters we need for our processing. The fact that the **Read** function that accepts one parameter is actually located in the ancestor window, not the descendant window, isn't an issue for us.

Function overloading allows you to use a much smaller function set with a much greater range of functionality. Its disadvantage is more run-time overhead each time the function is called, because the compiler has to check the arguments passed to execute the appropriate function.

Function Overloading without Using Inheritance

PowerBuilder 5.0 allows you to define multiple functions with the same name and different arguments at the same object level. This allows you to take advantage of function overloading without having to build a hierarchy of objects.

Let's take another look at our browse example. Let's say that we were starting out with the window that offers the user both an ASCII and a hex view of the data they are browsing. In this case, we can still simplify our processing by defining two window functions to read the file into the browse window. The first **Read** function takes a file name parameter and the second includes a type parameter:

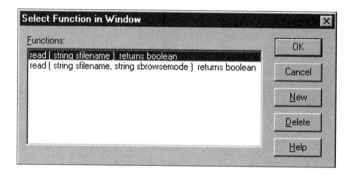

As you can see, the only distinction between the two **Read** functions is the parameters passed to them. However, each will process data differently. The advantage here is that each function can be simplified to perform a single task, thus reducing the length and complexity of your application's function scripts.

We've included this example in the **Ch01.pbl** library—the **w_browseagain** window. If you try running the window, you'll see that it works exactly as in the previous examples.

Summary

This chapter has introduced you to some of the basic object-oriented features of PowerBuilder 5.0. We've explained what objects and classes are and looked at how you create and destroy them. We also covered the PowerBuilder Object browser and explained the three main concepts of object-oriented programming: inheritance, encapsulation and polymorphism. Finally, we looked at the various ways of using function overloading.

In the next chapter we'll look in more detail at how PowerBuilder deals with objects.

Working with Objects

In this chapter, we'll continue to look at how object-oriented features are implemented in PowerBuilder 5.0. We'll look at the way objects communicate with each other and then discuss how you use events, functions and messages. We'll also look at the different types of variables that you can use in PowerBuilder, how and where you use them and how you can control access to them. Finally, we'll take a look at the differences between events and functions.

Inter-object Communication

Broadly speaking, PowerBuilder objects communicate in three ways, via:

- Global variables
- Instance variables and functions
- The message object

Let's take a look at each of these.

Global Variables

Using global variables is the easiest and most straightforward way of communicating between objects. When you declare a variable as global, any script from any object in the application can access that variable.

However, we don't recommend this method because a global variable can be accessed by all application objects, so any object can change its value. Unless you adhere to a strict set of naming conventions, global variables can also make application maintenance more difficult, as it can be difficult to keep track of what impacted the global variable at what point in the application. Finally, the use of global variables goes against object orientation's rule that data should be encapsulated in objects.

Instance Variables and Functions

This is the best way of implementing object-oriented programming principles. Declare instance variables and define functions that act on the instance variables with appropriate access levels. This gives you full control over variables declared for the object. It also means that if you need to make changes later, you only need to do so in one place. To execute one object's function from another object, use the following syntax:

```
Object_Name.{type}{calltype}{when}FunctionName( Arg1, Arg2, ... )
```

This syntax has changed from Version 4.0. Of note are the new **calltype** and **when** parameters, which allow you to control when the function is executed and when the physical reference to the object is resolved, i.e. at run time (dynamic) or compile time (static).

The Message Object

You may sometimes want to pass values as you're opening a window or return values after closing it. PowerBuilder provides several functions that allow you to do both of these:

```
OpenWithParm( WindowVariable, Parameter {,ParentWindowVariable})
OpenWithParm( WinVar, Parm, WindowNameString
             (,ParentWindowVariable})
OpenSheetWithParm(Windowvar, Parameter {, WindowNameString},
             MDIWindowName {, Position{, WindowArrangeStyle}} )
Windowname.OpenUserObjectWithParm ( UserObject, Parameter {, x, y })
WindowName.OpenUserObjectWithParm (UserObject, Parameter, ObjectType
                                        {, x, y })
CloseWithReturn( WindowName, Parameter )
```

The **message object** is a global variable that is available by default with all PowerBuilder applications. As its name suggests, it's used as an intermediate object to store messages that are passed between objects. For example, consider the first function in the list. When you open a window with this function, the parameter that's specified in the function is stored in the message object and you can access it in the opening window.

It has the following attributes:

Property	Data Type	Description
Handle	Long	The handle of the window or control.
Number	UnsignedInt	The event number (comes from Windows).
WordParm	Long	The word parameter for the event (comes from Windows). The parameter's value and meaning are determined by the event.
LongParm	Long	The long parameter for the event (comes from Windows). The parameter's value and meaning are determined by the event.

Table continued on following page

Property	Data Type	Description
DoubleParm	Double	A numeric variable.
StringParm	String	A string or string variable.
PowerObjectParm	PowerObject	Any PowerBuilder object type.
Processed	Boolean	Indicator of whether or not the script processed the event. The default is false.
ReturnValue	Long	The value you want returned to Windows when **Message.Processed** is true. When **Message.Processed** is false, this attribute is ignored.

If a string variable is passed to the message object, it's available in **Message.StringParm**; if it's an integer, it's available in **Message.DoubleParm**, and so on. We recommend that you declare instance variables at the called object and assign values from the message object to the instance variables as the first step in the open event of the called object. You should do this because the message object is global and other events might occur before you access the value in the message object, causing the value to be overridden.

As well as sending traditional data types to other objects, you can also send PowerBuilder objects through the message object. The PowerBuilder object is available in **Message.PowerObject**. This is sometimes useful if you want to send values of different data types to other objects. For example, let's consider again the first function listed above. It allows you to send only one parameter, but if you want to send several parameters of different data types, you can create a structure object, assign it values and then pass the structure object as the parameter to this function.

As well as using it indirectly, you can also access the message object's attributes directly. For example, if you didn't want the user to be able to close a window when they select Close from the control menu, you could use the message object to ensure that the window doesn't close. In any window, the **CloseQuery** event executes before the **Close** event. If **CloseQuery** doesn't execute successfully, the **Close** event isn't triggered. So, you can put code in the **CloseQuery** event to confirm whether the user wants to close the window and then return a true or false value to the message object, depending on the user's response:

```
Int lResponse
lResponse = MessageBox( "CloseQuery Event", "Do you want to close the window?", &
                                            Question!, YesNo!, 2 )
If ( lResponse = 1 ) Then
    Message.ReturnValue= 0
Else
    Message.ReturnValue= 1
End If
```

Events and Messages

Whenever an event occurs, Windows notifies the application by dispatching a message. For instance, when you move the mouse, Windows sends a **wm_mousemove** message to the active window. The application can respond to the message in two ways: it can execute event-handler code or it can ignore the message completely. If it ignores the message, Windows may perform a default action related to the particular event.

Looking at the above example again, when the user clicks on the window's Close button, Windows dispatches a message to the window notifying it of the user's request. You can place event handler code in the **CloseQuery** event to save the data or ask the user to confirm the close; you can even block the default Windows action and prevent the window from being closed. However, if no code exists in the **CloseQuery** event, Windows will perform the default actions, which include closing the window, deallocating the memory it used, etc.

You can divide Windows messages into three categories: informational, notification and action.

Message Type	Description
Informational	Informational messages return the current state of an object—whether an object is visible, its foreground color, etc.
Notification	Notification messages inform objects that something has been done to the object. For example, when you click on a command button, Windows tells the command button 'You have been clicked' by sending an appropriate message.
Action	Action messages do something to an object. For example, adding an entry in a list box or creating an object.

Event Mapping in PowerBuilder

From a Windows application perspective, events in the application are triggered by Windows messages. The application responds to the message by executing the code written to that event. Events in PowerBuilder, on the other hand, have a slightly more complex relationship with the application and the messages. In simple terms, a PowerBuilder event is mapped to a relevant Windows message, but there's also an extra layer in this event message mapping. Each event is mapped to a PowerBuilder event ID which is, in turn, mapped to the relevant Windows message. So, for example, the PowerBuilder **MouseMove** event is mapped to the **pbm_mousemove** event ID which is, in turn, mapped to the **wm_mousemove** Windows message.

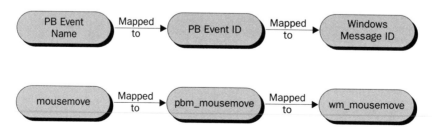

Event IDs are provided to allow developers to map standard Windows events to custom defined PowerBuilder object events. These custom events are known as **user events**.

User Events

PowerBuilder predefines event names for different controls and maps them to the appropriate event ID. For example, a command button has the following predefined events:

Event Name	Event ID
Clicked	pbm_bnclicked
Constructor	pbm_constructor
Destructor	pbm_destructor
DragDrop	pbm_bnDragDrop
DragEnter	pbm_bn_DragEnter
DragLeave	pbm_DragLeave
DragWithIn	pbm_bnDragWithin
GetFocus	pbm_bnGetFocus
LoseFocus	pbm_bnKillFocus
Other	pbm_Other
rButtonDown	pbm_rButtonDown

You can see from the table that PowerBuilder only predefines the events that are most frequently used for each object. The command button, for example, doesn't have a predefined **MouseMove** event, even though this event is a standard Windows event.

So what happens if you need this event, say to display Microhelp when the mouse moves over a command button? PowerBuilder allows you to define a user event for the command button and then map it to one of the available events.

To define a user event, you select Declare/User Events... from the menu in the appropriate painter. You'll see a dialog box similar to the one on the following page.

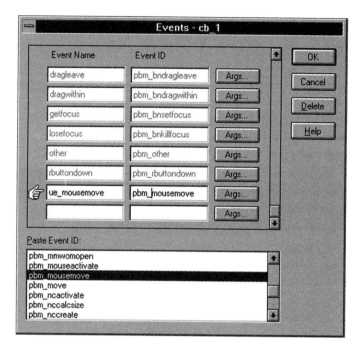

Just type in **ue_mousemove** as the Event Name and map it to the **pbm_mousemove** event ID in the Paste Event ID list box.

> You can map an event ID to only one event name at each object level and you can't unmap predefined events. If you don't want to do anything when an event occurs, you just don't write a script for that event.

You can define user events for any object, except those derived from the **DrawObject** class, i.e. line, oval, rectangle, etc.

Custom Event IDs

As well as the standard event IDs mapped to Windows messages, you can also map a user event to a custom event ID or, indeed, define a user event which isn't mapped to any event ID.

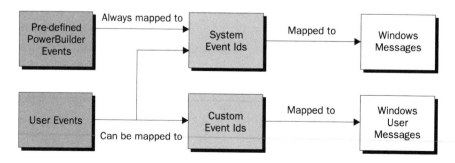

There are 75 custom events, with event IDs **pbm_custom01** to **pbm_custom75**. The custom event IDs are mapped to Windows user messages. For more information on Windows messages, refer to the documentation that comes with the Microsoft Windows SDK. When you define a user event and map it to one of these event IDs, the script doesn't execute automatically—you need to explicitly execute it.

Let's say we wanted an event that performs some post open processing, such as loading DataWindows, or starting a timer, to execute after our window opens. If the code were placed in the **Open** script, the window would not be displayed until the event had finished executing. In many cases, you want the window to display immediately, while background processing finishes the startup process.

To do this, we would define a user event based on one of PowerBuilder's custom events. The **Open** event of the window then calls the user event, using the **PostEvent** function, to begin running the script while the window is displayed. We'll look at the **PostEvent** function later in this chapter.

Parameterized Events

PowerBuilder 5.0 allows you to pass parameters to an event. This is a significant change for the product as it will allow it to more closely adhere to object-oriented design standards and techniques.

The Events dialog box now includes an Args... button to the right of each event name. Custom event IDs have two predefined parameters: **wparam** and **lparam**. All other event IDs have various parameters defined.

You can't change the parameter list for any event ID listed in the Paste Event ID list box, but if you define an event without mapping it to any event ID, you can define parameters to be passed to the event. PowerBuilder executes events that haven't been mapped to an event ID by dynamically generating an internal ID number for these events at run time and placing them in the message queue.

Passing Arguments to an Event

You can pass arguments to an event in three ways: by value, by reference or as read-only. When an argument is passed by value, PowerBuilder makes a copy of the argument, which means that any changes to the argument in the event script won't be reflected in the calling script. When an argument is passed by reference, any changes to the argument in the event script are reflected in the calling script. Passing an argument as read-only allows you to use the value of the argument in the event script, but you can't make changes to the passed value.

The **parameters** application in the **Ch02.pbl** library illustrates the difference between the three methods of passing arguments. We've declared three different user events: **ue_byvalue**, **ue_byref** and **ue_readonly**. Each of these accept a single argument, **argument1**, passed by value, reference and read-only respectively. The application consists of a window which has a drop-down list box, allowing you to select from the three different methods and a command button which calls the relevant user event.

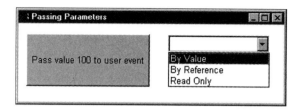

The code for the command button simply calls the relevant user event, passing a value of 100, and then displays the value once we've called the user event.

Here's the code for each user event:

```
int divider
argument1 = argument1 + 100
divider = argument1/10
messagebox ("User Event Script", divider)
argument1 = argument1 + 100
return 0
```

We simply make changes to the argument value, do some processing with it, display the result and then make more changes to the argument value, before returning to the calling script.

> You'll notice that the code for the **ue_readonly** event has the lines which change the argument value commented out. This is because when you pass an argument as read-only, you can't make any changes to the value in the user event. You can only use that value in any processing that you want to do. If you try uncommenting these lines, you'll find that the script won't compile.

You'll find that when you pass the argument by value, after you've executed the user event its value is still 100, even though it has been increased to 300 in the user event script. When the argument is passed by reference, the changes made to it in the user event are reflected in the calling script, so its value is 300. When the argument is passed as read-only, no changes are made in the user event script, so the value is still 100.

Event Return Values

Powerbuilder Version 5.0 allows an event to return a value. The return values for all event IDs listed in the Paste Event ID are defined as **Long**.

For any event that's mapped to an event ID, you don't need to code a **return** statement, even though the declaration indicates **Long** as the return value. If you execute a mapped event which has no code at all, the return value will be **NULL**. If the event has a script, but no **return** statement, the return value is **0**. If the script is commented but without code, the return value is again **0**.

However, if you declare an unmapped event, you must return some value with the **return** statement, otherwise you'll get a compiler error. You may have noticed that in the above example the final line of the user event scripts was **return 0**.

Triggering an Event

Events that are mapped to regular event IDs trigger their event handler automatically whenever they occur. For example, clicking on a command button automatically executes the script written for its **Clicked** event (**pbm_bnclicked** event ID). However, there are times when you'll want to trigger an event programmatically. Let's say you want to trigger the **Sort** event in a DataWindow control when the user selects the ue_sort option from the DataWindow's pop-up menu. To do this, you need to use the **TriggerEvent** function, which has the following syntax:

> **ObjectName.TriggerEvent(Event, { WordParm }, { LongParm })**

The **WordParm** and **LongParm** arguments are optional. Note that to trigger predefined events, you need to use enumerated data types. All predefined events are defined as enumerated data types. For example, there's an enumerated data type **Close!** for the **Close** event, **Activate!** for the **Activate** event, and so on. The following examples trigger the **Close** and **Activate** events for the **w_test** window:

```
Int li_retstat
li_retstat = w_test.TriggerEvent( Close! )
If li_retstat <> 1 Then
     //Error handling ...
End If

li_retstat = w_test.TriggerEvent( Activate! )
If li_retstat <> 1 Then
     //Error handling ...
End If
```

If you're triggering a user-defined event, you need to use the event name in quotations. The following example triggers the **ue_save** and **ue_retrieve** events for the **w_test** window:

```
Int li_retstat
li_retstat = w_test.TriggerEvent( "ue_save" )
If li_retstat <> 1 Then
     //Error handling ...
End If

li_retstat = w_test.TriggerEvent( "ue_retrieve" )
If li_retstat <> 1 Then
     //Error handling ...
End If
```

If the specified event's script executes successfully, **TriggerEvent** returns **1**. If there's no script or the event specified isn't valid (say you forgot to define the event or misspelled the event name whilst specifying it as the function argument), the return value will be **-1**. It's always worth checking this return value.

TriggerEvent executes synchronously, which means that it executes immediately. The command that follows will not execute until it has completed execution.

39

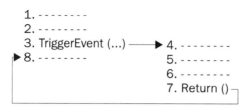

> If you want to execute an event asynchronously, you should use the
> **PostEvent** function which we'll look at in just a moment.

As you saw in the syntax, you can also send parameters to the event in **TriggerEvent**. These
parameters are stored in the message object—in the **Message.StringParm** and
Message.LongParm members.

Note that you can only pass two parameters to an event through this function. Another
disadvantage is that you can't trap the return value of the event. The value it returns is the
success of the function call, not the code returned in the event script.

An Alternative to TriggerEvent

Powerbuilder 5.0 offers an additional syntax for executing events and functions. Even though
Powersoft makes the point that this new syntax isn't a replacement but only an enhancement of
the old syntax, this is probably an understatement. After a while, you'll find that the new format
provides all the functionality of the previous one, with the addition of a number of important
enhancements. We've already looked at this new syntax when we were discussing functions:

```
{ObjectName.}{Type}  {CallType}  {When}  Function/Event  Name
                                           ({ ArgumentList})
```

The default behavior is to execute a function , but you can execute an event by specifying **EVENT**
as the **Type**. The **CallType** indicates whether it's a static or dynamic event (we'll explain these
in a moment) and **When** indicates whether you want to trigger or post the function or event. You
need to specify parentheses after the function or event name, just as you do when you call a
function. The following lines both trigger the **ue_save** event at the window:

```
Parent.Event Trigger ue_save()
Parent.Event ue_save()
```

The return value for **TriggerEvent** is always an integer, but the return value for this new syntax
depends on the return value type declared in the called function or event. So, if the event returns
a string value, you need to assign the return value to a string variable. It's good practice to check
the return value, but assigning it isn't mandatory.

```
String ls_status
ls_status =     Parent.EVENT STATIC TRIGGER ue_SendToMainFrame()
ls_status =     Parent.EVENT TRIGGER ue_SendToMainFrame()
Parent.EVENT STATIC TRIGGER ue_SendToMainFrame()
Parent.EVENT TRIGGER ue_SendToMainFrame()
```

All the above statements are correct. There's only the one limitation—the return value expression shouldn't return an array. **CallType** is static by default, which means the compiler checks for the presence of the calling function or event and its return value at compile time. If the function or event doesn't exist, or the assigned return value is incorrect, the compiler will generate an error.

Triggering Events Dynamically

Sometimes, the functions or events don't exist at compile time. Take the example of the generic function shown here. We've highlighted the important lines:

```
Window iWindow
datawindow l_dw
integer    li_NoOfControls, li_Counter, li_RetStatus

li_NoOfControls = UpperBound(iWindow.Control[])

For li_Counter = 1 to li_NoOfControls
      Choose Case iWindow.Control[ li_Counter ].TypeOf()
    Case DataWindow!
       l_dw = iWindow.Control[ li_Counter ]
       If ( l_dw.ModifiedCount()+ l_dw.DeletedCount() > 0 ) Then
            li_RetStatus = l_dw.Event DYNAMIC ue_PreSave()
          If li_RetStatus <> 0 Then Return -100
          li_RetStatus = l_dw.Update( True )
          l_dw.Event DYNAMIC ue_PostSave()
          If li_RetStatus <> 0 Then Return -100
       End If
    Case Else
       // Other code
    End Choose
Next

Return 0
```

This function saves all the DataWindows in the given window. It executes the **ue_presave** event for a DataWindow before it saves it and calls the **ue_postsave** event after it has saved it. We expect the DataWindow in the passed window to have both of these events at run time, so we can use the **DYNAMIC** keyword. This tells the compiler not to check for the existence of the named function until run time. If you tried compiling this code without the **DYNAMIC** keyword, you'd get two 'Unknown function' error messages.

If you're using the **DYNAMIC** keyword and the event *doesn't* exist at run time, the compiler won't generate an error that aborts the application. Instead it will return **-1** as the return value. So, again, make sure you check for return values.

Cascaded Functions and Events

One of the nicer new features available in PowerBuilder 5.0 is the introduction of **cascaded functions calls**, where the return value of one function or event becomes the object for the following call. An example of this syntax is:

Func1_ReturnsObject( ).Func2_ReturnsObject( ).Func3_ReturnsAnything( )

This syntax allows you to make nested function or event calls. In this situation, the return value of the first function or event must be an object, which becomes the object upon which the second function or event acts. The following example calculates the production for different types of machines:

```
// instance variables
Int      ii_hours
Int      ii_YarnType

NonVisualObject          lnc_object
nc_MachineObject         lnc_MachObj
Long                     li_Prod

lnc_MachObj = Create nc_MachineObject

// get an instance of the object
lnc_object  = lnc_MachObj.of_GetObject ( )

//call a function in the user object using the local instance
li_Prod = lnc_object.FUNCTION DYNAMIC of_GetProd (iValue)
if ( li_Prod < 1 ) then
        //Error Checking
end if

Destroy lnc_MachObj
```

When the **of_GetObject** function of the user object **nc_MachineObject** is called, it returns an instance of an appropriate user object, depending on the additional processing performed in the object. The second function, **of_GetProd**, which resides in the object selected by the first process, returns a result based on the parameters supplied.

The following code does exactly the same thing, but this time using nested function calls:

```
// instance variables
int      ii_hours
String ii_YarnType

nc_MachineObject         lnc_MachObj
Long                     li_Prod

lnc_MachObj = Create nc_MachineObject

// get an instance of the object
// and call a function using the returned instance
li_Prod = lnc_MachObj.FUNCTION DYNAMIC of_GetObj().of_GetProd( iValue )

If li_Prod = 0 Then
    // Error handling
End If

Destroy lnc_MachObj
```

Notice that we've used the **FUNCTION** and **DYNAMIC** keywords in this example. The **FUNCTION** keyword is introduced to tell PowerBuilder that we are going to call a function at run time. The **DYNAMIC** keyword is required because the function reference doesn't exist until an instance is returned from the **of_GetObject** function.

However, there's a problem with this second example: there's no way you can check whether the returned object is valid. So, make sure you check for the valid object and carry out any error handling in the called objects.

Using the **DYNAMIC** keyword for the first function or event from the left means that it will apply to all subsequent nested function or event calls. If you want to post the function or event call, you can do so only in the last function or event call.

Does TriggerEvent Really Trigger an Event?

When you use **TriggerEvent**, PowerBuilder executes the script for the specified event, but does this mean that **TriggerEvent** is really triggering the event? Let's look at a simple window **Close** event. When we trigger this event, we expect the window to close, but is this what happens? When we call **TriggerEvent**, PowerBuilder puts the message at the top of its internal message queue and then executes. It doesn't place the message in the Windows message queue. To really close the window, we need to call **Send** to send the close message to Windows. This is the syntax:

Send(Handle, MessageNo, LowWord, Long)

Handle is the handle of the window to which you want to send the message. You can get the handle of the window by calling the **Handle** function. The **MessageNo** is the Windows message number. For example, the following code in the **Clicked** event of a command button sends the close message to Windows and closes the parent window:

```
Send ( Handle( Parent ), 16, 0, 0 )
```

This triggers the window's **Close** event, which in turn triggers the **CloseQuery** event. If the **CloseQuery** event executes successfully, PowerBuilder executes the **Close** event script and closes the window.

All the Windows messages are listed in the **Winuser.h** header file which comes with Watcom C++ and other C++ compilers. The entry for **WM_CLOSE** looks like this:

```
#define WM_CLOSE                    0x0010
```

Converting this number from hexadecimal to decimal gives you 16, which is our message number. You can use Watcom's **Wspy.exe** utility to view all the messages that occur when an event is called.

Posting an Event

If you want to execute an event asynchronously (i.e. you don't need the current script to wait for the execution of the posted event to be completed), you can use the **PostEvent** function. Its syntax is the same as **TriggerEvent**:

```
ObjectName.PostEvent( Event, { WordParm }, { LongParm } )
```

A good example of where this can be used is when you want to open a window containing a DataWindow. You can populate the DataWindow in the **Open** event of the window, but this means a delay in the opening of the window, so you can use **PostEvent** to populate the DataWindow while the window opens.

When PowerBuilder encounters **PostEvent**, it simply posts the message in PowerBuilder's internal object message queue and starts executing the next command after the **PostEvent** function call. When all the messages before the posted message in the message queue have been executed, PowerBuilder executes the event specified in the **PostEvent** function. Typically, this event is executed at the end of the current script, though this isn't guaranteed. When it's executed depends on the messages pending in the message queue. In summary, the current script doesn't wait for the results of the event script execution specified in the **PostEvent** function call.

```
//Event:: Window Open Event
1. Dw_master.SetTransObject(SQLCA)
2. PostEvent(This, "ue_retrieve")
3. CheckMenuOptions()
                                        //Event:: ue_retrieve
                                   ──▶ 4. dw_master.Retrieve()
                                        5.   Return()
```

As we explained earlier, you can post events or functions with the new v5.0 syntax. Just use the **POST** keyword in place of **When**:

{ObjectName.}{Type} {CallType} {POST} Function/Event Name
({ ArgumentList})

Remember, the **PostEvent** function and the **POST** keyword simply execute the script for the specified event. To actually make the events happen, you can use the **Post** function in the same way that we explained earlier with the **Send** function.

You can see an example of using **TriggerEvent** and **PostEvent** in the **oop_pb_impl** application in **Ch02.pbl**.

Variables and Scoping

By default, all numeric variables are initialized to zero at declaration time, unless you give them a specific value. A string variable is initialized to zero length (i.e. **""**). Although you can store up to 60000 characters in a string variable, at declaration time it won't occupy that much space. When you assign it a value, its length is determined by the length of the value you specify.

You can declare PowerBuilder objects as variables in the same way you can with traditional data types. For example, the following code declares a window variable and a user object variable:

```
Window lWindow
uo_datawindow lDataWindow
```

When you declare a variable in an event script, it's destroyed as soon as the script completes execution. In other words, variables you declare in an event or function script are **local**. In PowerScript, a variable can have one of four levels of scope: local, instance, shared or global. The scope of a variable determines the areas of an application from which it can be accessed.

Scope of Variable	Description
Local	These variables are only available in the declared script and can't be accessed by any other script or function. They are destroyed when the script or function completes execution.
Instance	Each instance of an object has its own set of instance variables. They are available to all object level scripts and functions and they are destroyed when the instance is destroyed.
Shared	These variables are available to all object level scripts and functions. They are shared among instances of an object and remain in memory even after the last instance of an object is destroyed. These variables aren't available to an object's descendants.
Global	These are available to all scripts and functions in an application and are only destroyed when the application execution is over.

To declare variables with levels of scope other than local, you need to select the appropriate scope from the Declare menu.

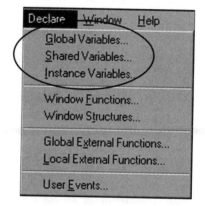

You might think it logical that in a descendant, a local variable would be available in the same event script as the ancestor, but you'd be wrong. Even though you can execute ancestor event scripts, ancestor and descendant event scripts are independent in that they don't have access to the local variables of other events and functions.

The content of an instance variable is independent in each instance of the object. In contrast, as the name suggests, a shared variable is shared among instances of the same object. You can't access a shared variable once you've closed all the instances of an object, but its value persists in memory. This means that when another instance is created, the value of the previous instance is carried forward into the new instance. Have a look at the **oop_pb_impl** application in **Ch02.pbl** to see how this works.

You can declare a global variable and a local variable with the same name. In earlier versions of PowerBuilder, you couldn't access a global variable in a script where there was a local variable with the same name. However, in this situation in Version 5.0, you receive an informational message from the compiler and you can access the global variable by using the double colon symbol (::).

In contrast, if you declare an instance and a global variable with the same name, referring to that name without a prefix means that you'll be referencing the global variable. To access the instance variable, you need to use the **This** keyword. The following snippets of code summarize these distinctions:

```
// Global and instance variable are declared with the same name.
This.var1 = 100        // Sets instance variable
var1 = 100             // Sets global variable
::var1 = 100           // Sets global variable
```

```
// Global, instance and local variable are declared with the same name.
This.var1 = 100        // Sets instance variable
var1 = 100             // Sets local variable
::var1 = 100           // Sets global variable
```

Access Levels: Instance Variables

Objects that are instantiated from the base classes support two types of variables: instance and shared. By default, these variables are accessible by other objects in an application, but you'll sometimes need to alter the availability of instance variables so that other objects can't change their values.

PowerBuilder provides **access levels** to solve this problem. You can define access to instance variables at three levels:

 Public

 Private

 Protected

> These user-defined access levels only apply to instance variables—other types of variables have access levels that you can't change.

Public, Private and Protected Access

These access keywords allow you to specify the visibility, or scope, of the properties and methods in the class.

A property or function declared with public access means that wherever the object is in scope, any code inside or outside the object can access that property or method. While public access might seem risky, you really need to allow the world outside the object to communicate with the object. You should use public access to define the **interface** to an object.

For instance, in the rapidly growing field of Windows ActiveX and Delphi VCL controls, these interfaces may be the only programming information you'll have on the object. When you buy a calendar ActiveX control, the documentation may only tell how to functionally use the object in an application and list a set of public interfaces to the control. We realize there must be many more properties and methods at work in the object, but they are hidden from us. Only the public interfaces are known.

If you do things properly, the hidden properties and methods aren't just undocumented, they're literally unavailable to you. The **Private** access keyword will ensure that no access is granted to a property or method from outside the object. Thus, even if the object is instantiated in your local script, there's nothing your code can do to alter the private properties or invoke the private methods of the object.

In a class definition, if you declare a property or method as protected, it means that only objects instantiated from that class or its descendants can access it.

An object instantiated from a descendant class can therefore access its own private and protected members and also its ancestor's protected members. This promotes reuse of code and enforces a common 'look and feel'. Note that if an ancestor wants exclusive control over a property or method, you can declare it to be private, in which case not even the descendants can mess with the data or invoke the function.

The following table summarizes the different types of access:

Access Level	Description
Public	Accessible by all objects in an application—this is the default access level for all user-defined objects. Global variables are always public.
Protected	Only accessible by that object and its descendant objects.
Private	Only accessible by other functions and scripts declared for the same object. Shared variables are always private.

Setting Access Rights

You set the levels of access for instance variables by specifying the keyword **Private** or **Protected** before the data type, for example:

```
Private Int ii_counter1, ii_counter2
```

Once you've specified an access level, all the variables that follow are assigned that access level until another access level is declared. So, in the following example, the first two variables are private, but the third is protected.

```
Private:
Int ii_counter1
Int ii_counter2

Protected:
Int ii_counter3
```

In PowerBuilder 5.0, the access level rules have been enhanced to give you more control over the protection of an object's data. The following table shows the additional restrictions that you can now apply to variables.

Modifier	Description
PrivateRead	Can only be read by the defining class.
PrivateWrite	Can only be modified by the defining class.
ProtectedRead	Can only be read by the defining class or its direct descendants.
ProtectedWrite	Can only be modified by the defining class or its direct descendants.

There's also a modified syntax to support these new restrictions:

{Visibility} {ReadAccess} {WriteAccess} <data type> <variable name>

Declaring a variable as **Protected PrivateRead PrivateWrite** effectively renders it invisible and prevents descendants from declaring the same variable. If you do try to declare an instance variable with the same name in a descendant, PowerBuilder will give you a compiler error:

Information C0148: The identifier 'i_test' conflicts with an existing property with this name. The new definition of 'i_test' will take precedence and the prior value will be ignored until this version of 'i_test' goes out of scope

It won't prevent you from saving the declaration, but if you try to read the variable in the descendant scripts, you'll see this error message:

Error C0158: The property "i_test" was found in class "w_parent", but insufficient rights are available to access it

If you try to modify the variable in the descendant scripts, you'll get the following error:

Error C0143: This property can only be modified by an event or function in its parent class

One word of warning to note is that you can declare *and* initialize an instance variable at the descendant level. Also, if the variable was assigned only **PrivateWrite** access in the ancestor, the new value that you assign it in the descendant *will* take affect. For example, suppose you declared the following instance variable at the ancestor level,

```
// Ancestor
Protected PrivateWrite int i_test = 100
```

and defined the same instance variable at the descendant level as follows:

```
// Descendant
/* You will get an informational message, but this won't prevent you from making
the declaration. */
i_test = 200
```

If you do this, you'll get a compiler error but won't be prevented from saving the declaration, so if you then use the variable in some script, the new value will be used. For example, the following code would display a message box with the value 200:

```
// In the script
// The MessageBox() displays 200
MessageBox( "Value in descendant", i_test )
```

The following table summarizes the possible combinations of scope and modifier:

	Visibility Modifier		
Read/Write Modifier	**Public**	**Protected**	**Private**
ProtectedRead	✓	✗	✗
ProtectedWrite	✓	✗	✗
PrivateRead	✓	✓	✗
PrivateWrite	✓	✓	✗

Access Levels: Functions

PowerBuilder allows you to declare two types of function: global and object. A function automatically becomes global when it's declared in the Function Painter. A global function is always public. To declare a function at the object level, you select <Object> Functions... from the Declare menu in the relevant painter. You can specify access levels for object functions in the function declaration dialog box, as shown here:

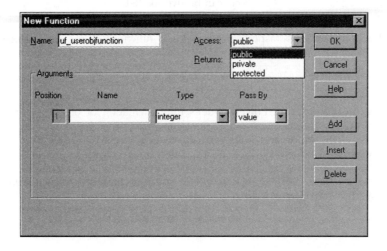

It makes sense that you can't specify read/write modifiers for functions.

Choosing between Events and Functions

We've spent some time discussing the various ways that PowerBuilder communicates between objects, the various ways it passes variables and how you can control the scope of variables in events and functions. We'll finish off the chapter with a table that highlights the differences between events and functions:

Event	Function
Executing a non-existent event returns a null value.	Executing a non-existent function generates an error that you need to take care of in the error handling.
An event is always public and can be called by any object.	You can specify access levels for a function.
You have the option of extending or overriding an event script in a descendant object.	Declaring the same function with the same interface in a descendant object always overrides the ancestor function.
Calling an event starts a search from the ancestor down to the object where it's called from.	Searching order for unqualified names follows this order: Global external functions Global functions Local external functions Object level functions (calling a function starts searching from the descendant upwards) System function
Events can't be overloaded.	Functions can be overloaded.

We'll look in detail at many of these aspects of events and functions in the coming chapters.

Summary

In this chapter, we've broadly covered PowerBuilder's implementation of object orientation and seen how objects communicate with each other using events and functions. We've also looked at how variables are passed between objects and how you can control access to variables by defining scope and access levels. We finished off with a look at the differences between events and functions.

In the next chapter, we'll take a detailed look at one of the foundations of object-oriented programming in PowerBuilder: user objects.

User Objects

PowerBuilder provides 'property and behavior rich' classes and controls, such as DataWindows, command buttons, transaction objects, single line edits, etc. The functionality that these classes provide can be extended or overridden by adding attributes and behaviors and building custom classes called **user objects**, which can be shared throughout a system, promoting code reuse.

PowerBuilder broadly classifies user objects into two categories: **class** and **visual**. As you would expect, class objects (or non-visual objects) have no visual properties or behaviors, whereas visual user objects have visual properties and behaviors.

User objects are one of the mainstays of object-oriented programming in PowerBuilder, so, in this chapter, we'll look at both class and visual user objects, creating some useful objects that you can reuse in your own applications.

Class User Objects

Class or non-visual user objects are typically used to encapsulate some business logic that you want to make available in your applications. They can be further categorized into standard, custom or C++ objects.

Standard Class

Standard non-visual user objects extend or override the functionality of standard PowerBuilder non-visual objects. When you create a standard class user object, you are asked to select a standard PowerBuilder object from which you want to inherit functionality.

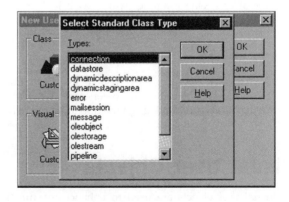

These are typically used for handling database connections, errors, e-mail interfaces and OLE connections. We'll look in detail at creating a couple of these later in the chapter and then discuss the OLE objects in later chapters.

When you create a standard class user object, it has access to all the properties and behaviors of the object it's derived from. PowerBuilder provides default global variables of the types **transaction**, **dynamicdescriptionarea**, **dynamicstagingarea**, **error** and **message**. You can replace the class of these global variables with any non-visual user object derived from the default classes. These variables are set in the properties sheet of the Application painter:

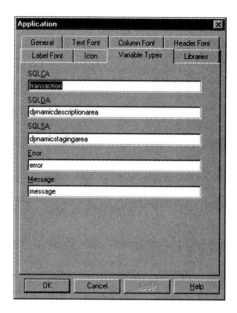

So, for example, we could create a standard class user object to handle errors in our application and, by substituting the name of our user object for the Message variable in the application's properties, any errors in the application would be handled by our user object, rather than the PowerBuilder system object.

Custom Class

Custom class user objects are derived from the PowerBuilder non-visual object. Non-visual objects provide an empty shell for abstracting and encapsulating various non-interface functionality. They are typically used to provide libraries of utility functions and to control the operation of other class user objects. One example (which we'll look at later in the chapter) is a database transaction manager.

C++ Class

C++ class user objects allow you to use DLLs and C++ code to provide functionality which requires greater speed than Powerscript itself can provide. These are typically used to do heavy number crunching and graphics operations, where the C++ code gives better performance than Powerscript. We'll look in detail at C++ user objects in the next chapter.

Visual User Objects

Visual user objects are used to enhance the functionality of common PowerBuilder visual controls or controls available from third parties. They can be further categorized into standard, custom and external.

Standard Visual

Standard visual user objects are derived from standard visual PowerBuilder controls. When you create a standard visual user object, you select which control you want to inherit functionality from.

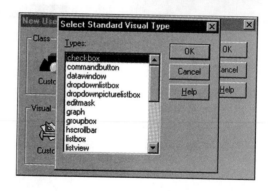

These are used to extend the functionality of the standard controls and add functionality specific to your needs.

> In the Window painter, you can customize the PainterBar or create a completely new toolbar to display all your standard visual user objects so that you can simply drag-and-drop them onto your windows.

Custom Visual

Custom visual user objects are user objects created by aggregating multiple controls or user objects to provide the desired functionality. Similar to standard visual user objects, you can use them as controls on windows or other custom user objects.

As an example, a common requirement in database applications is the need to scroll through records forwards, backwards, to the first record and to the last record. You could create this as a custom visual user object consisting of four command buttons with the required functionality:

You can then drop this user object on your windows when you need this functionality.

External User Objects

PowerBuilder is an open development environment and allows easy integration of external objects and controls. External visual user objects are derived from custom controls created as Windows DLLs. This means that you can integrate visual controls developed in other languages in your PowerBuilder applications. By creating a user object, you can extend the functionality of these controls as well as provide other objects with an interface to them.

The properties, methods and events of external user objects aren't available in the User Object painter, so you need to be familiar with them before you can create a user object. You have to specify the class name of the control when you select the DLL file.

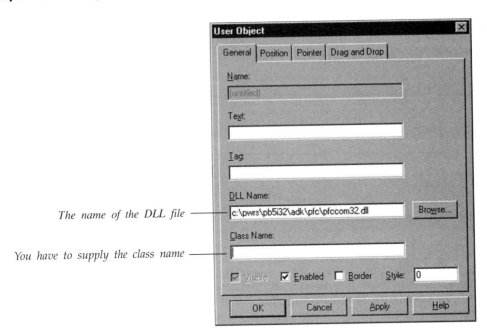

The name of the DLL file ——————

You have to supply the class name ——————

You can create custom events, functions, instance variables, etc., for this user object just as for any other user object.

VBX and OCX User Objects

VBXs are controls created around Microsoft's Visual Basic development tool. There remains a wealth of robust and appealing third party VBX controls on the market and if you install the 16-bit version of PowerBuilder 5.0, you still have the option of creating VBX user objects.

VBXs are not supported in the 32-bit version of PowerBuilder 5.0 for Windows 95 and Windows NT but there *is* support for **OCXs**, the 32-bit version of VBXs and recently renamed by Microsoft as **ActiveX** controls. Many quality VBXs have now been ported to OCX (or ActiveX) format. Although OCX doesn't appear as an option in the New User Object dialog box, they can be simply created using standard and custom visual objects. We'll look at these in detail in Chapter 6.

Good User Object Design

Using poorly designed user objects in an application is worse than not using any user objects at all! You should ensure that the user objects you design are generic and scaleable so that they can easily adapt to change. They should be easily portable across different modules in your application, as well as across different applications. A functional enhancement or requirement change shouldn't require unnecessary re-engineering of the object.

To design a good user object you have to have a good understanding of object-oriented topics, as well as the application and interpretation of these concepts in the PowerBuilder environment. Let's revisit some object-oriented concepts and review them in the context of designing good user objects.

Encapsulation

User objects should be well encapsulated with properties and functions correctly scoped as public, private or protected. The objects should have a well-defined interface for other objects to access their properties, states and behaviors. For example, if you have an object with a variable **var1** which can be addressed by other objects, you would define two functions:

 f_getVar1 to return its value.

 f_setVar1 to initialize it.

User objects should be provided with an initializing function if they need their properties to be initialized when they're instantiated.

Standard user objects have all the functions and properties of the ancestor object. You can create additional functions and properties and appropriately scope them.

Custom user objects, on the other hand, have a limited basic set of events, properties and functions. It's up to the architect to do a good job in encapsulating the functionality and providing a good interface to it. Visual custom user objects are more complex to construct than class custom user objects because they constitute interface components and users interact with them.

Polymorphism

You can design polymorphic behavior into user objects by using functions and events. Version 5.0 of PowerBuilder allows true function overloading, enabling you to implement polymorphic behavior using functions. The dot notation semantic of invoking functions enforces strong typing. In Version 5.0, this is no longer a limitation because functions can be triggered and posted like events. Triggering a function invokes it immediately, whereas posting a function puts it in the object's message queue and it gets executed when pending messages have been processed. With this new feature, user objects support implementation of polymorphic behavior through both subclassing and subtyping.

You can also implement polymorphic behavior in user objects using events. The biggest difference between events and functions is that events can be extended at the descendant level, whereas functions cannot. Events can also be completely overridden at the descendant level. Implementing polymorphic behavior in custom visual user objects requires a good design because objects inherited from them have access to events at the user object level and not to events of controls that constitute it.

We can illustrate this with an example.

Say we design a custom user object which has two DataWindows. The user can double-click on the left DataWindow, **dw_left**, and move the selected row to the DataWindow on the right, **dw_right**, and vice versa.

Now, suppose we have a constraint that some business logic has to be satisfied before a row can be moved. This business logic will be implemented in the control derived from this user object. The object inherited from this user object won't have access to the **doubleClicked** events of either DataWindow. We'll have to provide two custom events, **dwLeftDblClk** and **dwRightDblClk**, in the user object to provide the inherited control access to the **doubleClicked** events of both the DataWindows. We'll also need to provide two additional events, **dwLeftBusChk** and **dwRightBusChk**, to check the business logic.

In its **doubleClicked** event, the DataWindow on the left, **dw_left**, should first trigger the event **dwLeftBusChk** and then the event **dwLeftDblClk**:

```
----
----
parent.triggerEvent("dwLeftBusChk")
----
----
parent.triggerEvent("dwLeftDblChk")
```

The DataWindow on the right, **dw_right**, should first trigger the event **dwRightBusChk** and then the event **dwRightDblClk** in its **doubleClicked** event:

```
----
----
parent.triggerEvent("dwRightBusChk")
----
----
parent.triggerEvent("dwRightDblChk")
```

Controls derived from this user object can now extend the double-clicked behavior of either DataWindow and implement their own specific business rules.

Inheritance

You can create an object hierarchy by inheriting from existing user objects to create new ones. The user objects that you inherit from should be well constructed. They shouldn't be overly complex and should have a flexible interface. The classes that you build should be good abstractions and they should implement behavior that you can easily extend. Overriding functions and events in an ancestor is a sign of a poor abstraction and inflexible design. If you have to override any functions or events at the descendant level, you should re-examine the design of the object.

User Object Examples

We've looked at the various types of user objects that you can create and highlighted some of the characteristics of well-designed user objects. Let's put this theory into practice now by creating a range of different types of user objects which can be reused in your applications. Each of these is provided in the **Ch03.pbl** on the disk. There is also an application there (**userobj**) which illustrates how some of them can be used.

Database Transaction User Object

This user object will encapsulate functionality to perform database connections and transactions. You're probably familiar with the idea of storing database connection parameters in an **INI** file that you can distribute with your applications. You can then query this **INI** file using the **Profilestring** function and fill in a login window when users log into a database. We'll use the same idea for our user object, encapsulating this functionality in the object and adding other functionality to handle the database connection and beginning, committing and rolling back database transactions.

This is the **nvo_transaction** user object in the **Ch03.pbl** library. If you open up the user object, you'll see that it has no visual components and indeed it isn't possible to add any visual components to it because the Controls menu is completely grayed out.

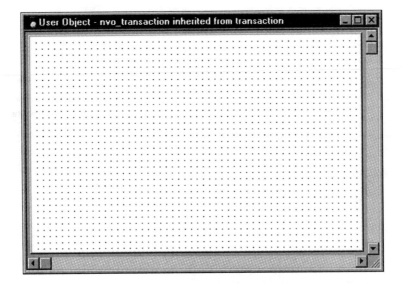

All the functions that we want the database to perform are coded as user object functions:

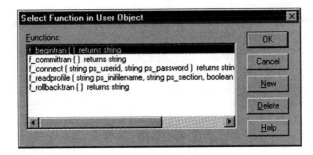

We'll look at each of these in turn.

Reading Database Connection Parameters

This is the **f_readProfile** function. The **INI** file name and the section name in the **INI** file are the two parameters required, both of which are passed by value. The function returns **0** if it succeeds and **−1** if there is an error.

```
/****************************************************/
function:        f_readProfile
parameters:      ps_IniFileName        string
                 ps_section            string
                 pb_autoCommit         boolean
return value:    0                     success
                 -1                    failure
/****************************************************/
setPointer(HourGlass!)
int li_rc
//set the attributes of the transaction object
this.database = profileString(ps_IniFileName, ps_section, "database", "")
this.serverName = profileString(ps_IniFileName, ps_section, "serverName", "")
//check for valid attributes
if this.database = "" or this.serverName = "" then
    li_rc = -1
else
    //set the dbms and the autocommit mode
    this.dbms = "Sybase"
    this.autoCommit = pb_autoCommit
end if
return li_rc
```

The code simply reads the database and server name values from the **INI** file, using the **profilestring** function. If values are found, it sets the **dbms** value to "Sybase" and sets **autocommit** to true or false, depending on the value passed to the function.

You could easily adapt this code to handle ODBC database connections or other server connections, such as Oracle or SQL Server.

Connecting to a Database

The **f_connect** function establishes the connection to the database. This function requires two parameters specifying the user name and the password of the database user. Both the parameters are passed by value and the function returns either an empty string or an error message. The script for this function is as follows:

```
/****************************************************/
function:        f_connect
parameters:      ps_userID             string
                 ps_passWord           string
return value:    ''                    success
                 ls_errMsg             failure
/****************************************************/
setPointer(hourGlass!)
string ls_errMsg
//set the 1D and the PassWord
this.logID = ps_userID
this.logPass = ps_passWord
//connect to the database
connect using this ;
//check the return code
if this.sqlCode <> 0 then
        ls_errMsg = this.sqlErrText
end if
return ls_errMsg
```

Beginning, Committing and Rolling Back a Transaction

The three other functions—**f_beginTran**, **f_commitTran** and **f_rollbackTran**—all return an empty string or an error message if an error occurs. These functions are implemented using the first format of dynamic SQL—**Execute immediate "A SQL string"**

The script for the function **f_beginTran**, which starts a database unit of work, is as follows:

```
/******************************************************/
function:        f_beginTran
parameters:      <NONE>
return value:    ''              success
                 ls_errMsg       failure
/******************************************************/
setPointer(HourGlass!)
string ls_errText
//begin the transaction
execute immediate "begin transaction" using this ;
if this.errCode = -1 then
   ls_errText = this.sqlErrText
end if
return ls_errText
```

The script of the function **f_commitTran**, which applies changes to the database since the beginning of the current unit of work, is:

```
/******************************************************
function:        f_commitTran
parameters:      <NONE>
return value:    ''              success
                 ls_errMsg       failure
******************************************************/
setPointer(HourGlass!)
string ls_errText
//commit the transaction
execute immediate "commit transaction" using this ;
if this.sqlCode = -1 then
   ls_errText = this.sqlErrText
end if
return ls_errText
```

The script of the function **f_rollbackTran**, which rolls back a database unit of work, is:

```
/******************************************************
function:        f_rollbackTran
parameters:      <NONE>
return value:    ''              success
                 ls_errMsg       failure
******************************************************/
setPointer(HourGlass!)
string ls_errText
//rollback the transaction
execute immediate "rollback transaction" using this ;
if this.sqlCode = -1 then
```

```
      ls_errText = this.sqlErrText
   end if
   return ls_errText
```

> PowerBuilder automatically issues a 'begin transaction' command to the database and begins a database unit of work if the **autoCommit** property of the transaction object is set to true. If it is, you only have to program logic to end the unit of work—to rollback or commit the transaction based on its failure or success. You have to build logic to start and end the database unit of work only if the **autoCommit** property of the transaction object is set to false.

You can use this object to establish all the database connections in your application to a Sybase SQL Server database. It's well encapsulated and insulates objects in your application from accessing its connection attributes and using dynamic SQL to begin and end database transactions. It has a simple interface which other objects in your application can use to access the functionality provided by **nvo_transaction**. You can make this object sophisticated enough to be used in establishing multiple database connections, as well as connecting to various database engines.

To use the transaction object to handle database connections, you would simply replace the SQLCA global variable **transaction** with **nvo_transaction** in the application properties.

Reference Data Cache User Object

The datastore object is a new feature in PowerBuilder 5.0; it's a DataWindow without any visual properties or behaviors. It can be effectively used to cache data in memory.

There are many instances in database applications where the same set of reference data is used in different reports. In previous versions of PowerBuilder, you could implement an invisible DataWindow control on a window to maintain that dataset. But remember, the DataWindow is a visual control with a large footprint and it can only exist as a control on a window or a custom visual user object. Also, you can instantiate it dynamically by using the **OpenUserObject** set of functions, which require a window as a holder. You can't instantiate it using the **Create** statement.

It's good practice to minimize database access in a client-server database application. This not only reduces network traffic, but also reduces utilization of database resources. You can improve the performance of database queries by reducing the number of joins required in building the result data set. These issues can be addressed by caching static data in your application and by reusing the same data set wherever required.

We've constructed a datastore user object to cache all the reference data in an application. This is the **nvo_referencedata** user object in the **Ch03.pbl** library. This object will retrieve all the reference data in the format: code type, code value, decode.

First, we constructed an external DataWindow, **d_reference_data**, with three columns:

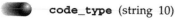 **code_type** (string 10)

code_value (string 20)

decode (string 50)

We then attached this DataWindow object to the user object.

The user object should have functions to provide other objects with code values and decodes for a particular code type. It should also have the ability to report errors.

The function that provides all code values and decodes for a particular code type should either provide the data as a tab-delimited string or accept a DataWindow as a parameter and directly copy the data into it. The first format of the function **f_getReferenceData**, in which it returns a tab-delimited string (**code_type~tcode_value~tdecode**), is:

```
/*****************************************************
function:        f_getReferenceData
parameters:      ps_codeType       string value
                 ps_refData        string ref
return value:    0 or number of rows
                 -1                failure
*****************************************************/
setPointer(HourGlass!)
string ls_data
long ll_rows
//set the filter
if setFilter("code_type='" + ps_codeType + "'") = 1 then
   if Filter() = 1 then
      //get the rows
      ll_rows = rowCount()
      if ll_rows > 0 then
         //get the data
         ps_refData = describe("datawindow.Data")
      end if
   else
      ll_rows = -1
   end if
else
   ll_rows = -1
end if

return ll_rows
```

The second format of the function accepts a DataWindow as a parameter and sets the data directly in it. The script of this function is:

```
/*****************************************************
function:        f_getReferenceData
parameters:      ps_parmType            string value
                 pdw_TargetDataWindow   target dw value
return value:    0 or number of rows
                 -1                failure
*****************************************************/
setPointer(HourGlass!)
string ls_data
long ll_rows
//set the filter
if setFilter("code_type='" + ps_ParmType + "'") = 1 then
   if Filter() = 1 then
      //get the rows
```

```
            ll_rows = rowCount()
            if ll_rows > 0 then
                //get the data
                if THIS.RowsCopy (1, ll_rows, Primary!, pdw_TargetDataWindow, &
                    pdw_targetDataWindow.rowCount() + 1, Primary!) = -1 then
                    ll_rows = -1
                end if
            end if
        else
            ll_rows = -1
        end if
    else
        ll_rows = -1
    end if

    return ll_rows
```

From the scripts shown above, it's obvious that the function **f_getReferenceData** is overloaded—it will behave differently depending on the parameters passed to it.

nvo_referencedata requires a script in the **dbError** event to report errors encountered while retrieving data from the database. The script in the **dberror** event is:

```
/******************************************************
script:            dberror
parameters:        sqlDbCode    long
                   sqlErrText   string
                   sqlSyntax    string
                   buffer       dwBuffer
                   row          long
return value:      0
                   1
******************************************************/
setPointer(hourGlass!)
string ls_errMsg
//report the error
ls_errMsg = "Error number: " + string(sqldbCode) + "~r~n" + &
            "SQL: " + sqlSyntax + "~r~n" + &
            " Error: " + sqlErrText
MessageBox("Database Error", ls_errMsg)
//suppress the system message
return 1
```

You can instantiate the user object, **nvo_referenceData**, as a global in your application if objects in different modules need access to reference data that it caches. This user object also insulates your application from the physical implementation of reference tables in your database.

Database Transaction Manager

If your application connects to only one database, you can instantiate **nvo_transaction** globally. All objects in your application can use that global instance for all database activity. But what if your application has to connect to multiple databases?

In an object-oriented application, you should create a 'database transaction manager' to encapsulate functionality to create and initialize multiple instances of **nvo_transaction**. All objects in your application should use methods of the database transaction manager object to access a transaction object. This insulates objects in your application from the implementation details of how the application establishes multiple database connections.

The database transaction manager should have methods to initialize all database connections, disconnect all or a particular database connection and provide access to a transaction object for a particular database connection to a requesting object. You shouldn't have to hard-code database transaction objects in your application. Objects shouldn't directly reference transaction objects in **nvo_transaction** to connect to a particular database. The database transaction manager should be sophisticated enough to allow the objects in your application to be able to access a 'physical' transaction object by providing a 'logical' reference to it.

This is the custom class user object **nvo_transManager**. We've created a structure **st_transaction** to associate physical transaction objects with their logical names and defined an array of the type **st_transaction** as a private instance variable, **ist_transaction[]**.

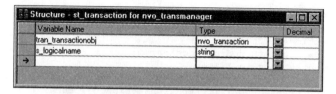

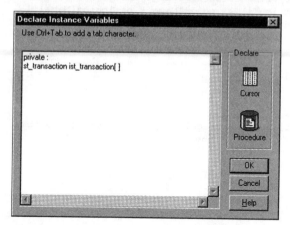

There are three functions declared, one of which is overloaded:

- **f_createTransactionObj** to initialize all database connections.

- **f_getTransObj**, which returns the physical transaction object for a specified logical connection.

- **f_disconnect**, which disconnects either all database connections or a specific database connection if a parameter is passed to it.

f_createTransactionObj

The parameters to this function include the name of the **INI** file which defines the connection parameters, the names of all the sections in the **INI** which define the connection parameters, the corresponding logical name for each connection, the user name and password, a flag to configure the **autocommit** attribute of each connection and a variable passed by reference indicating the error message if an error is encountered. The script of this function is:

```
/*****************************************************
script:              f_createTransactionObj
parameters:          ps_iniFile              string
                     ps_section[ ]           string
                     ps_logicalName[ ]       string
                     ps_userName             string
                     ps_password             string
                     pb_autoCommit[ ]        boolean
                     ps_errMsg               string ref
return value:        0                       success
                     -1                      error
*****************************************************/
setPointer(HourGlass!)
int li_numConnections, i, li_rc
li_numConnections = upperBound(ps_section)
for i = li_numConnections to 1 Step -1
    ist_transaction[i].tran_transactionObj = create nvo_transaction
    if isValid(ist_transaction[i].tran_transactionObj) then
        ist_transaction[i].s_logicalName = ps_logicalName[i]
        if ist_transaction[i].tran_transactionObj.f_readprofile(ps_inifile, &
ps_section[i], pb_autocommit[i]) = -1 then
            li_rc = -1
            ps_errMsg = "Could not initialize database connection: " + &
ps_logicalName[i]
            exit
        else
            ps_errMsg = &
ist_transaction[i].tran_transactionObj.f_connect(ps_userName, ps_password)
            if ps_errMsg <> "" then
                li_rc = -1
                exit
            end if
        end if
    else
        ps_errMsg = "Could not create transaction object for connection: "+ &
ps_logicalName[i]
        li_rc = -1
        exit
    end if
next

return li_rc
```

This function iterates over each element of the array **ps_section[]**. Each element represents a section in the **INI** file indicated by the variable **ps_iniFile**, which provides values used by a transaction object to connect to a database. This function also creates an instance of **nvo_transaction** in each iteration of the loop and invokes the method **f_readProfile** in each instance to initialize it from the appropriate section in the **INI** file.

f_getTransObj

The object **nvo_transManager** maintains a pool of transaction objects and encapsulates all database connections from application classes. Application classes can access a transaction object by invoking this method and passing the desired transaction object's logical tag.

The script for this function is:

```
/*****************************************************
script:             f_getTransObj
parameters:         ps_logicalName    string
                    ptran_transObj    nvo_transaction    ref
return value:       0                 success
                    -1                error
*****************************************************/

int li_numConnections, i, li_rc
boolean lb_transLocated
li_numConnections = upperBound(ist_Transaction)
for i = 1 to li_numConnections
    if Upper(ps_logicalName) = Upper(ist_transaction[i].s_logicalName) then
        lb_transLocated = TRUE
        ptran_transObj = ist_transaction[i].tran_TransactionObj
        exit
    end if
next

if not lb_transLocated then
    li_rc = -1
end if

return li_rc
```

f_disconnect

This function is overloaded so that it can either disconnect all database connections or disconnect a specified database connection. Here are both the flavors of the function:

```
/*****************************************************
script:             f_disconnect
parameters:         ps_errMsg    string ref
return value:       0            success
                    -1           error
*****************************************************/

setPointer(hourGlass!)
int li_numConnections, i, li_rc
li_numConnections = upperBound(ist_transaction)
for i = 1 to li_numConnections
    if isValid(ist_transaction[i].tran_transactionObj) then
        ist_transaction[i].tran_transactionObj.f_rollbackTran()
        disconnect using ist_transaction[i].tran_transactionObj ;
        if ist_transaction[i].tran_transactionObj.sqlcode <> 0 then
            ps_errMsg = ps_errMsg + "Error disconnecting transaction: " + &
ist_transaction[i].s_logicalName + " " + &
ist_transaction[i].tran_transactionObj.sqlErrText
```

```
                li_rc = -1
            exit
        else
            destroy ist_transaction[i].tran_transactionObj
        end if
    end if
next

return li_rc


/****************************************************
function:        f_disconnect
parameters:      ps_logicalName      string
                 ps_errMsg           string ref
return value:    0                   success
                 1                   error
****************************************************/
setPointer(hourGlass!)
nvo_transaction l_transaction
int li_rc
if f_getTransObj(ps_logicalName, l_transaction) = -1 then
    ps_errMsg = "Unable to reference transaction object for " + &
                    ps_logicalName
    li_rc = -1
else
    l_transaction.f_rollbackTran()
    disconnect using l_transaction ;
    if l_transaction.sqlcode <> 0 then
        ps_errMsg = "Error encountered while disconnecting " + &
            ps_logicalName + " " + l_transaction.sqlErrText
        li_rc = -1
    end if
end if

return li_rc
```

We've shown in this example how we were able to integrate an existing user object, **nvo_transaction**, with **nvo_transManager** and create a powerful database transaction manager.

Prompt for Save User Object

A common requirement in many database applications is a facility for the user to be prompted to save changes when a window is closed. We've built a custom class user object, **nvo_promptSave**, to provide this functionality.

The user object has just the one function, **f_promptSave**, which checks the DataWindow controls passed to it as parameters for unapplied changes. It prompts the user to save the unapplied changes and offers three options: Yes, No and Cancel.

```
/*********************************************************
function:           f_promptSave
parameters:         p_dwControl[]    datawindow
return value:       1 if user selected Yes
                    2 if user selected No
                    3 if user selected Cancel
                    -1 if an error occurs
*********************************************************/
setPointer(hourGlass!)
int li_rc, i, li_numDw, li_modCount, li_delCount
li_numDw = upperBound(p_dwControl)
for i = 1 to li_numDw
   li_modCount = p_dwControl[i].modifiedCount()
   li_delCount = p_dwControl[i].deletedCount()
   if li_modcount = -1 or li_delCount = -1 then
      li_rc = -1
      exit
   elseif li_modcount > 0 or li_delCount > 0 then
      li_rc = MessageBox("Save Changes", "Changes not saved, save changes now?", &
Question!, YesNoCancel!)
      exit
   end if
next

return li_rc
```

We'll explain integration of this object in a window in a later section.

DataWindow User Object

We've created a standard visual user object derived from a DataWindow. This is the **uo_DW** user object. We've added extra functionality which includes the ability to highlight a selected row, report database errors and prompt the user for confirmation whenever its **Update** method is invoked.

We've coded its **Clicked** event to select the clicked row and deselect any other selected row:

```
/*********************************************************
event:          clicked
parameters:     xpos         int
                ypos         int
                row          long
                dwo          dwObject
return value:   0            continue
                1            stop processing
*********************************************************/
setPointer(HourGlass!)
if row > 0 and row <> getSelectedRow(0) then
   selectRow(0, FALSE)
   selectRow(row, TRUE)
end if
```

Database error handling is done by the script in the **dberror** event. This event is automatically triggered whenever a database error occurs in it. The script reports the database error text, the SQL command being executed when the error occurred and the database-specific error number.

```
/*****************************************************
   event:              dbError
   parameters:         sqldbCode          long
                       sqlErrText         string
                       sqlSyntax          string
                       buffer             dwBuffer
                       row                long
   return value:       0            display default error msg
                       1            do not display the error message
   *****************************************************/
setPointer(hourGlass!)
string ls_errText
ls_errText = "Error No: " + string(sqlDbCode) + "~r~n" + &
            "Msg: " + sqlErrText + "~r~n" + &
            "SQL Command: " + sqlSyntax
messageBox("Database Error", ls_errText)
return 1
```

This object should also prompt the user to confirm a save whenever the save behavior is invoked. You can invoke the save behavior of a DataWindow by calling its **Update** method. The functionality can be provided without changing the DataWindow's interface, by overloading the **Update** method.

> This function applies just to the simplest form of the DataWindow **Update** function where there is an implicit **AcceptText** and the **Update** flags are automatically set, i.e. **dw_1.Update (true, true)**. To handle those cases where you may not want to do an **AcceptText** or automatically reset the **Update** flags (i.e. when updating multiple tables), you'll want to have overloaded **Update** function(s) to accept and handle these conditions explicitly.

The script of this function is as follows:

```
/*****************************************************
   function:           update
   parameters:         <NONE>
   return value:       -1          error
                       1           successful
                       0           User canceled
   *****************************************************/
int li_rc
if messageBox("Save Confirm", "Apply changes to the database", &
                Question!, YesNo!) = 1 then
   li_rc = super::update()
end if

return li_rc
```

To use this user object in your own applications, you just drop it onto a window and set its DataWindow Object Name property to the name of the DataWindow object that you want it to display.

Tab User Object

The tab folder is a powerful way of organizing views of data. In previous versions of PowerBuilder, you had to build your own tab class as a custom user object. Version 5.0 provides a standard tab object.

We've built a visual user object derived from the standard tab control. When another tab is selected, the generic functionality provided in this object prompts the user to save any unapplied modifications in any DataWindow in the currently selected tab page.

The design of this user object, **uo_saveTab**, uses the non-visual custom user object **nvo_promptSave**. In the **constructor** event of **uo_saveTab**, we've created an instance of **nvo_promptSave** and assigned it to the instance variable **invo_promptSave**, defined in **uo_saveTab**.

```
/********************************************************
event:          constructor
parameters:     <NONE>
return value:   <NONE>
********************************************************/
invo_promptSave = create nvo_promptSave
```

The **destructor** event destroys this object:

```
/********************************************************
event:          destructor
parameters:     <NONE>
return value:   <NONE>
********************************************************/
destroy invo_promptSave
```

Whenever a tab folder is changed, this object should be able to check for any DataWindow changes that haven't been saved to the database. The event **selectionChanging** gets triggered in the tab object when a user selects another tab. The event has two parameters—**oldIndex** and **newIndex**—which indicate the index number of the currently selected tab and the newly selected tab. The script checks whether the current tab page has any DataWindows and, if it does, it checks whether they have any changes that haven't yet been saved:

```
/********************************************************
event:          selectionChanging
parameters:     oldIndex    int
newIndex        int
return value:   0   nothing to do
                1   if user selected Yes
                2   if user selected No
                3   if user selected Cancel
               -1   if an error occurs
********************************************************/
```

```
object l_object
int li_numControls, i, j, li_rc
datawindow l_dataWindow[]
if oldindex > 0 then
   li_numControls = upperBound(this.control[oldindex].control)
   for i = 1 to li_numControls
      l_object =  this.control[oldindex].control[i].TypeOf()
      if this.control[oldindex].control[i].TypeOf() = dataWindow! then
         j ++
         l_dataWindow[j] = this.control[oldindex].control[i]
      end if
   next
   if j > 1 then
      li_rc = invo_promptSave.f_promptSave(l_dataWindow)
   end if
end if

message.processed = TRUE
message.returnValue = li_rc
```

This event sets the **message.returnValue** property to indicate the choice made by the user to manage the flow of control at the inherited level.

This example shows how a class visual user object can be integrated with a custom user object.

RichTextEdit User Object

PowerBuilder 5.0 provides a new RichTextEdit object class, which allows you to implement rich text functionality in your application. It provides some word processing capabilities, such as word shrinking and wrapping, font selection, font style selection, underlining, etc. PowerBuilder applications can now provide functionality to create rich text (**RTF**) documents and manipulate existing **RTF** documents.

uo_richTextEdit is a standard visual user object based on the RichTextEdit control. This object provides generic functionality to view and merge **RTF** files and save them. It also provides a dialog to the user to allow them to select and open a file and merge it with an existing **RTF** file in the control or replace the contents. It also provides the user with a dialog screen to specify the file name to save the text in.

We've set the properties that we want to enforce in the **constructor** event of this object. All RichTextEdit controls should be resizable, display a ruler bar, be able to word wrap, display a tab bar, provide a pop-up menu for selecting properties and display a toolbar. We've also added a vertical scrollbar to move through the document.

```
/*****************************************************
event:            constructor
parameters:       <NONE>
return value:     <NONE>
*****************************************************/
setPointer(hourGlass!)
this.resizable = TRUE
this.rulerBar = TRUE
```

```
this.wordWrap = TRUE
this.tabBar = TRUE
this.popMenu = TRUE
this.toolBar = TRUE
this.VScrollBar = TRUE
```

Opening and Displaying an RTF Document

This is the overloaded function, **insertDocument**, which prompts the user to select a file and checks whether the contents of the file are to replace the existing text, be appended to the text or be inserted into the text at the current insertion point.

```
/****************************************************
function:         insertDocument
parameters:       <NONE>
return value:     1 success
                  0 cancel
                  -1 error
****************************************************/
setPointer(hourGlass!)

integer li_rc, li_selectNum
string ls_pathName, ls_fileName, ls_ext, ls_currentFieldName
boolean lb_clearFlag
fileType l_fileType

li_rc = GetFileOpenName("Select File", ls_pathName, ls_fileName, &
        "*.RTF,*.TXT", "RichText(*.RTF),*.RTF,Text(*.TXT),*.TXT")
if li_rc = 1 then
    ls_ext = right(upper(trim(ls_fileName)), 3)
    if ls_ext = "RTF" then
        l_fileType = FileTypeRichText!
    elseif ls_ext = "TXT" then
        l_fileType = FileTypeText!
    end if
    if ls_ext <> "RTF" and ls_ext <> "TXT" then
        messageBox("Error", "Please select a text or rich text file")
        li_rc = -1
    else
        ls_currentFieldName = trim(this.inputFieldCurrentName())
        li_selectNum =  MessageBox("File Location", &
            "Place file at insertion point " + ls_currentFieldName + &
            "?", Question!, YesNoCancel!)
        if li_selectNum <> 3 then
            if li_selectNum = 2 then
                lb_clearFlag = true
            end if
            li_rc = super::insertDocument(ls_pathName, lb_clearFlag, &
                l_fileType)
        end if
    end if
end if
return li_rc
```

73

Saving the Current Text

This is handled by overloading the **saveDocument** function to prompt the user with a dialog to specify the save file name:

```
/*****************************************************
function:        saveDocument
parameters:      <NONE>
return value:    1            success
                 0            cancel
                 -1           error
*****************************************************/
setPointer(hourGlass!)

integer li_rc
string ls_pathName, ls_fileName, ls_ext
fileType l_fileType

li_rc = GetFileSaveName("Save File", ls_pathName, ls_fileName, &
          "*.RTF,*.TXT", "RichText(*.RTF),*.RTF,Text(*.TXT),*.TXT")
if li_rc = 1 then
    ls_ext = right(upper(trim(ls_fileName)), 3)
    if ls_ext = "RTF" then
        l_fileType = FileTypeRichText!
    elseif ls_ext = "TXT" then
        l_fileType = FileTypeText!
    end if
    if ls_ext <> "RTF" and ls_ext <> "TXT" then
        li_rc = SaveDocument(ls_pathName, l_fileType)
    else
        li_rc = SaveDocument(ls_pathName)
    end if
end if

return li_rc
```

You can use this user object by simply placing it on a window and calling the **insertDocument** and **saveDocument** functions from command buttons or from menu options.

Type Ahead User Object

We've created a generic custom visual user object, called **uo_typeAhead**, which searches a DataWindow column for a row that matches the specified data. It performs this search as each character is entered by the user in a SingleLineEdit control. This control provides a drop-down list box which allows a user to select a DataWindow column to search in and a SingleLineEdit field, where the user can enter the data to search for.

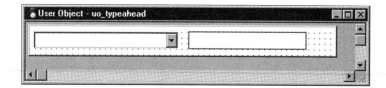

uo_typeahead is composed of a drop-down list box control, named **ddlb_colList**, and a SingleLineEdit control, named **sle_Data**. The interface of this user object allows users to specify the DataWindow for the search and the display names and column names of the DataWindow columns.

We've declared a structure, **st_columns**, to relate the DataWindow column display name to the actual name and declared three private instance variables:

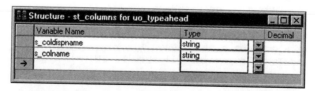

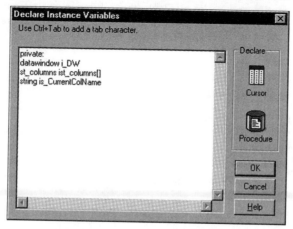

The function, **f_setDW**, initializes the DataWindow variable:

```
/***********************************************************
function:        f_setDW
parameters:      <NONE>
return value:    <NONE>
***********************************************************/
i_DW = p_DW
```

This object requires a function which provides column names for **ddlb_colList**. The function **f_setColAttrib** sets the column name as well as the column display names.

The display names are shown in **ddlb_colList**, but the object uses the column names to find the matching row in the DataWindow **i_DW**. The structure **st_Columns** stores the display name and column name pairs and the function **f_setColAttrib** initializes an array of the type **st_Columns** and sets the column display names in the **ddlb_colList**.

```
/****************************************************
function:          f_setColAttrib
parameters:        ps_colDispName[]  string
                   ps_colName[]      string
return value:      <NONE>
****************************************************/
setPointer(hourGlass!)
int li_numColumns, i
li_numColumns = upperBound(ps_colDispName)
for i = li_numColumns to 1 step -1
    ist_columns[i].s_colDispName = ps_colDispName[i]
    ist_columns[i].s_colName = ps_colName[i]
    ddlb_colList.addItem(ist_columns[i].s_colDispName)
next
```

ddlb_colList should identify and make available the column name currently selected in an instance variable. This is where the string instance variable comes in. The **selectionChanged** event of **ddlb_colList** identifies the current column name and assigns it to the instance variable **is_currentColName**.

```
/****************************************************
event:             selectionChanged
parameters:        index        int
return value:      0            continue processing
****************************************************/
setPointer(HourGlass!)
int i, li_numCols
string ls_colDispName
ls_colDispName = trim(this.Text(index))
if ls_colDispName = "" then
    is_currentColName = ""
else
    li_numCols = upperBound(ist_columns)
    for i = 1 to li_numCols
        if ist_columns[i].s_colDispName = ls_colDispName then
            is_currentColName = ist_columns[i].s_colName
        end if
    next
end if
```

The SingleLineEdit, **sle_data**, should have functionality to search the DataWindow **i_DW**'s column **is_currentColName** for the row that has the data that matches the data entered by the user. This functionality should be dynamic, i.e. the search should occur as each character is entered. The matching row should also be highlighted in **i_DW**. We've created a user event, **keyUp**, in the control **sle_data**, mapping to the Windows message **pbm_keyUp**. This event is triggered whenever a nonsystem key is released.

```
/****************************************************
event:             keyUp
parameters:        key          keyCode
                   keyFlags     unSignedLong
return value:      long
****************************************************/
```

76

```
    string ls_text
    long ll_rowNum, ll_totRows
    ls_text = this.text
    ll_totRows = i_DW.rowCount()
    if ll_totRows > 0 then
        ll_rowNum = i_DW.Find(is_CurrentColName + "='" + ls_text + "'" , 1, &
                ll_totRows)
        if ll_rowNum > 0 then
            i_DW.selectRow(0, FALSE)
            i_DW.selectRow(ll_rowNum, TRUE)
        end if
    end if
end if
```

uo_typeahead has a simple interface. All you have to do is initialize it from the **constructor** event at the inserted level. This object is well encapsulated and generic in nature.

Integrating User Objects in Your Application

The design of user objects should be generic and there should be no hard-coded logic regarding the object. They may be instantiated or exist at run time.

You can't statically integrate class user objects with windows or user objects at design time. You have to instantiate them at run time by using the PowerScript command **create objname**. Always remember to destroy any object explicitly created by using the PowerScript command **destroy objname**.

```
    anyUserObject l_anyUserObject
    l_anyUserObject = create anyUserObject
    l_anyUserObject.triggerEvent("xyz")
    --------
    --------
    destroy l_anyUser Object
```

Version 5.0 also has a new function, **create using className**, to instantiate class user objects. You don't have to hard-code the object name of the class to be instantiated if you use this function:

```
    powerObject l_anyUserObject
    string ls_className
    ls_className = "anyUserObject"
    l_anyUserObject = create using ls_className
    l_anyUserObject.triggerEvent("xyz")
    --------
    --------
    destroy l_anyUserObject
```

In Version 5.0, custom class user objects also have a new property, named **autoInstantiate**. If this property is enabled in this class, you don't have to explicitly instantiate an object of this class. The first reference to it automatically instantiates it.

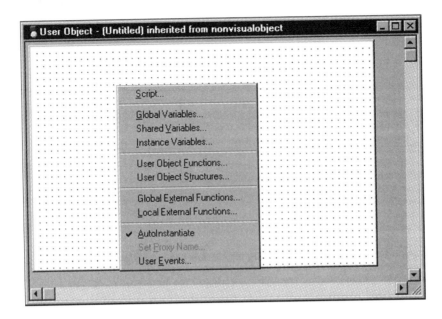

You can statically bind custom and standard user objects to windows or other user objects at design time. You can also instantiate them at run time by using the **openUserObject** and **openUserObjectWithParm** functions and close them using the **closeUserObject** function.

Summary

In this chapter, we've constructed different types of user objects which you can use in your own applications. The examples demonstrate good user object design and programming techniques. We've also constructed user objects which have a **using** relationship with other user objects. This illustrates how user objects can associatively help in implementing higher level user objects.

In the next chapter, we'll look at the one type of user object we didn't cover here: the C++ class user object.

C++ Class User Objects

In the previous chapter, we looked at user objects and how you can use them in your applications. What we didn't talk about was C++ user objects.

In this chapter, we'll take a detailed look at this more complicated type of user object—we'll look at what C++ user objects actually are, why you might want to use them in your applications and how you create them.

What is a C++ Class User Object?

A C++ class user object is one of the non-visual types of PowerBuilder user object. It has no visual component to it—there is no control associated with it and it includes only variables and functions.

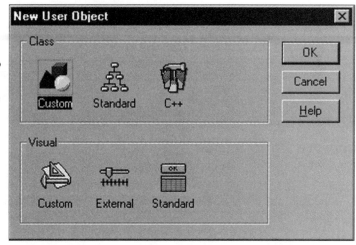

> Note that you can only create C++ user objects with the Enterprise edition of PowerBuilder, or using the Advanced Developer's Kit.

PowerBuilder introduced the ability to create a C++ DLL from within PowerBuilder in Version 4.0. Creating a C++ user object involves linking your PowerBuilder application to a Windows DLL (dynamic link library), and the Enterprise edition includes a selection of tools to create DLLs as part of the Watcom Integrated Development Environment (IDE). These tools include a text editor, resource editor, debugger, compiler, linker and skeleton code generator. They enable you to create user objects in PowerBuilder and declare functions that are coded in C++.

How C++ User Objects Differ from other User Objects

As a non-visual user object, a C++ user object can't be dropped onto a window like other PowerBuilder controls such as CommandButtons, CheckBoxes, RadioButtons, etc. Instead, you create an instance using the **CREATE** command and, when you have finished using it, destroy it using the **DESTROY** command.

The structure of a C++ user object is different from the structure of other PowerBuilder objects. You declare the function names, arguments and return values in PowerBuilder, and code the actual logic in C++. This is different from, say, a standard user object. In a standard user object, all the code and logic is written using PowerScript and it resides within your PowerBuilder application. In a C++ user object, the functional logic code is written in C++ and resides outside the PowerBuilder application. If you install your PowerBuilder application without the DLLs it references, you'll get an error.

That said, though, there are also several similarities between the structure of a C++ user object and other PowerBuilder objects. You can declare instance variables, user functions and user events for your C++ user object just as you do for any other PowerBuilder object.

Why Use a C++ User Object?

As you would expect, C++ user objects offer all the usual benefits of objects such as allowing you to use inheritance, to encapsulate functions and make them reusable in other applications, etc. The benefits they add over and above other objects, though, are as follows:

 They encapture the raw processing power and flexibility of C++ and so enable you to improve performance.

 They allow you to reuse existing C++ class objects. This saves you development time and cost, and allows you to extend your PowerBuilder application.

 They provide flexibility and control—C++ lets you get at the internals of the system in a way that scripting languages can't.

Improve Performance

C++ is a programming language that offers you better processing power, flexibility and performance than PowerScript, which is a scripting language. Executing mathematical, arithmetic functions and complex calculations in C++ is faster than using PowerScript—what takes minutes to execute using PowerScript would take only seconds to execute in C/C++. For this reason, C++ user objects give you tremendous power to extend your PowerBuilder application.

You can use C++ for processing intensive tasks while your PowerScript code takes care of what it does best, including user interface development, database connection and data presentation. For example, if you need spell checking capability in your PowerBuilder application, you can create a C++ based spell checker user object. Spell checking is a processing intensive task and so is better executed in C++ than PowerScript. Moreover, if you create a spell checker DLL, you can use it not only in your PowerBuilder application but also in C, C++, Visual Basic or Delphi applications. A spell checker written in PowerScript, on the other hand, isn't reusable across different applications. It remains restricted to the PowerBuilder environment.

As another example, suppose you're designing a PowerBuilder front end that requires the users to enter the addresses of customers including zip code, city and state. To expedite data entry, you can integrate a zip code lookup class library with your PowerBuilder application. The user enters the zip code and the application automatically populates the city and state fields with matching entries. Or the user enters the city and state and the application retrieves the matching zip code and places it in the zip code field on the data entry screen. Searching for a city and state that matches a given zip code, or vice versa, is a mathematically intensive task. It means searching and sorting through a large database of zip codes, cities and states. This type of task is better suited to C++ than PowerScript.

Reuse Existing Libraries

There are many class libraries written in C++. The fact that you can reuse these libraries with your PowerBuilder application saves you a lot of time and effort.

So, instead of writing your own spell checker, if you have the source code available, you could integrate the class library of a third-party spell checker. You can extend existing class libraries by adding new classes and modifying existing ones. You integrate existing source code using the built-in Watcom C++ editor provided with the Enterprise edition of PowerBuilder.

Flexibility and Control

C++ provides access to the internals of the machine, giving you greater flexibility to carry out complex tasks.

Consider this example: you're designing a PowerBuilder front end to some mainframe data. What you want to do is design a friendly GUI so that, instead of using the cryptic mainframe commands, users can point and click to access the data. How do you establish a link between your PowerBuilder application and the mainframe data behind the scenes? One way to do this is use a third party DLL, such as **Hllapi.dll**. This is a Windows DLL that can be called by any Windows application to communicate with a mainframe. PowerBuilder doesn't have any built-in functions or user objects that you can use to access mainframe data, so you couldn't link your PB application with the mainframe data using PowerScript code. You need an intermediate link—a DLL.

Dynamic-link Libraries

As we mentioned earlier, creating a C++ user object involves linking your PowerBuilder application to a Windows DLL (dynamic link library), which is a set of functions. You can create your own DLLs to extend the capabilities of the base libraries of any Windows application. A Windows application calls DLLs only at run time. This helps reduce the size of your **EXE** file. It also makes your Windows application modular in nature—you can reuse the same DLLs across several different Windows applications, thus saving you valuable time and memory space.

Windows comprises three main DLLs: **Gdi32.dll**, **User32.dll** and **Kernel32.dll**. These are the basic set of functions for the Windows operating system, though they are only a tiny subset of all the system DLLs provided by Windows. They are also supported by other file types; for example, **Krnl386.exe** supports the **Kernel32.dll**. Other common libraries that can be found on most systems include **Winmm.dll** (multimedia extensions) and **advapi32.dll** for manipulating the system registry. The default location for these DLLs is the **System** subdirectory of your Windows directory (i.e. **C:\Windows\System**).

You can also create your own DLL's that will carry out specific tasks required for your application. As we mentioned earlier, these will typically be complex functions that would be too slow to do in PowerScript. Other times, you may feel the need to write your own DLLs for wrappers. A wrapper function is used to access some of the underlying Windows DLL functions that would not normally be available to PowerScript. You could create a wrapper to use this otherwise forbidden function and present it to your PowerScript code in a useable form.

Linking Libraries

When you create an executable program, you need to link the libraries that you are using to your source programs. You can do this in two ways: statically or dynamically.

Static Linking

If you use the static linking method, all functions from the library that are referenced in the program become part of the executable. This means that you get a large executable file that requires more RAM and disk space. A large executable file takes more time to load into memory. If you create ten different programs that use the same library, the functions in the library will be copied into ten executables. Executing all these programs takes more memory. Also, with static linking, code can't be shared between applications.

Dynamic Linking

With dynamic linking, the functions in the library aren't part of the executable file. Instead, the executable file contains references to the functions. This means that even if you create ten different programs that use the same library, you only need to create one DLL, so you save memory and disk space. At execution time, DLLs are loaded into memory once and can be shared between programs. A program can even unload the DLL if it's not needed at any given point in time and thus free up some memory. A DLL's primary purpose is to reduce the load image of an **EXE** as well as share resources across multiple **EXE**s or instances of an **EXE**. One more thing to note is that you can update these DLLs without relinking, since the executable contains references, not the actual code.

To run a program that uses a dynamic library, the library must be present on the disk, in either the current directory, a directory accessible through the **PATH** string in MS-DOS, the Windows directory, or the **System** subdirectory of the Windows directory.

The Contents of a DLL

A DLL is an executable file. It contains the following functions: **Entry**, **LibMain** and **Exit**.

The Entry Function

Once the Windows loader has loaded a DLL into memory, it transfers execution to the DLL's entry-point function, which performs whatever initialization is necessary for the DLL to function properly. When you're developing a C++ class in PowerBuilder, Watcom C/C++ provides a DLL entry function called **LibEntry**, which is located at **C:\Watc\Lib286\Win\LibEntry.obj**.

> The name of **LibEntry.Obj** will, of course, change depending on how you install PowerBuilder and the platform it's installed on.

LibEntry's most important task is to initialize the DLL's local heap if it has one. Without a local heap, the DLL can't use any of Windows' local memory management APIs. Once it has initialized the DLL's local heap, **LibEntry** usually calls a programmer-specified function to perform any additional initialization required by the DLL.

You may wonder why we call a programmer-specified function when we could just perform all initialization in **LibEntry**. The reason for this is that, for performance purposes, **LibEntry** is written in Assembly language. This means that any changes or additions to the **LibEntry.obj** have to be made in Assembly language and, as you are no doubt aware, it's easier to program in a high level language, such as C or C++, than in Assembly language.

So it's just easier to write the minimum code necessary in **LibEntry** using Assembly language and then call a function that can be written in a high-level language. Anyway, PowerBuilder releases you from all these tasks by providing the **LibEntry.obj** file which takes care of every thing related to initialization. **LibEntry.obj** is a run-time object file that is linked by the built-in C++ compiler at build time.

If this function fails, Windows unloads the DLL from memory. If all goes well, it calls **LibMain**.

The LibMain Function

LibMain is a programmer-supplied initialization function called by **LibEntry**. Since **LibEntry** performs initializations that are common to all DLLs, you can write your DLL-specific initialization in **LibMain**. And, as this is a separate function from **LibEntry**, you can write it in a high-level language instead of writing in Assembly language.

When writing C++ classes in PowerBuilder, Watcom C/C++ creates a file **lmain.cpp**. This file contains two functions: **LibMain** and **WEP**. You shouldn't modify these files unless you have a good understanding of C++ (really, you shouldn't modify them at all).

```
/* This file is generated by PowerBuilder.
 * You may modify it in any way you wish but do not remove
 * Libmain and WEP.  Without them you will be unable to link your DLL.
 */

#include <windows.h>
#include "pbdll.h"


int PB_EXPORT LibMain( HANDLE hmod, WORD dataseg, WORD heap, LPSTR cmdline)
{
    hmod = hmod;                    // these assignments generate no code
    dataseg = dataseg;              // but prevent compiler warnings about
    heap = heap;                    // unreferenced variables
    cmdline = cmdline;
    return( 1 );
}
```

If **LibMain** returns false, Windows unloads the DLL from memory.

> You should note that you can't have multiple instances of the same DLL in memory and that **LibEntry** and **LibMain** are only called once, no matter how many applications are sharing the same DLL. If you want to do additional initialization for each instance of your application, you should provide an exported function and call that function instead.

85

You might want to use **LibMain** to load resources such as bitmaps or icons, or else to create data structures that the DLL manages. Note, though, that you shouldn't write code in **LibMain** that depends on other DLLs having being loaded previously. This is because, when several DLLs need to be loaded at one time, Windows does not load them in any guaranteed order.

The Exit Function

WEP (Windows Exit procedure) is the last function of a DLL to be called before Windows unloads the DLL from memory. The purpose of **WEP** is to perform any cleanup that a DLL needs to do before it's unloaded. Each DLL's **WEP** is called only once. When a DLL's usage count drops to zero, the Windows loader calls the DLL's **WEP** and then unloads the DLL. The usage count for an implicitly loaded DLL will be zero when all instances of all applications that are currently using it exit. The following code lists the **WEP** code that is generated by Watcom C/C++ while you create a C++ class user object from PowerBuilder.

```
int PB_EXPORT WEP( int res )
{
    res = res;
    return( 1 );
}
```

> In Windows 3.0 this function is required for all DLLs, but it's optional in Windows 3.1 and upwards.

Programmer-defined Functions

These are the functions in which you can actually implement the functionality you want—they're the real workhorses of the DLL.

When declaring functions within a DLL, you should follow certain conventions, as specified in the Windows SDK. For example, you need to use the ANSI keywords: **_far**, **_pascal** and **_export**.

The **_FAR** declaration helps Windows change the code segment of any program as required by the memory manager.

> Note that the references to specific key words such as **_FAR** or **_NEAR** are not applicable in a 32-bit environment.

_PASCAL function calls are more efficient than C function calls as they leave the responsibility of managing parameters and the cleaning up of the stack to the called procedure. Under C function calls, the calling procedure has to take care of this. Thus, **_PASCAL** function calls eliminate any duplication of code, since there can be multiple instances of one procedure calling a single instance of another procedure. The **_PASCAL** calling convention stores each parameter on the stack in the order in which they are coded in the function call. The C convention places the parameters in the exact opposite order. The reason for the C convention difference, is that it allows for a variable number of parameters by ensuring that the first parameter is always at a fixed positive offset from the stack pointer (SP). The **_PASCAL** convention makes no such assurance, so if a parameter isn't passed, the addresses computed for those that are passed will be erroneous. In the case of PowerBuilder, your DLL must use the same convention as PowerBuilder itself in order for parameter data to be passed from the PowerBuilder program to your DLL. PowerBuilder requires that you use the **_PASCAL** calling convention due to the manner that this convention stores parameters on the stack.

The **_EXPORT** keyword tells the compiler which functions in the DLL should be made visible and accessible to the world outside. PowerBuilder's class library code generator provides the **PB_EXPORT** definition. This provides the correct calling sequence and keywords for all functions accessed by PowerBuilder.

There are two varieties of programmer-defined function that implement the functionality of DLLs: exported and non-exported.

Exported Functions

Exported functions define the programming interface of a DLL and are meant to be called by applications and other DLLs. They usually represent the highest abstraction level a DLL provides to its callers. To implement these high-level services, exported functions often call non-exported functions that perform the necessary operations to support their functionality.

You must declare exported functions as **_far** because they don't reside in the segments from which they are called. However, they may use any naming and parameter passing conventions that pass parameters on the stack. Two popular conventions are **_pascal** and **_cdecl**. You can't use conventions that pass parameters in the CPU's registers because prolog code uses the CPU's registers when the function is called. PowerBuilder uses the **_pascal** calling convention, since this convention avoids passing parameters in the CPU registers. Also note that exported functions that return floating-point values, or structures and objects larger than four bytes, must use the **_pascal** calling convention.

The header file **pbdll.h** consists of a macro as shown below:

```
#define PB_EXPORT        __pascal __export
```

If you look at the **LibMain** listing that we gave earlier, you'll see that **LibMain** is declared as an exported function by placing **PB_EXPORT** before it. Similarly, when you declare a function in PowerBuilder for use in a C++ class, PowerBuilder includes **pbdll.h** in the **#include** section in the generated code and also places **PB_EXPORT** in the function declaration.

Non-exported (Internal) Functions

Internal functions can only be called by other functions within the same DLL; applications and other DLLs can't call them and don't need to be aware that they even exist.

Internal functions in DLLs can use any naming and parameter-passing conventions supported by your compiler. You declare these functions in the C++ code, not in the PowerScript.

Memory Models

Memory models limit the size of the program and data by describing the number of bytes used to address data and call functions in the program. A memory model consists of a code model and a data model. The PowerBuilder C++ class builder creates DLLs based on the large model, which means that it makes use of far pointers for code as well as data. It also means that all data and code segments include explicit segment and offset values. This model allows for code size up to the amount of available memory, but limits any single data item to the 64K barrier. As PowerBuilder uses the large memory model, any DLL that requires a reference to a value in the PowerBuilder heap must also be of this model.

PowerBuilder and C++ Data Types

The following table lists the PowerBuilder and corresponding C++ data types.

PowerBuilder Data Type	C++ Data Type	Description
Boolean	bool	2-byte signed integer
char	char, byte	1-byte
date, time, datetime	Not available	-
double, decimal	double	8-byte double precision floating point number
int	int	2-byte signed integer
long	long	4-byte signed integer
real	float	4-byte single precision floating point number
string	lpint, lpword, lplong, lpdword, lpvoid	4-byte far pointer
ulong	dword, unsigned, long	4-byte unsigned integer
unit	word, handle, hwnd	2-byte unsigned integer

Creating C++ Classes

Creating a C++ class user object using PowerBuilder involves the following steps:

1 Create the user object.

2 Declare instance and shared variables.

3 Declare user object functions.

4 Write code for the declared functions in C++.

Let's start with a simple example of creating a C++ DLL that returns the factorial value of a given number.

Click the User Object painter button and select **New**. Then select the C++ User Object icon and provide a DLL name (for example, **pb_fact1.dll**). This is the DLL that PowerBuilder will create once you save the user object.

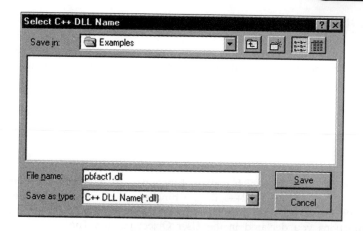

The painter is no different from the standard user object painter, except that there is one more icon on the Painter Bar—to invoke the Watcom editor. Declare the function as follows by selecting Declare/UserObject Functions... from the menu.

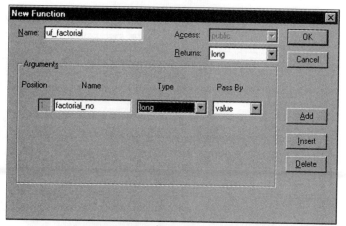

When you click the OK command button, control returns to the User Object painter. We're going to write the actual logic in C++, so save the user object as **cuo_factorial** and then click on the C++ Editor button to invoke the Watcom IDE:

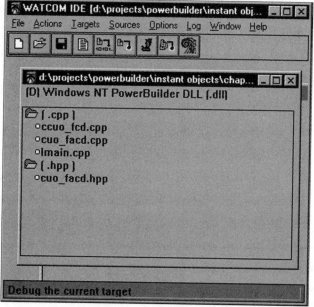

Interface Files

When you create a C++ user object, PowerBuilder creates various templates which you can use to type in and compile your C++ code. It generates the following files for you.

- **.hpp** files
- **.cpp** files

.hpp files

The **.hpp** files are header files which contain functions and data member definitions. The extension is **.h** in C and **.hpp** in C++. To use functions declared in these files, you refer to them in **.cpp** files with the **#include** directive. PowerBuilder automatically generates this file by declaring the functions you declared in the User Object painter. The code is as follows:

```
/* WATCOM Interface Generator   Version 1.0 */
/* This file contains code generated by PowerBuilder.
 * Do not modify code delimited by comments of the form:
 * // $PB$ - begin generated code for object <>.  Do not modify this code
 * // $PB$ - end generated code for object <>.
 * This file contains the the C++ class definition for your user object.
 */

#include <string.hpp>
#include <windows.h>

// $PB$ - begin generated code for object <cuo_factorial>. Do not modify this code
class cuo_factorial {
public:
    virtual long uf_factorial( long factorial_no );
// $PB$ - end generated code for object <cuo_factorial>.
public:
    virtual ~cuo_factorial() {}
    /*
     * PUT YOUR DECLARATIONS HERE
     */

};
```

.cpp Files

These are the actual source code and are similar to **.C** extension files in C programs. In C++, the source file extension is **.cpp**. PowerBuilder generates three files for us:

- **Lmain.cpp**, which contains the **LibMain** and **WEP** functions that are required for the DLL.

- A file that contains the PowerBuilder interface. PowerBuilder doesn't make calls to the functions directly, but uses this file instead. This file name is typically prefixed with **c**. Don't change anything in this file. The code is as follows:

```
/* WATCOM Interface Generator    Version 1.0 */
/* This file is generated by PowerBuilder.
 * Do not modify this file.
 * This file contains interface code called by PowerBuilder.
 */

#include <pbdll.h>

#include "cuo_faCD.hpp"

extern "C" {
long PB_EXPORT cuo_factorialuf_factorial( cuo_factorial *this_hdl, long
                        factorial_no );
cuo_factorial *PB_EXPORT cuo_factorial_CPP_CONSTRUCTOR();
void PB_EXPORT cuo_factorial_CPP_DESTRUCTOR( cuo_factorial *this_hdl );
}

long PB_EXPORT cuo_factorialuf_factorial( cuo_factorial *this_hdl, long
                        factorial_no ) {
    return( this_hdl->uf_factorial( factorial_no ) );
}

cuo_factorial *PB_EXPORT cuo_factorial_CPP_CONSTRUCTOR() {
    return( new cuo_factorial );
}

void PB_EXPORT cuo_factorial_CPP_DESTRUCTOR( cuo_factorial *this_hdl ) {
    delete this_hdl;
}
```

The third file, in our case **cuo_facd.cpp**, is where you write the actual logic for
the functions declared in the User Object painter. The code generated by
PowerBuilder looks like this:

```
/* WATCOM Interface Generator    Version 1.0 */
/* This file contains code generated by PowerBuilder.
 * Do not modify code delimited by comments of the form:
 * // $PB$ — begin generated code for object <>.  Do not modify this code
 * // $PB$ — end generated code for object <>.
 * This file contains the bodies the functions for your user object.
 */

#include <pbdll.h>

#include "cuo_faCD.hpp"

// $PB$ — begin generated code for object <cuo_factorial>. Do not modify this code
#if 1
long cuo_factorial::uf_factorial( long factorial_no ) {
// $PB$ — end generated code for object <cuo_factorial>.
//====================================

    /*
     * PUT YOUR CODE HERE
     */
```

```
        return( 0 );
}
#endif // PowerBuilder code, do not remove
```

Don't remove any lines generated by PowerBuilder other than replacing the 'Put your code here' comments with actual code.

To edit this file, double-click on the file name. Add the following code:

```
/* WATCOM Interface Generator    Version 1.0 */
/* This file contains code generated by PowerBuilder.
 * Do not modify code delimited by comments of the form:
 * // $PB$ — begin generated code for object <>.  Do not modify this code
 * // $PB$ — end generated code for object <>.
 * This file contains the bodies the functions for your user object.
 */

#include <pbdll.h>

#include "cuo_faCD.hpp"

// $PB$ — begin generated code for object <cuo_factorial>. Do not modify this code
#if 1
long cuo_factorial::uf_factorial( long factorial_no ) {
// $PB$ — end generated code for object <cuo_factorial>.
//===================================

long var1, var2;

    if ( factorial_no > 10 || factorial_no < 0 )
        return( -1 );
    else
    {
        var1 = factorial_no;
        for ( var2 = factorial_no - 1; var2 > 1; var2— )
            {
                var1 *= var2;
            }
        return ( var1 );
    }
}
#endif // PowerBuilder code, do not remove
```

Using Your User Object

Once you're done writing your functions, exit from the editor and use the Watcom compiler to link and compile the code into a DLL—select **Actions/Make All** from the menu. Then exit from the Watcom IDE.

To use your user object in a window, you simply include its instance in the window and access the instance—declare a variable of the user object type and use the **CREATE** command to create an instance of the user object in the window.

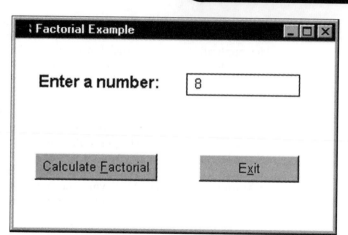

Paint a window like the one shown here and write the following code for the Calculate Factorial command button.

```
cuo_factorial  lcuo_func1
Long           lFactor

lcuo_func1 = Create cuo_factorial

//
// typically you would test before calling the function
// in this example we show that the DLL is returning an error
// value as designed.
//
lFactor = lcuo_func1.uf_factorial( Long( sle_1.Text ) )
if ( lFactor > -1 ) then
    MessageBox( "Factorial value of " + sle_1.Text, String( lFactor) )
else
        MessageBox( "Invalid Value provided", "Please Select A " + &
                    "Value From 0 to 10." )
end if

Destroy lcuo_func1
```

You can now test the window out.

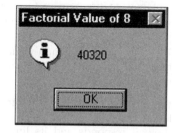

When you're done using your user object, use the **DESTROY** command to deallocate its memory.

```
DESTROY lcuo_func1
```

As you can see, the Enterprise edition of PowerBuilder eliminates the need for a separate C++ compiler to write DLLs for your application. PowerBuilder provides a one-stop center to write your PowerBuilder applications and external functions as a Windows DLL. When creating such a DLL, PowerBuilder automatically generates some of the necessary files for you thus saving time and effort. You can create and test your DLL from your PowerBuilder environment without having to switch to a separate C++ compiler.

> Note that the Watcom compiler that is provided with PowerBuilder 5.0 for 32-bit systems, only supports Pentium Optimization settings (only those libraries are provided). You can change the IDE settings to optimize for another CPU, but if you do your code will fail to link (with little or no warning as to why). Also, you may encounter problems when linking the DLL from within the IDE; in this case, you may want to resort to a batch file.

Debugging DLLs

To debug a DLL, open the user object and invoke the C++ editor. Select Targets/Debug from the menu. This option invokes the Watcom debugger. The debugger for Windows 95/Windows NT is GUI based and as such is a great improvement on the old DOS version. It comes with a symbols file for PowerBuilder and actually allows you to walk through the internals of the PowerBuilder product, along with your own code.

From the Modules window, double-click on the file in which the actual code is placed, i.e. `cuo_facd.cpp`. This will display the code in the main window. Click on the square brackets on the line where you want to put break and select Run/Go from the menu. This will bring the control back to PowerBuilder. Close the User Object painter and click on the run icon. As soon as the code reaches the line on which you put the break, control switches to Watcom debugger where you can execute step-by-step by pressing the *F10* function key.

Limits of a C++ User Object

C++ user objects can add power and flexibility to your applications, but remember that you do need prior knowledge of how to program in C++, which, it has to be said, has a longer learning curve than PowerScript. There are also a few limitations which you should bear in mind:

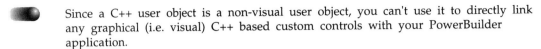 Since a C++ user object is a non-visual user object, you can't use it to directly link any graphical (i.e. visual) C++ based custom controls with your PowerBuilder application.

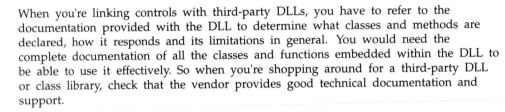 When you're linking controls with third-party DLLs, you have to refer to the documentation provided with the DLL to determine what classes and methods are declared, how it responds and its limitations in general. You would need the complete documentation of all the classes and functions embedded within the DLL to be able to use it effectively. So when you're shopping around for a third-party DLL or class library, check that the vendor provides good technical documentation and support.

You can only write user events for the limited number of events that occur to the user object as a whole. These user events include:

```
Constructor

Destructor

DragDrop

DragEnter

DragLeave

DragWithin

RButtonDown
```

In addition to these events, you can write custom user events for the user object as a whole.

Other Issues to Consider

There are some project sites that maintain all the source code and that need to create the executable on their machine in batch mode; they don't want to do any GUI process and later they want to compare their executable file with the file we created byte by byte. To allow them to create the executable and DLL, you need to provide all the C++ source files and the make file as a DOS batch file.

If you come across this situation, capture the log file created by Watcom when you select Make All and submit the file to the production center. While creating the DLL, you will see this log file at the bottom of the main window:

```
Connecting...
cd c:\workdir
wmake -f c:\workdir\pb_fact1.mk -h -e
wpp ccuo_fcd.cpp -i=D:\WATC\h;D:\WATC\h\win -fhq -w4 -e25 -zq -otexan -d2 -zu -
bt=windows -ml
wpp cuo_facd.cpp -i=D:\WATC\h;D:\WATC\h\win -fhq -w4 -e25 -zq -otexan -d2 -zu -
bt=windows -ml
wpp lmain.cpp -i=D:\WATC\h;D:\WATC\h\win -fhq -w4 -e25 -zq -otexan -d2 -zu -
bt=windows -ml
wlink SYS windows dll op m d all op st=8192 libf libentry.obj op maxe=25 op q op
symf @pb_fact1.1k1
wrc -q -ad -s2 -s0  pb_fact1.dll
wfscopy pb_fact1.dll D:\WATC\binw\pb_fact1.dll
Execution complete
```

Remove the top and bottom line from the file and save this as a batch file with the **.bat** extension.

You'll also need to think about the path for the DLL file. When you create the user object, you specify the location and DLL file name in the Select C++ DLL file dialog box. If you simply specify the DLL file name, PowerBuilder will store the full path in its definition, as shown below:

```
string LibraryName="c:\workdir\pb_fact1.dll"
```

It will also look for the same path at execution time, which isn't what we want. Specifying **.\pb_fact1.dll** in the dialog box will overcome this problem. If you have already created the .DLL, before you create the final executable file, export the user object, edit the path and import it back.

Summary

In this chapter you have learned the basics of working with C++ class user objects. We looked at Windows DLLs and saw how to create and use C++ DLLs from within your PowerBuilder environment.

PowerBuilder's C++ user object greatly expands the capabilities of the PowerBuilder product. As a developer, you will run into any number of situations where your program must access peripheral devices, non-standard data, legacy systems, or perform heavy duty calculations. In most 4GL environments, you must resort to external calls to DLLs in these situations. With PowerBuilder's C++ user object, however, you have the capability to address these challenges directly from within the product.

Object-oriented Menus

Everyone who has used a Windows application is familiar with menus. Whether they're menu bars (with drop-down or cascading menus) or pop-ups, menus enable users to interact with the graphical user interface and access the functionality of an application.

A good menu layout can make all the difference between an easy to use application and a confusing jumble of options that immediately intimidates the user. When you're designing your application framework, you should take the time to also think about the menus. Menus not only allow users to control the behavior of the windows, but also lead them through the work cycle. Remember, the menu answers the question "What can I do right now?" A user wants to open a body of work, do something valuable with it, then leave. Your application requirements determine the universe and the menu has to interpret those laws to inform the user what he or she can do.

Creating menus in PowerBuilder is a straightforward process—the Menu painter includes tabs to set the menu item names and MicroHelp, style, keyboard shortcut and toolbar options. We won't go into detail about creating menus in this chapter, but we'll look at:

- How windows and menus interact
- Implementing menus in an MDI application
- Implementing static menus in an application
- Implementing dynamic menus in an application

Menu Types

Menus can be classified in two broad categories: **menu bars** and **pop-up menus**.

Menu bars are the primary menu interface for graphical user interfaces and can be provided on all types of window, except child windows and response or modal windows. Each menu item provides access to a grouping of subordinate menu items, which can further provide access to a cascading hierarchy of menu items.

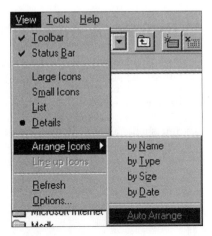

You can use pop-up menus on any type of window. They are floating menus which appear when a user (right)-clicks on a hot spot and should provide access to context-sensitive functionality, i.e. the menu items that appear should be dependent on the hot spot on which the user clicked. Pop-up menus are normally displayed at the location of the pointer and provide the user with easy access to commands.

As we mentioned earlier, we're not going to talk you through the Menu painter, because it's pretty intuitive to use, even if you're not already familiar with it. We'll discuss other issues about creating menu bars later in the chapter. We will, however, talk briefly about how to create pop-up menus, as this is less straightforward.

Creating Pop-up Menus

To create pop-up menus, you use the menu function **PopMenu**, which requires two parameters: the x and y coordinates of the menu's location. To display the menu at the location of the mouse pointer, you can use the **PointerX** and **PointerY** functions to return the current mouse x and y coordinates.

The simplest way to create a pop-up menu is to designate a column of the current window's menu for pop-up purposes. For example, if you wanted the window's Edit menu to appear as a pop-up menu when the user right-clicks on a control, you could put the following code in the **rbuttondown** event:

```
m_window_menu lm_Menu
lm_Menu = Parent.MenuID
lm_Menu.m_Edit.PopMenu(Parent.PointerX(), Parent.PointerY())
```

A more flexible way to create a pop-up menu is to create a menu in the Menu painter, instantiate it and then pop it up. Of course, if you do this, you'll have to write the scripts for the menu items.

```
m_popup_menu lm_Menu
lm_Menu = Create m_popup_menu
lm_Menu.m_menuitem.PopMenu(Parent.PointerX(), Parent.PointerY())
Destroy lm_Menu
```

Alternatively, you could create pop-up menu items with the same menu item names as the window's menu, then create a menu function that matches the name of the clicked menu item with its mate on the window menu and triggers it.

Window/Menu Interaction

When you're designing an application, you should treat menus as interface objects. You shouldn't embed application or business logic in any menu script or function. Instead, when users click on a menu item to initiate some functionality, this user interaction should be passed on to a window to be 'interpreted'.

You should use windows as controller objects. They serve as a placeholder and integrator for controls, objects and menus which collaborate to provide the application functionality.

Referring to a Window from a Menu

Menus that are part of a usable menu hierarchy must refer to their parent windows in a generic manner, so don't hard-code any names. A menu is an object like any other and, in all cases, a menu object is associated with a window object to provide functionality, in the same way that a window object is assigned to an application object. PowerBuilder provides menus with a pointer to the parent window and you can use the keyword `ParentWindow` in menu scripts to refer to the parent window.

> Don't get `ParentWindow` confused with `Parent`, which window controls use as a generic reference to the window. Menus are not window controls—they're separate objects that are merely associated with the window.

A menu can't call any user-defined functions in a static manner if the `ParentWindow` keyword is used in its parent window. `ParentWindow` is classed as a window and PowerBuilder can't resolve references to functions that may or may not exist on the generic window class' descendants.

The easiest way for a menu to communicate with its parent window is by triggering events and functions in it. You have to be careful when you're triggering functions because, to use `ParentWindow`, you have to use the **DYNAMIC** keyword. This will cause an error if the function doesn't exist in the menu's parent window at run time.

```
ParentWindow.triggerEvent(eventName)
```

or

```
ParentWindow.Function DYNAMIC TRIGGER f_foo( )
```

When you're triggering events, you can pass additional parameters to the parent window by using the **WordParm** and **LongParm** parameters.

Triggering events and functions (using the **DYNAMIC** keyword) ensures loose coupling between windows and menus. Adopting this practice requires each menu's parent window to have an event or function available for each enabled menu item. This ensures that menus are used only as interface or GUI objects.

> Remember that the new keyword, **DYNAMIC**, allows a reference to be resolved at run time instead of compile time. This can have a number of advantages, such as allowing you to code the call, then the function afterwards. However, it can also lead to errors, as a reference may be missed at compile time.

Referring to a Menu Item from a Window

Windows programs rarely have to refer to menu items directly, but two common instances when they do are when you implement application security and use the function **OpenSheet**.

Let's have a look at these cases.

Restricting Access to Menu Items

Suppose that you need to provide for certain menu items in an application to be disabled or hidden, depending on a user's access level.

You should build menus as well-encapsulated objects. This implies that it would be bad practice to have windows directly reference attributes of menu items. Menu security should be implemented as menu behavior incorporated in the menu hierarchy. This menu/window interaction should be ideally coupled at the base window/base menu level.

The base menu should have a public function, say **mf_secureMenu**, which sets properties of menu items based on a security level parameter, say **li_securityLevel**. This function should be overloaded by each descendant menu. The descendant function, **mf_secureMenu**, should set the attributes for menu items introduced at that level and then call the ancestor **mf_secureMenu** function using the **super::** keyword; i.e. **super::mf_SecureMenu**. The base menu and base window should be loosely coupled and security should be initiated by triggering the menu security function, **mf_secureMenu**, from the base window's **Open** event.

```
menu l_menu
int li_securityLevel
//some processing
l_menu = this.menuID
l_menu.Function DYNAMIC TRIGGER mf_secureMenu(li_securityLevel)
//some processing
```

Using OpenSheet

The **OpenSheet** function requires a parameter to indicate the number of the menu item under which you want to add the names of any open sheets. You can either hard-code this number or derive it at run time.

```
OpenSheet ( sheet {, windowtype }, mdiframe {, menuitem
{, arrangeopen } } )
```

> Menu items in PowerBuilder have a hierarchical relationship. Each menu item can be accessed from the Item[i] property of its parent menu item. For example, if you have a menu with three menu items, such as **File**, **Window** and **Help**, you can access these items from the Item[1], Item[2] and Item[3] properties of the menu. You can access menu items that appear in the **File** drop-down menu from the Menu[1].Menu[1], Menu[1].Menu[2], Menu[1].Menu[3], etc., properties of the menu.

The **Item[]** property of a menu is an unbounded array. This array specifies the menu items in a menu object and provides access to the properties of each menu item. Let's use this to determine the number of a menu item so that we can use it in conjunction with the **OpenSheet** function. The script for the function, **mf_getMenuItemName**, is shown on the following page. Call this function with the text of the menu item under which you want the sheet title to appear and it will return the menu item number to be used in the **OpenSheet** call.

```
/**********************************************************
Function Name:    mf_getMenuItemName
Parameters:       ps_menuItemName    string
ReturnValue       li_menuItemNum     int
**********************************************************/
// (Note: the text must match exactly.
// if the menuitem text has an accelerator key,
// the '&' must also be in ps_menuItemName.
// e.g. typically, "&File" would match, but "File" would not.

int li_menuItemNum, li_Items, i
setPointer(HourGlass!)
ps_menuItemName = trim(ps_menuItemName)
if ps_menuItemName <> "" then
    li_items = upperBound(this.menuID.item)
    for i = 1 to li_items
      if upper(this.menuID.item[i].Text) = upper(ps_menuItemName) then
         li_menuItemNum = i
      end if
   next
end if
return li_menuItemNum
```

Alternatively, you can save yourself this extra work by relying on Windows conventions which state that in an MDI application, the second menu bar item from the right will always be Window. This is the default position, no matter which variety of the **OpenSheet** function you use.

Implementing Menus in an MDI Application

In the MDI presentation style, multiple sheets or documents are arranged in a frame. The frame always has a menu and each sheet can either use the frame's menu or have its own. If the sheet has a menu, this will override the frame's menu; if the sheet doesn't have a menu, it uses the frame's menu.

In the figures shown here and on the following page, Sheet1 has its own menu; Sheet2 doesn't, so it uses the MDI frame's menu.

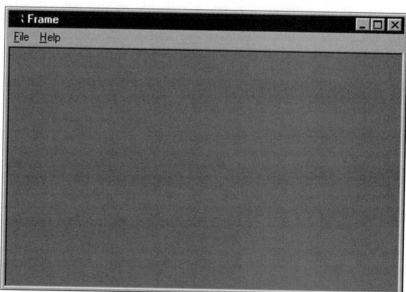

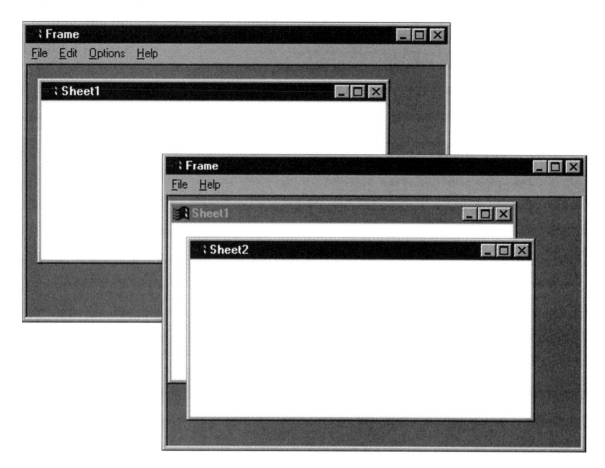

Toolbars behave slightly differently to menus in an MDI frame. The MDI frame's toolbar doesn't get replaced with the sheet's toolbar. Instead, if both the frame's menu and the sheet's menu have a toolbar implemented, both are displayed. If you only want to see the sheet's toolbar, you have to hide the frame's toolbar programmatically.

Using ParentWindow in an MDI Application

In the previous section we discussed messaging between menus and windows. In an MDI application, you should only use the **ParentWindow** keyword in menu scripts if all the sheets in the application have a menu attached to them. If any sheets do not have their own menu, they will use the frame's menu, so the **ParentWindow** keyword will refer to the MDI frame. In this situation, you should use the **getActiveSheet** function to message the MDI frame and sheets appropriately. Let's review this with an example.

The frame window, **w_frame**, has a menu, **m_frame**, associated with it. Window, **w_sheet1**, has the menu, **m_sheet1**, associated with it and **w_sheet2** has no menu associated with it—it will use the frame's menu **m_frame** when it's the active sheet. In this situation, messages from **m_frame** could be passed to **w_sheet2** by using **w_frame** as the 'message broker'. Let's review how the menu item **m_frame.m_file.m_open** is implemented. The script in the **Clicked** event of this menu item should just trigger the **ue_open_sheet** event in the **ParentWindow**.

```
parentWindow.triggerEvent("ue_open_sheet")
```

The script in **ue_open_sheet** event of **w_frame** should make a decision whether the message was meant for it or for a sheet using its menu. This script has to determine the active sheet and relay the message to it.

```
window l_window
l_window = getActiveSheet( )
if isValid(l_window) then
    l_window.triggerEvent("ue_open_sheet")
else
    //some processing
end if
```

Designing Menus

Your application can include menus that are built in two different ways. Static menus are created using the Menu painter and are based on an inheritance hierarchy. They can be inherited in a similar way to other objects and, in the descendant menu, you can add new menu items or modify existing ones and create, extend or override ancestor scripts.

Dynamic menus, on the other hand, are created programmatically and generated at run time. We'll take a look at both of these.

Static Menus

The Menu painter allows you to design and create menus, with one significant limitation which we'll look at in a moment.

The menus that you implement in your application should provide a uniform look, which means that menu options shouldn't change radically as users navigate through different screens in the application. At the same time, you don't want to re-invent menus from scratch whenever you have to construct a new one. You should have a flexible menu hierarchy that allows you to implement new menus very easily.

However, designing a flexible menu hierarchy is as challenging as designing a window hierarchy. In general, menus shouldn't embed any application logic and shouldn't refer to specific application classes or objects.

To design an effective menu hierarchy, you have to standardize all messages that are communicated by menus to windows. For example, all windows that require their menus to have a Close menu item selection should standardize on **ue_close** as the event or function which the menus will trigger when a user selects that menu item. This means that you have to standardize events or functions on all windows in your application as far as window/menu interaction is concerned. This results in a standard interface between menus and windows in the application and makes it possible to implement a menu hierarchy. You need to define these standards in an ancestor class of the window and menu to prevent run-time surprises.

Initiating Modules from a Menu

Let's consider the case where the action of selecting a menu item initiates a module instead of invoking a behavior of the active sheet. For example, in the following figure, the menu items Inventory and Accounting provide access to two different functional modules in the application.

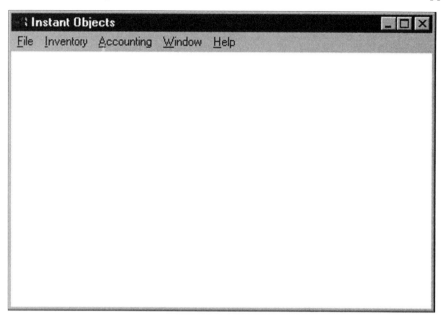

It's not practical for all windows to have knowledge of every module in your application—think of all the code you would have to add each time a module was added or modified, not to mention the fact that this would go against almost every rule of object-oriented design.

Instead, you should allow menus direct access to the MDI frame (there are many solutions to this design problem, but this is the simplest). Menu items which initiate functional modules would only communicate with the MDI frame. This would involve declaring the MDI frame as a global and having the script directly trigger functions or events.

```
gw_MDIFrame.triggerEvent("inventory_open")
```

To use a function instead of an event, you can design an abstract factory class and couple your base window with this object. An **abstract factory** is a class that provides a standard interface to initiate and access different application modules. We'll discuss this design pattern in detail in Chapter 8. The base window will have to provide a public interface to the abstract factory.

```
int f_createModule(string ps_moduleName)
```

This ensures a standard interface between menus and windows. The script in the Inventory menu item has to trigger the function, **f_createModule**, in the parent window.

```
ParentWindow.Function DYNAMIC TRIGGER f_createModule("inventory")
```

Menu Painter Limitations

The Menu painter has a limitation on inserting menu items between existing menu items at the descendant level. For example, take this menu:

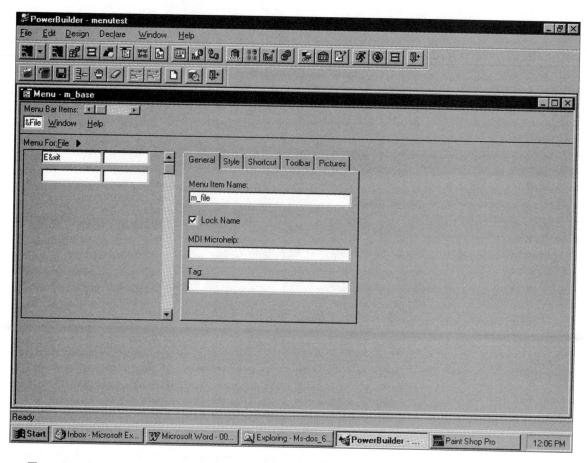

There is only one menu item, **m_exit**, that drops down from **m_file**. However, suppose you want to inherit from this menu and, in the descendant menu, you need the additional menu items **m_open**, **m_close**, **m_save** and **m_saveAs** to appear above **m_exit**.

The Menu painter doesn't allow you to insert menu items between those that are created at the ancestor level.

107

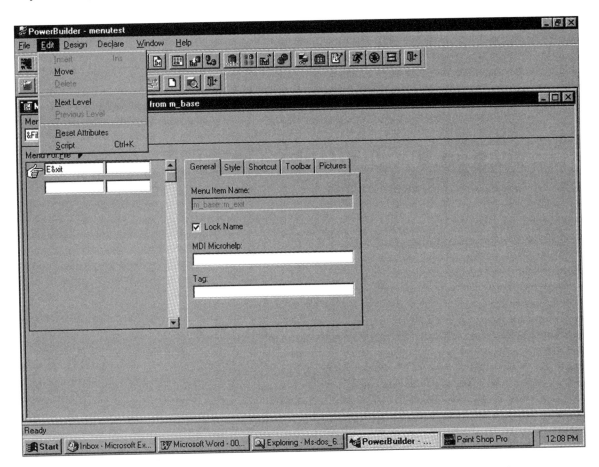

PowerBuilder does provide a Shift Over/Down property for each menu item. Setting this property makes the menu item shift down at run time if other menu items are added in the descendant menu. Still, this only gets round the limitation in cases of very simple menu inheritance.

The other solution to this problem is to provide dummy menu items at the base menu level. You should set the Visible property of these menu items to false.

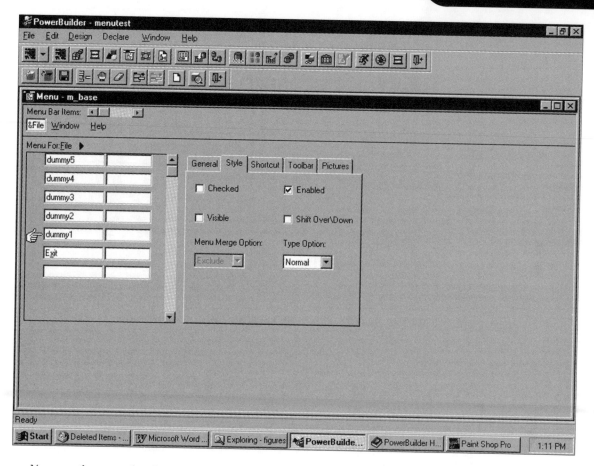

You can then use the dummy menu items as the Open, Close, Save and Save As menu items at the descendant menu by modifying their text and Visible property.

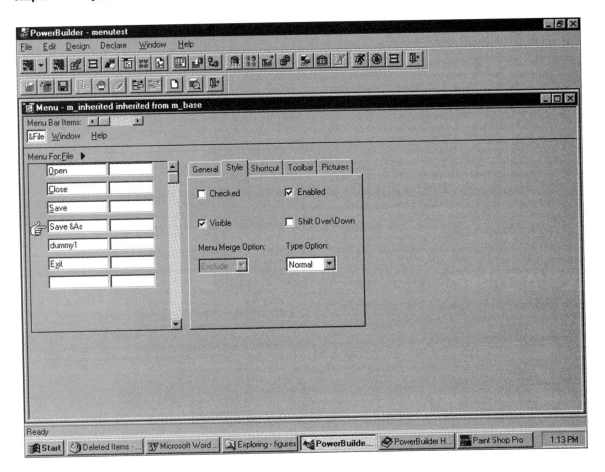

Dynamic Menus

If an application has a lot of screens, it could contain a lot of menus, which not only increase the amount of code to be maintained, but also the number of run-time dynamic libraries in the application. Static menus also make it difficult to customize the menus at run time. Dynamic menus provide a solution to these problems.

An application's menu hierarchy should ideally consist of static and dynamic menus, the combination providing a flexible menu architecture. You should only create menu items which can change at run time dynamically, because doing this for them all can slow down your application. Generating a menu at run time involves allocating memory for each menu item.

Let's implement a simple dynamic menu to explain the concept involved. Start by setting up two menus, named **m_template** and **m_generator**. The menu **m_template** consists of one item, named **m_dummy**. The other menu, **m_generator**, also consists of one menu item, **m_placeholder**. The menu, **m_template**, is the menu that should be assigned to any window that requires a dynamic menu. This menu will be extended at run time to include additional menu items. The menu, **m_generator**, is the menu that is used to allocate memory and create the additional menu items. Let's implement a dynamic menu with three top level menu items: File, Window and Help. File has an additional drop-down menu item: Exit.

110

Create a window, **w_dynamic_menu**, and assign it the menu, **m_template**. The script in the **Open** event of **w_dynamic_menu** will have to allocate memory and create the additional menu items. Here's the script:

```
/****************************************************************
 Event Name:     open
 Parameters:     <NONE>
 ReturnValue     <NONE>
 ****************************************************************/
m_generator l_generator[]
int li_numMenuItem = 3, i
string ls_title[4] = {"&File", "&Window","&Help", "&Exit"}
string ls_event[4] = {"File","Window", "Help", "Exit"}
menu l_menu

l_menu = this.menuID

for i = 1 TO li_numMenuItem
   if i > 1 then
      l_generator[i] = create m_generator
    l_generator[i].ITEM[1].text = ls_title[i]
      this.menuID.item[i] = l_generator[i].ITEM[1]
   else
      this.menuID.item[i].text = ls_title[i]
   end if
next

l_generator[4] = create m_generator
l_generator[4].item[1].text = ls_title[i]
this.menuID.item[1].item[1] = l_generator[i].item[1]

this.menuID.Item[1].Hide()
this.menuID.Item[1].Show()
```

> The **Hide** and **Show** functions force the menu to redraw and show the menu items that were created dynamically. Note that the script shown above is geared towards creating a specific menu and isn't generic in design.

This gives us the menu we were after:

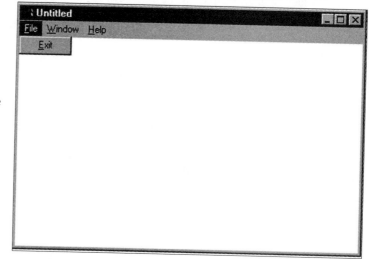

Designing a menu hierarchy consisting of static and dynamic menu items requires you to define the rules that should be used at run time to create the dynamic menus and the interface between the menu and windows.

The 'rules' that you have to define for creating menus at run time include the properties of the menu item, including the label or text, whether or not it's disabled, the bitmap for the toolbar button for this menu item, etc. The dynamic menu item also needs to know its location in the menu hierarchy and what it has to do when a user clicks on it.

Once you've defined a dynamic menu item's physical location and properties, how do you define what it does when the user clicks on it? Well, first you need to standardize the interface between the menus and windows in your application. Earlier, we established a scenario where the menu item either triggers an event on the parent window or calls a particular function in it. We'll have to modify the menu, **m_generator**, to demonstrate how a dynamically created menu item interacts with a window when a user clicks on it.

Create two private instance variables in **m_generator**, called **ib_callFunction** and **is_message**. The first indicates whether the **Clicked** event of the dynamic menu item should trigger an event in the parent window or call a function in it. The second indicates the event to be triggered or the parameter to be passed to the function. You have to create a function to initialize these variables and place the logic to implement the clicked behavior in the **Clicked** event of **m_generator.m_placeHolder**. Here's the script for this event:

```
/******************************************************************
  Event Name:    clicked
  Parameters:    <NONE>
  ReturnValue    <NONE>
******************************************************************/
if is_message <> "" then
  if ib_callFunction then
    ParentWindow.Function DYNAMIC TRIGGER f_createModule(is_Message)
  else
      ParentWindow.triggerEvent(is_Message)
    end if
end if
```

Have a look at the example on the disk (**Ch05.pbl**) to see this in action.

So, to summarize, the 'rules' have to provide information about:

- The menu associated with a window class
- The menu items to be created dynamically
- The properties of the dynamically created menu item
- Whether the menu has to trigger an event or call a function when clicked

Have another look at the script that we showed earlier that created menu items at run time. This should be made generic and designed so that it uses the 'rules' to modify and configure a window's menu at run time.

You should create a class user object to encapsulate the functionality to create and manipulate menu items and couple it with the base window in your application. You can define the rules for creating menus in tables in a relational database or in ASCII files. The class user object will read them at run time to augment the menu object of a window.

Summary

Programmers often overlook menus as they're designing an application. Static menus are faster to create at run time, but inherited menus in PowerBuilder have a lot of limitations. This chapter serves to introduce you to creating menu items at run time.

A menu architecture should consist of static menus which are extended at run time by creating menu items. An application can also allow its users to customize menus if it has the functionality to create menu items at run time.

Object Linking and Embedding

Object linking and embedding, or OLE, is one of the key components in Microsoft's enterprise computing strategy. Originally conceived as a technology to allow applications to share functionality and data, it has matured into a standard for inter-component communications both on the desktop and across the network.

OLE allows one application to use the functionality of another. In this chapter, we'll look at the history and some of the features of OLE and then see how you can put OLE to practical use in your applications.

An Overview of OLE

OLE is a manifestation of the Common Object Model (COM), a specification that defines a common method for communication and resource sharing across applications.

COM is a technology through which compliant applications can provide interfaces to one another at run time. COM provides application components or independent processing entities that can be plugged together to make or enhance applications. It accomplishes this by defining a binary interface for objects that's independent of a programming language. Objects conforming to COM can communicate with each other without programming using specific information about each other's implementations.

OLE is a set of object services built on top of COM. OLE objects provide services to their clients through interfaces, which are static in nature and don't support the concept of a class or inheritance. OLE services include features such as in-place editing, OLE controls and OLE Automation.

PowerBuilder takes advantage of OLE to enhance its internal object-oriented capabilities. Whereas PowerBuilder provides structural and development object-oriented facilities, OLE provides run-time objects that can be plugged into applications. The merging of these two concepts provides the developer with an advanced arsenal of tools that allows him or her to quickly develop sophisticated and efficient applications.

OLE allows applications that have no predefined knowledge of each other to interact and share information. Using OLE, a developer can create application objects that expose an interface to other applications. These application objects or **components** can then be linked together to form complete applications. This type of plug-and-play environment leads to robust, feature-rich applications built upon existing (and proven) technology.

History of OLE

The original goal behind OLE was to simplify computing on a system running Windows. Around the time of Windows 3.1, most personal computer users were accustomed to a file-based view of their system. The file-based view essentially defined all data as 'files' that are loaded into applications where they're used. Microsoft and the industry wanted and needed a much simpler approach.

This led to the introduction of the 'document-centric' computing concept, which was based, in part, on the Apple Macintosh interface. A document-centric system meant that the user didn't need to be concerned about which application was running or which file was loaded. OLE-enhanced or **compound** documents had the ability to contain data of many different formats, along with information that identified the type of data stored. The user only needed to know which document they were working on. So, as opposed to loading Microsoft Word and then loading a file into Word, the user could simply select a word-processing document. When the document was activated, it contained all the necessary details to start any associated applications that were required to present the information it contained.

As the technology matured, the true potential of OLE began to be realized. As well as simply enhancing documents, OLE offered a common interface that could be used by independent applications to share information. The focus of OLE development and use rapidly shifted from enhancing documents to creating inter-operable applications.

OLE is now at release level 2.0 and the new version shows a startling shift in emphasis of OLE technology. OLE 2.0 goes beyond its acronym—object linking and embedding has developed into a fully-fledged inter-component resource and data-sharing mechanism.

Linking and Embedding

When incorporating an object into an application, you have the choice of either linking it or embedding it. The application that has the object embedded or linked into it is called the OLE **client** or **container object**. The application that created the embedded/linked object is the OLE **server**.

When an object is linked, the application stores a reference to the data, rather than the data itself. With an embedded object, a copy of the original object is physically stored with the application in which the object is embedded, along with all of the information needed to manage the object. As a result, the object becomes a physical part of your application—the data is actually stored in your PowerBuilder **PBL** file and compiled into your PowerBuilder executable.

When you're deciding between linking or embedding an object, there are several things for you to consider:

- Will anyone else have access to data contained in objects outside of your application?
- Is the data contained in your objects of a static nature?
- Is the size of your application important?
- Is there a chance of someone moving files containing objects?
- Is speed important?

The following table highlights some of the differences between linking and embedding when you're considering these questions:

Topic	Linking	Embedding
Effect of changes on the source object	If objects are changed outside your application, the object in your application will be updated automatically.	An embedded object can only be edited from within your application.
Application size	Using linked objects will keep the size of your application down, as the objects are not stored within it.	Embedded objects are stored within your application, so the file size is bigger.
Effect of moving the source object	When you use linked objects, your application contains a reference to the linked file, so if the file is moved, the link will be severed.	This isn't a problem with embedded objects as the object is stored within the application.
Application speed	Linked objects are only loaded into your application when they are required, so start-up speed should be quicker. However, working with a linked object reduces the speed of your application, because the container has to link to the file.	Start-up speed will be slower because the file is bigger, but working with the embedded objects is quicker because the object already exists in your application.
Type of editing	Linked objects can't be activated in-place for editing. Only off-site activation is allowed.	In-place and off-site activation is allowed.

OLE Features

To support the document-centric idea, OLE provided several advanced features, including **drag-and-drop editing** and **in-place visual editing**.

Drag-and-drop Editing

Drag-and-drop eliminates the traditional barriers between applications. It enables you to freely drag information to and from a variety of applications. Rather than having to deal with moving a data file from one 'directory' to another and then merging the file into an application, you are supplied with a intuitive, visual means for sharing data between applications. Drag-and-drop makes compound documents easier to create and manage because it provides an interactive model that more closely resembles how people interact with physical objects.

OLE supports the following types of drag-and-drop:

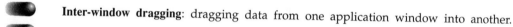 **Inter-window dragging**: dragging data from one application window into another.

Inter-object dragging: objects nested within other objects can be dragged out of their containing objects to another window or to another container object.

Dropping over icons: objects can be dragged over the desktop to system resource icons such as printers and mailboxes. The appropriate action will be taken with the object, depending on the type of resource the icon represents.

In-place Visual Editing

In-place visual editing allows you to select an OLE object and interact with it in the application in which it is embedded. You don't need to switch to a different application to work with the information presented.

When you edit in-place, all menus, toolbars, palettes and other controls necessary to interact with the embedded object temporarily replace the existing menus and controls of the active window. In effect, the object application appears to 'take over' the current application window. When you return to the client application, its menus and controls are restored.

Visual editing can include a variety of operations, depending on the capabilities of the object. Embedded objects can be edited, played, displayed and recorded in-place. Linked objects, on the other hand, can be activated in-place for operations such as playback and display, but they can't be edited in-place. When a linked object is opened for editing, the object application is activated in a separate window.

An Object's Data

OLE associates two major types of data with an object: **visual representation data** and **native data**. An object's visual representation data is the information needed to render the object on a display device, while its native data is all the information needed for an application to edit the object. The visual representation data will typically always be present, but the native data depends on what method of OLE was used: linking or embedding. In linking, you'll see the data (visual representation), but you may not be able to do anything with it unless the source is available. In embedding, you will also see the data (visual representation), but the native data will activate the object's service assuming that the application that created the object is available.

OLE Components vs. PB Objects

OLE uses the terms **object** and **component** interchangeably—OLE is often referred to as Microsoft's answer to object orientation. To the user, there's really no distinction between the concept of a component and an object, because the two primary benefits of both are that they can be reused in many different applications and share data with each other. However, as a PowerBuilder developer, it's important to understand the differences between the two terms.

Generally speaking, a system is object-oriented if it exhibits the characteristics of an object as defined by the object model:

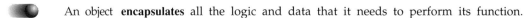 An object **encapsulates** all the logic and data that it needs to perform its function.

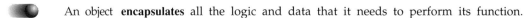 Each object has an interface that is used to interact with the outside world.

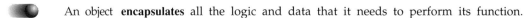 This interface consists of properties and methods.

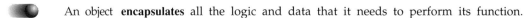 Objects can be inherited from one or more parent objects.

PowerBuilder is a good example of an object-oriented system. At its most detailed level, PowerBuilder supplies all of its functionality in terms of objects. Each object has properties consisting of public variables and methods consisting of public functions and events. These objects can be inherited from ancestors to create application-specific objects for use by the developer.

OLE provides components which are run-time or binary objects. A run-time object simply means that it exists as a process in memory. Because it's a binary (or compiled) object, its interfaces are static in nature. OLE components exhibit much of the object-oriented behavior that we've defined. They have properties and methods and they encapsulate all the data and logic needed to perform their functions.

The difference is that an OLE component is a run-time object—we can't change its interface or expand and enhance its functionality through inheritance. A PowerBuilder object is derived from a class that the developer creates or is provided by the PowerBuilder product. Once a PowerBuilder object has been created at run time, it takes on much of the same characteristics of an OLE object.

Using OLE in PowerBuilder 5.0

There are several ways of using OLE with PowerBuilder. These include:

- Using OLE controls (insertable controls)
- Using OLE with DataWindows
- OCXs (or ActiveX controls)
- OLE Automation

In the rest of this chapter, we'll look at examples of the first three of these implementations. Chapter 7 discusses OLE Automation.

OLE Controls

PowerBuilder provides support for OLE objects (known as **insertable objects**) and OCXs (custom OLE controls). To use these objects in PowerBuilder, you insert them into a PowerBuilder **OLE control**, which acts as a container.

OLE controls provide a means to enhance the PowerBuilder development environment with functional components that can be plugged into an application. They are a superset of the OLE 2.0 specification, supporting all of the features of OLE, along with several enhancements that allow for a tighter integration with development tools such as PowerBuilder.

In essence, an OLE control is an embedded object with support for properties and methods. You can think of an OLE control as an interface device that transforms different external events into useful programmatic events. When one of these events occurs, the control **client** (the application in which the control is embedded) can execute code to perform some action.

OLE controls communicate with the client application using standard OLE 2.0 communication protocols. The advantage of this approach is that controls created by different developers will all work together, sending and receiving data in a consistent manner.

Placing an OLE Control on a Window

Placing an OLE control on a window is little different to placing a normal control. When you select the OLE control from the drop-down list of window controls, you'll be presented with a dialog box requesting some information concerning the OLE control that will be placed on your window.

119

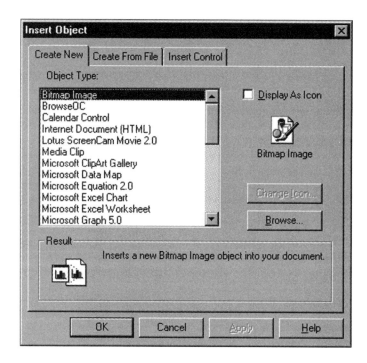

The first option in the Insert Object dialog box allows you to create an OLE control based on an OLE type that has been registered on your system. Windows keeps track of all OLE types that are added to your system. As new applications that are OLE-aware are installed, they update the Windows registry, which contains information related to your system and the software installed on it. We'll take a look at the Windows registry in the next chapter.

The second option allows you to create a control based on a file. This option will establish the control type based on the application reference Windows has assigned to the file you select. If no specific reference has been assigned, Windows will provide a generic type for the file that you select (usually text).

It's important to note that these first two options create a container control and place an OLE object within it. The control acts as a client to the embedded OLE object and allows you to communicate with the server application using standard OLE server/client protocols. You can, therefore, make changes to the object you create, using all the functionality of the server application.

The third option allows you to insert an OCX control on your window. We'll look at this option later in the chapter.

OLE Control Properties

Like all other window controls, an OLE control has various properties that you can set.

120

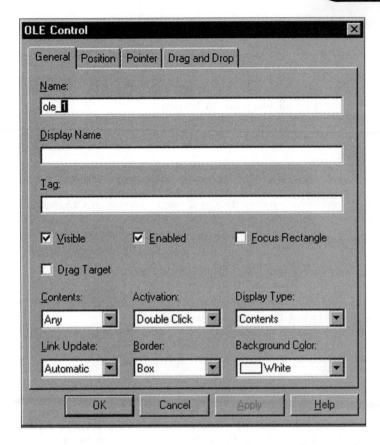

These include the control name, display name, tag, etc. There are also several special entries that apply to OLE objects specifically. The first property of interest is Contents.

Contents

You can set Contents to any of three options:

●	Any	Allows linked or embedded objects to be inserted.
●	Embedded	Allows only embedded objects to be inserted.
●	Linked	Allows only linked objects to be inserted.

The default for this property is Any, which means that either method is allowed. This is the most likely setting you will use, as it provides you with the most flexibility.

Activation

This property determines how an OLE server is activated. You can set the Activation property to:

●	Double Click	The server is activated by double clicking on it.

	Focus	The server is activated whenever the control receives focus.
	Manual	The server is activated by code.

Activation via Focus is the least desirable option. In most cases, it will take a few moments for an OLE application to load and display its data. If this has to occur each time the control gains focus, your program's performance will likely take a beating.

If you specify Manual, you need to take care of activating the server programmatically, for example:

```
result = ole_1.Activate(Offsite!)
```

Activate is the PowerBuilder function that you use to invoke an OLE server. When this function is called, you have two options that allow you to select how a server is activated: **Offsite!** or **InPlace!**. The **Offsite!** enumerated variable opens the server in its own window. This option supports OLE version 1.0 functionality and is always used when a linked OLE server is activated.

A more functional approach is to call the **Activate** function with the **InPlace!** enumerated variable argument. Here, the OLE server is opened in-place, which means that it is displayed within the frame of the OLE control inserted into your PowerBuilder window. You can invoke the OLE server in-place only when the content is embedded.

We've included an example on the disk in the **Ch06.pbl** library, which has an embedded Excel spreadsheet and allows you to activate it either in-place or offsite.

> **We should make a note of caution here. PowerBuilder's support for in-place automation can lead to difficulties. If the control placed in a PowerBuilder window doesn't account for the extra space required by the activated OLE server, the display can become jumbled.**

As we mentioned earlier, a side effect of in-place editing is that your PowerBuilder application's menu and the OLE server's application menu merge. This allows for a clean interface between the two applications, but you must take it into account when you develop the menu for your application.

Display Type

This property is used to specify whether you want to see the actual contents of the OLE object or an icon representing the server application. Certain objects, such as a sound file, will always display as an icon, as the data can't be visualized in a meaningful way.

If you choose to display the OLE object as an icon, you have the option of selecting which icon to display. Typically, the OLE sever application provides you with a default icon, but may include one or more additional icons to be used to represent the application. To choose a different icon, select the Change Icon button on the Insert Object dialog and provide the name and location of the file containing the alternative icon you want to use.

> Note that you can't change the icon displayed after the control has been inserted. The **Display Type** property only specifies that data or an icon is displayed, not what icon to display.

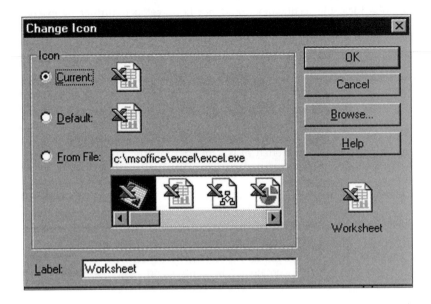

Link Update

This option is applicable only for linked types. Link Update tells OLE what to do if a link to a data file is broken. If set to Automatic, the system will attempt to find the file on your system. If it can't find the file, it will display a dialog to the user. If this property is set to Manual, you'll need to use the **UpdateLinksDialog** function to reset the link each time it's broken.

OCX Controls

As extensions to the existing OLE 2.0 specification, the OCX control architecture is built on proven technology and an industry-wide standard. Both 16- and 32-bit components can be developed using the same OCX control source code, by simply recompiling under Windows 3.1 or Windows NT and Windows 95. The new architecture also opens up the possibility of OCX controls being available in the future on additional operating systems such as the Macintosh or UNIX.

To really understand what an OCX control is, we need to look at what a **custom control** is. The custom control isn't unique to OLE; they were originally developed as a mechanism to expand upon the base functionality provided by the Windows operating system. They were first introduced with the release of Microsoft Windows Version 3.0. A custom control was defined at that time as a DLL that exported a set of functions. They were made available from third-party developers. These predeveloped custom controls were useful, but most C developers preferred to write their own and, as you can imagine, no standard interface was adhered to.

A new custom control architecture, called the **VBX**, was then defined specifically to support Visual Basic. Its purpose was to offer the features of specialized Windows controls, targeted specifically at the Visual Basic development environment. The VBX became incredibly popular and thousands of

VBXs, from simple buttons to complicated networking controls, popped up for a wide range of uses. These custom controls greatly enhanced the capabilities of the Visual Basic product and, due to their increasing popularity, support for VBXs was added to Powerbuilder with release 4.0.

The VBX, however, is a limited interface, specifically designed for Visual Basic. As such, although founded on a solid idea, the technology could not be developed further or extended to additional environments. With the advent of OLE, a new foundation for component reusability was devised. OLE provides a much more flexible environment for building powerful, reusable software components.

An OCX is an OLE In Process object (an OLE object that loads into the address space of its container) with some extended functionality. It has support for properties and methods through **IDispatch** (a standard interface used by all OLE 2.0-compliant objects), support for property pages using **ISpecifyPropertyPages**, support for type information with **IProvideClassInfo** and support for events through **IConnectionPointContainer**, along with individual connection points for each event set. Controls often also support property change notification.

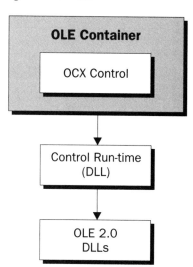

The diagram opposite illustrates a high level view of an OCX and its dependencies. A control container exposes an interface for each control embedded in the container. The control and container communicate through this interface. The control relies on a control run-time dynamic-link library (DLL) to provide an implementation of the control-specific interfaces. The control run-time DLL relies on standard OLE 2.0 DLLs.

OLE custom controls communicate with client applications using standard OLE 2.0 communication protocols. The advantage of this approach is that controls created by different developers will all work together, sending and receiving data in a manner that is consistent with all other controls.

The advent of the OCX brings about a real possibility of the widespread use of component-based application development. This essentially means pulling together functional application components from various sources to create complete applications. Rather than developing each interface, process and method over and over again, predeveloped and tested components are plugged together to create applications.

> Microsoft recently renamed their OCX technology ActiveX, much to the confusion of the development community. New controls may well be referred to as ActiveX controls, but they are essentially exactly the same as OCX controls. PowerBuilder still uses the term OCX, so we'll refer to these types of controls as OCXs. Just remember that wherever you see the term OCX, you can substitute the term ActiveX.

Inserting an OCX Control on a Window

When you insert an OCX on a window, you give your application the ability to interact with an OCX control's interface much the same as it would with one of PowerBuilder's own internal controls.

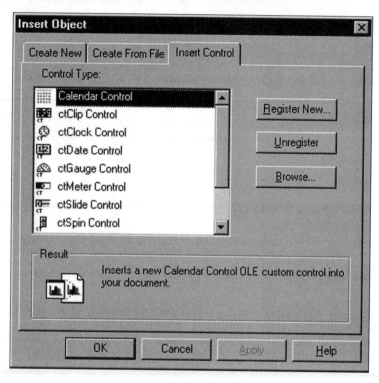

When you're inserting an OCX, you have the option of registering a control (if this has not already been done) using the **Register New...** button. This can be helpful when you're installing new OCX controls onto your system. The **Insert Object** dialog provides you with a display of all of the controls that are currently registered. The **Browse** button will load PowerBuilder's Object browser which displays the current registry settings for the selected OCX. You can also remove controls from the registry using the **Unregister** button.

We'll discuss the Windows registry in the next chapter.

OCX Control Properties

When an OCX control is inserted into a PowerBuilder object, it's treated slightly differently to a normal OLE object. If you view the standard properties of an OCX control using the **Properties...** menu selection, you'll notice that they are identical to most other objects, but that the OLE-specific properties are no longer supplied.

There is also a new option (**OCX Properties**) that provides you with access to the OCX control's properties. These properties can be set just as they would be for a standard PowerBuilder control. For example, the following screenshot shows the available OCX properties for the ctClock OCX that is installed with PowerBuilder.

125

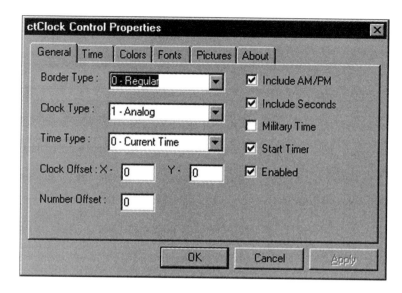

You can see that this includes various options allowing you to set properties of the clock, such as type of clock and type and format of the time.

Using an OCX

Before you can really take advantage of a control, you must first determine what features and facilities it offers. The OLE tab on the object browser allows you to look at all the properties, events and functions available in the OCXs on your system:

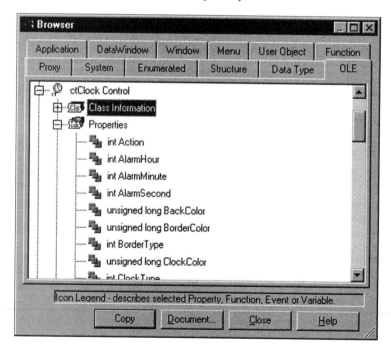

Here you can see some of the properties of the ctClock OCX. We can call these properties through the PowerBuilder interface to the object (using the keyword **Object**) and control them just like the properties of any other internal PowerBuilder control. For example, the following line of code would change the **ClockType** property:

```
ole_control.object.ClockType = 1
```

Events and functions are referenced in exactly the same way. The class information refers to how the object was registered on your system. It includes a GUID, which is a unique ID assigned to the control's OLE interface and a program ID, which identifies the application used to present the control. Along with this information is the name of the in-process server used to support the OCX, as well as a unique ID for a supporting type library (if one is provided).

Once we've placed the control in the window workspace, it looks like any other window control. However, unlike other controls, what is actually placed on the window is a 'container' control into which the OCX control is inserted. This works like a DataWindow object, where a placeholder is put on a window and a DataWindow object is then inserted into it. The container control is used to communicate with the actual OCX control, which is accessed using the object method.

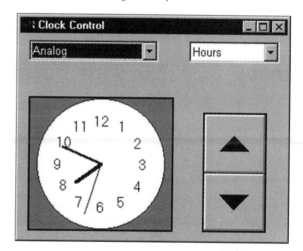

There's an example on the disk, in the **ch06.pbl** library. This uses the ctSpin OCX to control the time displayed on the ctClock OCX.

The first drop-down list box allows you to switch between analog and digital clock display by setting the **ClockType** property of the clock control:

```
If this.text = "Digital" then
    ole_clock.object.ClockType = 0    //set display to digital
else
    ole_clock.object.ClockType = 1    // set display to analog
end if
```

The second drop-down list box allows you to specify whether you want to change hours, minutes or seconds on the clock and this value is used in the **Click** event of the spin control:

```
int timeincrement

/* Check which button has been clicked and set increment acordingly */

If nbutton = 0 then
    timeincrement = +1
else
```

```
        timeincrement = -1
    end if

    /* Check the value in the timeunits drop down list box and change the appropriate
    property on the clock */

    Choose Case ddlb_timeunits.text
        Case "Hours"
            ole_clock.object.CurrentHour = &
                ole_clock.object.CurrentHour + timeincrement
        Case "Minutes"
            ole_clock.object.CurrentMinute = &
                ole_clock.object.CurrentMinute + timeincrement
        Case "Seconds"
                ole_clock.object.CurrentSecond = &
    ole_clock.object.CurrentSecond + timeincrement
    End Choose
```

We first check the value of **nbutton,** which determines which button on the spin control has been clicked, and set the increment to either +1 or -1. We then check which units we should change and set the relevant property of the clock control, either **CurrentHour**, **CurrentMinute** or **CurrentSecond**. That's all there is to using OCXs.

Using OLE 2.0 with DataWindows

PowerBuilder 5.0 provides three different ways to use OLE in DataWindows. We'll look at each of these in turn.

DataWindow OLE Presentation Style

With PowerBuilder 5.0, you have a new OLE 2.0 DataWindow presentation style, which allows you to edit data in a DataWindow in the editor of your choice. For example, you can query a database or other file and have the information displayed in the format of your choice, be that an Excel graph or Worksheet, a Word document or whatever.

The easiest way of seeing how this works is to look at an example. For this example, we want to access sales data that is stored in a tab-delimited file—**SampData.txt**. We want to display this data and allow users to manipulate it using Excel's functionality.

Create a new DataWindow and choose the External source and the OLE 2.0 presentation style:

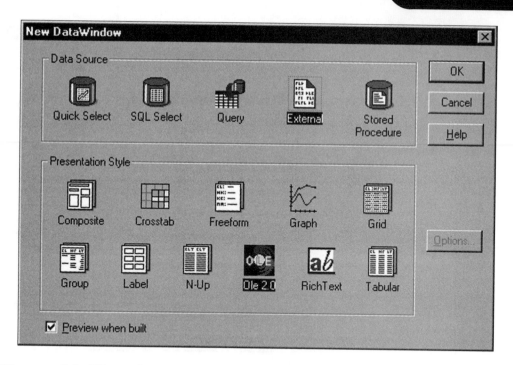

When you click OK, you'll be prompted for the Result Set Description. For our example, the data consists of the following elements:

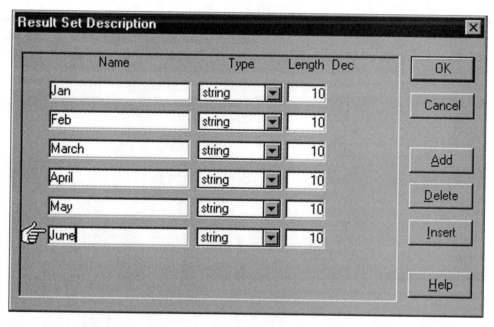

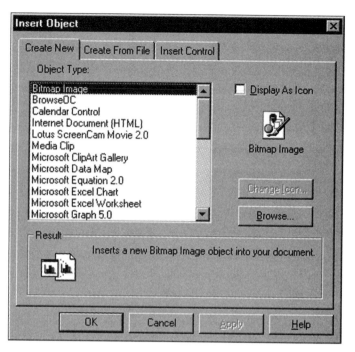

Now that a description of the data has been provided, pressing OK will bring up the following dialog requesting the type of OLE object to use:

You can now select any object type, depending on what you have installed on your machine—in this case, select Microsoft Excel Worksheet. With the type selected, PowerBuilder will activate the object. The worksheet is as yet empty; we'll import the data at run time.

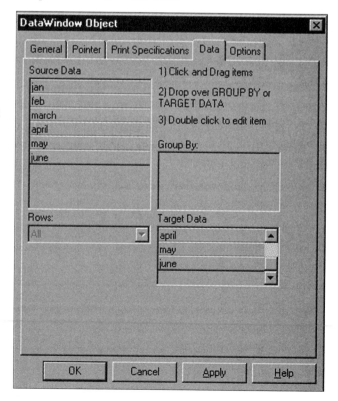

Now Powerbuilder needs to know what columns you want to be sent to the Excel object. Display the OLE Object Properties dialog with the Data Tab presented. The Data Tab allows you to select the columns to be displayed by dragging them from the Source Data list and dropping them on the Target Data entry box. Drag each column that you want displayed to the Target Data entry box and press OK when finished.

Now save the DataWindow and drop it onto a PowerBuilder window. When you run the window and import the external data into the DataWindow using **ImportFile**, your data will be displayed using the OLE object. If you double-click on the DataWindow, it will launch Excel, allowing you to modify its attributes.

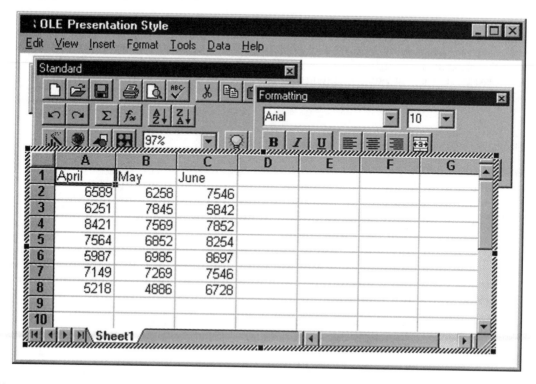

You can see this example working in the **Ch06.pbl** library on the disk.

> **Note that the OLE DataWindow presentation style is a new feature of Powerbuilder 5.0. You may find that things don't appear to work as expected. For example, both Microsoft Word and Microsoft Excel OLE objects can display unusually large text on some systems and with Microsoft Graph, the correlation between the result set description, target data set and the data displayed in the OLE object can be tenuous. I would advise you to use this new feature with caution in the initial release.**

Placing OLE Objects in a DataWindow

The OLE 2.0 presentation style allows you to display all of the data set retrieved by the DataWindow using the OLE server. However, sometimes you may want to display the data initially in a standard DataWindow and, when the user selects an object on the DataWindow, display the data using an OLE server. You can do this by placing an OLE 2.0 control in any one of the traditional presentation style DataWindows.

131

Once you've painted the DataWindow, use the Objects menu and select OLE Object. Insert the new OLE control on the DataWindow and the OLE Object's property sheet will appear with the Data tab selected. You can use this tab to select the data fields that will be displayed by the embedded OLE object.

This is much the same as using the OLE DataWindow presentation style, except that, here, the OLE object is displayed alongside the data in the DataWindow. The data displayed in the OLE object will be linked to the original set of data. However, whereas with the OLE presentation style the OLE object is associated with all rows, when you insert an OLE object into a DataWindow, you can associate it with individual or groups of rows. To link it to the current row, you change the Layer property on the Position tab to Band; this will then allow you to select Current Row for the Rows property on the Data tab.

Using OLE Blobs in a DataWindow

When you're working with OLE, your application may need a method to store OLE objects in a format that's more dynamic than embedding can allow. To handle this, PowerBuilder takes advantage of the special **blob** (binary large object) data type. The blob data type is used to store large amounts of data, for example chapters of a book, images, audio data, video files, etc.

PowerBuilder supplies a special OLE database blob type column that allows a DataWindow to store an embedded OLE object as a blob in a database. An OLE database blob is treated differently to other data types because of the special nature of a blob object. A blob is simply a binary object of some type and, as such, PowerBuilder needs some help defining what to do with it before you can select it for use in a DataWindow.

In our case, the blob is an OLE object. To tell Powerbuilder this, you must select the OLE Database Blob item off the Objects menu to insert an OLE blob column. We'll see how this works in a moment.

> The advantage of the OLE database blob object is that the data in the embedded object can be changed dynamically, as those changes will be stored along with the object in the database blob column.

In the **Blobsamp.db** database on the disk supplied with this book, there is a column that is the long binary data type called **Comments** in the **Contacts** table. Let's take a look at how we might select data from this column and display it in the DataWindow, as well as how we can update this column.

Connect to the database and then start the DataWindow painter. Select the Quick Select data source, along with the Tabular presentation style. Next select the **Contacts** table and whichever columns you want to display. Then, in design view, select Objects/OLE Database BLOB from the DataWindow painter design menu and place the new object in the detail band to the right of the last column. You'll be prompted for the blob definition like this:

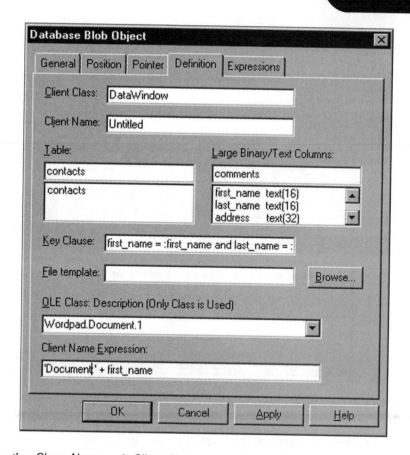

You can leave the Class Name and Client Name set with the defaults. These two values are used by some OLE servers to display in the OLE server windows, but we won't use them here.

A primary key was defined in the table, so PowerBuilder automatically populates the Table and Large Binary/Text columns for you. Otherwise, you would have to select contacts for the table and comments for the Large Binary/Text columns prompt.

> Note that if no primary key was defined, you wouldn't be able to update the table.

The value in the Key Clause is used by PowerBuilder in the **WHERE** clause of the **UPDATE**/ **DELETE** statement to update the database table. The File template property allows you to provide a default template to use every time you invoke the OLE server. A default template is used to define a standard presentation form for your result set. You can leave this empty for now.

Select the OLE server name from the drop-down list box. The value in the Client Name Expression is a string expression that is used to identify the row and column number in the DataWindow for the OLE server. When you invoke the OLE server from the DataWindow, the result of the Client Name Expression is displayed.

To see how it works, go to preview mode. Double-click on the database blob column to view the contents of that column of the database. You can add new comments and edit the existing ones.

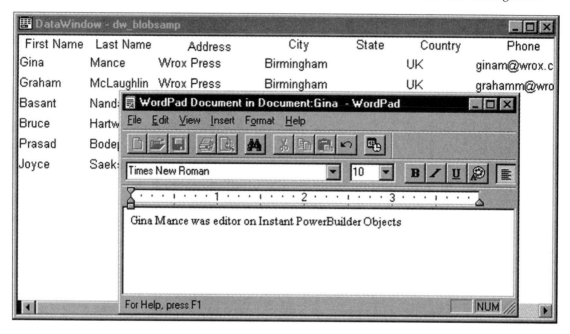

When the user double-clicks on this column, PowerBuilder automatically invokes the OLE server. If you want to invoke the OLE server programmatically, you can use the **OLEActivate** function.

```
Dw_1.OLEActivate(GetRow(), 2, 0)
```

The last argument to the **OLEActivate** function is the OLE server verb. The OLE server verb is a specific command sent to the server when it's activated. In most cases this is simply 0. To find supported verbs that you can use with the **OLEActivate** function, use **RegEdit/V** to review the registry entries for the OLE server that will be activated. We will look at the registry in more detail in the next chapter.

Summary

In this chapter, we've looked at several features of OLE and how you can take advantage of them in your PowerBuilder application. OLE is a powerful technology that allows you as a developer to significantly increase the functionality of your application with a minimum of work.

Enhancing your product by linking into existing products not only allows your application to provide additional features, but allows you to take advantage of your investment in existing applications. The true strength of OLE lies in its ability to improve the user's productivity—users can focus on the task at hand without having to worry about the data's origin, format and location.

In the next chapter, we'll look at OLE Automation and see how you can use this powerful facility to further enhance your PowerBuilder applications. We'll also take a closer look at the Windows registry and see how it affects how you use OLE in your applications.

OLE Automation

In the last chapter, we discussed the activation of an OLE server from a PowerBuilder application and the use of OLE controls. However, with OLE you can do a lot more than simply extend control functionality and activate server applications.

In this chapter, we'll look at OLE Automation and at the Windows registry.

OLE 2.0 Automation

OLE Automation is a Windows protocol intended to replace DDE. As with DDE, an application can use OLE Automation to share data or control another application. Once you've connected to a server, you can use a command set exposed to your application by the server to manipulate the object. This is a task you can perform behind the scenes, out of the user's sight.

This technology is useful if you need to use the features of one application in another. OLE Automation allows you to integrate features from both applications in a single procedure. For example, a PowerBuilder application can use Microsoft Excel as a financial calculation engine— whenever the PowerBuilder application needs to a perform a financial calculation, it simply calls one of Excel's functions, passing the data to be calculated as parameters. Excel performs the calculation and returns a result to the PowerBuilder application. Applications can greatly extend their capabilities through this transparent use of another application's features.

There are two sides involved in OLE Automation: the server and the client:

The server is the application or component that is controlled through its exposed interface. The exposed interface is referred to as an **object model**. An object model is a hierarchical collection of interface elements that are exposed to external applications. Access to any specific object in the hierarchy requires that all higher objects in it be instantiated. For example, the Excel object model exposes an application object, followed by a workbook object in its object hierarchy. In order to access a worksheet, the application object and the workbook object must have already been instantiated.

The client (or controller) is another application or development tool that controls the automation server by accessing its exposed interface. This is the real power behind OLE Automation. For example, in the arena of applications, a tool such as PowerBuilder can be used to present detailed graphs using Excel's graphing facilities.

PowerBuilder and OLE Automation

OLE Automation allows you to access the functionality of another application from within PowerBuilder without having to display that application. The work is done behind the scenes and the user need not even know that another application is involved. You do this by creating programmable OLE objects using PowerBuilder's OLEObject object type.

> The OLEObject object acts as a proxy for a remote OLE object. A proxy is a mechanism by which you can represent the external object in your code; all communication between the external object and your application is performed through the proxy.

We'll illustrate how you can put OLE Automation to use in PowerBuilder by showing a number of examples. We'll start with a couple of examples where Excel is the OLE server and PowerBuilder is the OLE client or controller and then look at using a PowerBuilder object as the OLE server.

Using Excel as an OLE Server

In this example, we'll be accessing an Excel spreadsheet to do some calculations for us and then use the result in our PowerBuilder application. We'll use OLE Automation to move the data to Excel. Note that, to run this and the following example, you'll need Excel 5.0 or higher.

The **Ch07.pbl** application supplied on the disk includes **w_excelsample**. This uses Excel to calculate the number of days, months and years between two dates. The sample application sends data to Excel, along with several formulae and then reads the resulting data and displays it on a PowerBuilder window.

To start, we create a simple form for the user to enter a Start Date and an End Date, as well as display the result of the Excel calculation.

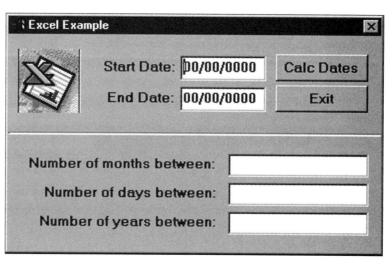

After entering the requested information, the user selects the Calc Dates command button. The command button contains all the code needed to access Excel. We'll look at this now.

Setting up Communication with the Server

Our first step is to define two variables of type OLEObject which we'll use to communicate with the Excel OLE server. The first variable is used to store a reference to the Excel application object, while the second is used to interact with a specific worksheet object. We'll also need another two variables to track return codes:

```
OLEObject  obExcel        //reference to Excel
OLEObject  obSheet        //Reference to Excel Sheet
Long       lResult        //result codes
Any        aResult        //PB undefined var
```

Of these, the variable of interest is the **aResult** value declared with a type of Any.

Any is a new variable type provided by PowerBuilder 5.0, that in many ways mimics Visual Basic's 'variant' data type. It's used for an OLE object that returns an undefined data type value to a client application. You can use this special type to capture this value in your PowerBuilder application and then convert it to a more suitable value.

As you can guess, you should use the Any type in moderation. One of the drawbacks of this new type is that, if an operation is performed on it that isn't valid for the value actually stored, a run-time error will occur. In addition, if you attempt to convert the type to a format with which the value in the variable isn't compatible, a run-time error will occur.

> If you look at the code supplied on the disk, you'll see that there is also a fifth variable. We need this to be able to take account of the way Excel calculates dates. Excel treats a date as a number starting at 1900 and increasing over time. As such, it doesn't directly support a date before 1900-01-01. **dMinDate** is used to make sure that the user enters a date after 1900, so that Excel will be able to perform the correct calculations.

Now that we have variables to work with, we can create the two objects that we'll need.

As do all OLE server applications, Excel exposes an interface to external applications. This interface consists of Excel's object model, which provides access to some 100 OLE Automation objects that you can use in your code. With this level of functionality, there really is no limit to what you can do with Excel using a tool like PowerBuilder.

Of all the OLE objects exposed, you can only create three directly in your code. They are:

- **Application** The application object is the highest object in Excel's object hierarchy. It's used to make the initial connection between your application and Excel.
- **Sheet** A sheet is one of Excel's primary presentation forms.
- **Chart** Excel charts are used to produce graphs based on data values provided either by your application or on a sheet.

Our example will use a reference to the application object to create an instance of a worksheet. We can then use this worksheet for our calculations.

Our first step is to instantiate two OLEObject type objects, using the **CREATE** statement.

```
    obExcel = CREATE OLEObject
    obSheet = CREATE OLEObject
```

Now we need to connect to an instance of Excel. PowerBuilder gives you two options. One is to create a new instance of the OLE server and return a reference to the new instance. You do this using the **ConnectToNewObject** method of the OLEObject object. The second option is to connect to an existing instance of an OLE server, using **ConnectToObject**. For this example, let's look at connecting to a new instance of a server.

ConnectToNewObject accepts a class name as a parameter and creates a new OLE object in the specified server application. If the application isn't already running, it will start a new instance.

```
    lResult = obExcel.ConnectToNewObject ( "Excel.Application" )
```

Here we create a new instance of the Excel application object, which always creates a new instance of Excel. If we were to create a new instance of a worksheet object initially, a new instance of Excel would not be started if Excel were already running.

ConnectToNewObject returns an error code value that we can test in our application. In this case, anything that isn't a zero is a problem. Note, however, that only the predefined functions of the OLEObject object return standard values; any other function you call will produce a result that's dependent on the server application, not PowerBuilder.

With that said, we can call a function in Excel that adds a new workbook. We'll use the first sheet of the created workbook as our calculation work space.

```
    aResult = obExcel.Workbooks.add()
    obSheet = obExcel.ActiveWorkBook.Worksheets(1)
```

Notice here that we use the variable of type Any to capture the return value for the **Add** call. That's due to that fact that Excel doesn't provide a defined type for this return value. The return value is actually a handle to the instantiated worksheet object created in Excel. However, we use the Any type, because Excel's interface doesn't provide type information and PowerBuilder will produce a run-time error if we attempt to assign the resulting value to a long or integer type variable.

The **obSheet** variable is then assigned the value of the first active worksheet, which, as we just created a new workbook, will be a blank sheet that we can use for our calculations. Note that we can't use the result of the **ADD** function for our processing, as that's a reference to a workbook, not a worksheet. A workbook is a collection of worksheets and doesn't provide worksheet functionality.

Our next step is to test the return value to verify that a valid handle to an instantiated object was returned using the **ISValid** PowerBuilder function. If we don't have a valid return value, we have to take a few extra steps to make sure that our objects are cleaned up and the server application released. The **DisconnectObject** method is provided by the OLEObject object to remove the link between your PowerBuilder application and the OLE server application. Once the link has been removed, we remove the objects from memory using the **DESTROY** command.

> Note that if you don't disconnect from the OLE object and destroy the references, PowerBuilder will gradually eat up your system's resources, producing unpredictable results.

```
if ( ISValid(aResult) = FALSE or isValid( obExcel ) = FALSE ) then

    //
    // Houston, we have a problem...
    //
    obSheet.DisconnectObject()
    obExcel.DisconnectObject()
    DESTROY obSheet
    DESTROY obExcel
    MessageBox( "OLE Error", "Unable To Add Excel Sheet, Code: " + &
                String( lResult ) )
    Return
end if
```

Passing Data between Client and Server

If we make a connection to Excel, we're then free to pass data back and forth. For our example, we'll send the dates entered by the user to the Excel spreadsheet. To do this, we take advantage of the **Range** method of the Excel worksheet object.

```
obSheet.Range("A1").Value = Parent.em_start.text
obSheet.Range("A2").Value = Parent.em_end.text
```

The **Range** function is quite flexible in that we're free to pass data either to individual cells or to multiple cells. In our example, we pass text strings representing the values entered. As Excel will recognize the format of the data, enforced by a entry mask in the PowerBuilder control, there's no need to convert the data to a date type.

Finally, we pass the formulae that will be used to calculate the values we need.

```
obSheet.Range("B1").Value = "=(YEAR(A2)-YEAR(A1))*12 + MONTH(A2)-"+ "MONTH(A1)"
obSheet.Range("B2").Value = "=A2-A1"
obSheet.Range("B3").Value = "=YEAR(A2)-YEAR(A1)"
```

Just as we supplied Excel with data, we can read data from Excel.

```
sle_Months.Text = String(obSheet.Range("B1").Value)
sle_Days.Text   = String(obSheet.Range("B2").Value)
sle_Years.Text  = String(obSheet.Range("B3").Value)
```

Here, we again take advantage of the **Range** method. As the data returned from our calculations is numeric in nature, the sample takes the extra step of converting it to a string type, before presenting the resulting value.

Removing the Connection

With our results presented to the user, we can remove our connection the Excel server and remove Excel from memory.

```
obExcel.ActiveWorkbook.Close( False )
obExcel.Quit

//
// disconnect
```

```
//
obSheet.DisconnectObject()
obExcel.DisconnectObject()

//
// kill references
//
DESTROY obSheet
DESTROY obExcel
```

You should note here that we use different methods to close the various objects. To remove the workbook, we use the **ActiveWorkbook** method to determine which workbook to close and the **Close** method to close it. The **Close** method accepts a Boolean value that determines whether or not a Save dialog is displayed when unsaved data is found on a worksheet of the workbook.

However, the application object uses the **Quit** method to exit the attached instance of Excel. This is important to note, as each OLE server object may require a different method call for similar operations. Here again, the call made is based on the server application, not PowerBuilder.

Using Excel's Charting Capabilities

The following example again uses Excel as the server to PowerBuilder's client. This time, however, we'll call on Excel's charting features.

In **ch07.pbl**, **w_chartsample** contains a DataWindow that presents some numeric sales data:

Sample Sales Report					
	CA	TN	FL	NY	IL
Jan	5847	4589	5896	6589	6258
Feb	4587	4268	3895	6251	7845
March	5789	6895	6359	8421	7569
April	4589	4682	7842	7564	6852
May	6895	5993	4879	5987	6985
June	5214	5569	6882	7149	7269
July	3598	3699	3987	5218	4886

Chart   Exit

We want to present this data in graphical form to the user, providing an overview of the sales data. We would also like the graph presented to rotate 360 degrees during presentation to provide an aesthetically pleasing effect—the user has indicated the graph will be used during the annual sales presentation to a number of line managers.

PowerBuilder's graphing capabilities, though adequate for most purposes, are not able to meet our needs in this case, so we need to turn to Excel.

Creating the Chart

Our first step is to link our application to Excel. As in our first example, we create two object variables that will reference the Excel application. The difference here is that one of the variables references the Excel chart that we'll create, as opposed to a worksheet.

```
PRIVATE:
    OLEObject    obExcel    //reference to Excel
    OLEObject    obChart    //reference to Chart
    Integer      iRotate    //Rotation
```

Here we create our object references as private instance variables. In this example, we need to work with the object in multiple controls, so a local variable in a control script would go out of scope as we worked in the different controls. As well as the object variables, we declare an integer variable that we'll use to determine the current chart rotation ratio.

The charting process starts when the user presses the Chart command button. The **Clicked** event of the command button makes an initial connection to Excel through the **ConnectToNewObject** function.

With a connection established, we add a new workbook to place our chart data on and then populate the first sheet of the workbook with the data that we'll use to create our graph.

```
obExcel.Workbooks.Add()

For iCounter = 1 To (iMaxRows)
    For iInner = 1 To (iMaxCols)
    saBuffer[iCounter, iInner] = dw_data.GetItemString(iCounter, iInner )
    Next
Next
```

You'll notice in this section of code that the data from the PowerBuilder DataWindow is collected into a multidimensional array. The reason for this has to do with PowerBuilder's implementation of OLE Automation and performance. We'll take a look at this issue in a moment.

With the data from our DataWindow loaded into an array, we now have to move it to Excel. We can do this with a single line of code.

```
obExcel.Range("$A$1:$F$9").Value = saBuffer
```

Notice that we pass the entire array to Excel. Excel's **Range** method is quite flexible in that it allows an application to pass structures of data that match the area specified in the **Range** method's parameter list. In this case, the **Range** method's parameter value specifies a grid of six columns and nine rows. As our PowerBuilder array dimensions match this selection, we can pass the data to Excel using a single reference to our array.

143

However, there's another reason why passing a complete array of data is of value here. PowerBuilder's implementation of OLE Automation isn't as robust as it might be. For example, PowerBuilder doesn't take advantage of the type libraries provided by OLE-compliant applications, such as Excel.

> A type library is a special file included with the OLE server product that identifies its exposed interface. This information can be used by a client application to take advantage of a technique known as early binding. Early binding essentially means that a development tool can use this library information to resolve references to the OLE server application's interface during compilation. As such, your client application doesn't need to resolve each reference made at run time, increasing its performance significantly.

Without this option, we need to make as few references to the OLE server application as possible, thus reducing the amount of time PowerBuilder spends resolving references. If we had to pass the data to Excel cell by cell, our application would be unacceptably slow. Even passing data row by row would require at least nine references, forcing PowerBuilder to resolve a reference for each row. Unfortunately, PowerBuilder doesn't retain information concerning references. As such, each time we make a call to an OLE server method or property, even if it's the same call over and over, PowerBuilder will resolve the reference as if it were the first time.

With the data now in Excel, we tell Excel that we'll use the data in our chart by selecting it using the **Select** method:

```
obExcel.Range("$A$1:$F$9").Select          //Select the area
```

With our data selected, we need to create a new chart, define its default attributes and present it to the user.

```
obChart.Type = -4101                //What chart
obChart.HasLegend = FALSE           //No Legend
obExcel.Visible = TRUE              //Make Excel Visible
obChart.Visible = TRUE              //Want to see it
```

This code supplies the type of chart to display, indicates that we don't want a legend on the graph and then makes both Excel and the chart visible to the user. The resulting graph looks like this:

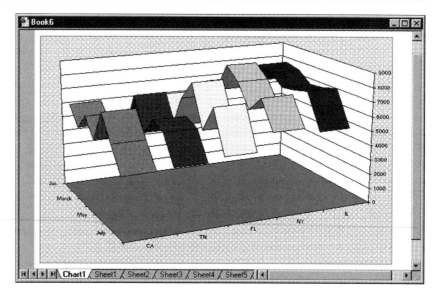

As you can see, we can produce a professional graph with minimal coding.

Rotating the Chart

However, we were asked make the graph rotate while it was being displayed. This turns out to be surprisingly easy.

Our first step is to define a timer on our PowerBuilder window. PowerBuilder allows you to define a timer that will trigger the window's **Timer** event at a specified interval. We'll use the timer to rotate the graph five degrees every two seconds, which will provide the illusion of a slowly rotating image, while not locking up the PowerBuilder application.

To activate a timer, we call the **Timer** function, specifying the interval between events and the window on which to trigger the **Timer** event. In this case, we want a two second delay between events and the event to execute on the parent window, which, in this case, is the PowerBuilder display window.

```
Timer( 2, Parent )
```

Each time the **Timer** event executes, the rotation of the graph is adjusted using:

```
obChart.Rotation = iRotate
iRotate = Mod( (iRotate + 5), 360 )
```

Here, the **iRotate** instance variable keeps track of the current rotation value and then is used to calculate a new value based on a total possible value of 360. The **Rotation** method is provided by the Excel server and performs all the necessary calculations required to reposition and redraw the graph.

Closing the Connection

As you can see, with some basic PowerScript code, you can take advantage of the advanced capabilities of Excel to enhance your application. All we have left to do is clean up the connection when the user is ready to end the presentation. The Exit button's **Clicked** event takes care of closing down the connection to Excel and destroying the object variables.

```
if ( isValid( obExcel ) ) then
        obExcel.ActiveWorkbook.Close( False )
        obExcel.Quit
        obChart.DisconnectObject()
        obExcel.DisconnectObject()
end if

Timer(0, Parent )

DESTROY obChart
DESTROY obExcel
```

If the user clicks Exit without displaying a graph, we don't need to close Excel, so our first step verifies that the Excel object is valid. If it is, we close the Excel workbook, followed by Excel itself and then we can remove our references and release our PowerBuilder objects. You should remember to turn off the timer by calling the **Timer** function with a zero interval.

Using PowerBuilder as an OLE Server

PowerBuilder provides for full access to OLE Automation capabilities, which means that you have the capability not only of working with other applications on your system, but also with other PowerBuilder objects. Using this technology, we can segment PowerBuilder functionality into reusable objects that can communicate with one another to perform tasks.

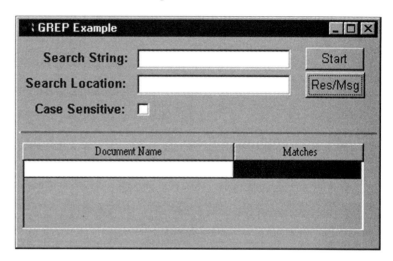

To illustrate OLE Automation in PowerBuilder, we'll take a look at the **Grep** example on the disk.

This example provides a 'front-end' PowerBuilder module that the user uses to enter search criteria. The front-end then connects to a 'back-end' module, sending it the criteria supplied by the user. The back-end uses this information to scan through text files at the location specified by the user and to search for the string supplied.

The **Grep** front-end allows the user to supply a string to search for, as well as a path or search location. The search can also be case-sensitive. The lower half of the dialog is used to present the results of the search to the user.

The Client

Let's start by taking a look at how the front-end application works. The real work of this application is in the **cb_Start** command button's script. The user clicks the **cb_Start** command button when they're ready to start a new search.

```
OLEObject oleServer        //Server reference object
OLEObject oleGrep          //Reference to GREP Class
Long      lRetValue        //Return value
String    saFileNames[]    //File Names
Int       siFileHits[]     //File hits
```

Our first step is to define a number of variables that we'll need for our processing. Here we define two **oleObject** object variables. The **oleServer** object variable is used to instantiate an instance of the PowerBuilder OLE Automation server, while the other is used to instantiate an instance of our **Grep** non-visual class user object. We'll look at why we use two variables for this example in a moment. We use the string and integer arrays to store the file names and number of search items found.

```
oleServer = CREATE OLEObject
lRetValue = oleServer.ConnectToNewObject ( "Powerbuilder.Application" )
if ( lRetValue < 0 ) then
     MessageBox( "Server Error", "Can't connect to PowerBuilder Server" )
     Return
end if

//
// set the library list (these will need to come from an INI)
//
oleServer.LibraryList = "oleserver.pbd"

//
// we are using compiled code
//
oleServer.MachineCode = FALSE
```

Here, we instantiate an OLEObject object which is used to communicate with the OLE server that is supplied with PowerBuilder. We connect to the PowerBuilder OLE server in much the same way that we establish a session with any other OLE server on our system. You use the familiar function, **ConnectToNewObject**. Using this object, we can then set a number of parameters that PowerBuilder requires when accessing PowerBuilder OLE objects. The two most important, and those used here, are the **LibraryList** and **MachineCode** properties.

   LibraryList contains a list of library objects to be searched when creating classes. These libraries can be Powerbuilder PBD libraries or DLL files generated by a compiled **.pbd** file.

   MachineCode is a Boolean attribute that specifies whether the libraries listed are PowerBuilder **.pbd** files, which are actually PowerBuilder code compiled into pCode. If set to true, the libraries must be PowerBuilder libraries that have been compiled into machine code.

Our next step is to instantiate an OLE object with the **CREATE** statement and then connect to the PowerBuilder automation server. We can then use this object to define the library list and machine code type parameters needed by the server when instantiating PowerBuilder classes.

```
//
// create a reference to the GREP Server class
//
oleGrep = oleServer.CreateObject( "grep" )
if ( isNull( oleGrep ) ) then
     MessageBox( "Server Error", "Can't create Grep Class" )
     DESTROY oleServer
     Return
end if
```

With a reference to the PowerBuilder server established, we can create an instance of our class, which is the 'back-end' of our process. Here, we see why we need two object variables. The sample establishes a reference to the PowerBuilder server and then creates an instance of a specific class using that reference.

> You could register your class as an independent OLE object and then connect directly to it—we'll look at how you would do this at the end of the chapter. However, this requires you to have previously registered your OLE class. Here, as we are in a development mode, it would be cumbersome to re-register the object each time an update was made (not to mention filling up the registry).

```
//
// set properties
//
oleGrep.pLocation( sle_Location.text )
oleGrep.pSearch( sle_Search.text )
oleGrep.pIsCase( cbx_isCase.Checked )
```

With a reference in place, we can now set the properties defined in the OLE object, using the values supplied by the user. The OLE object exposes a **Location**, **Search** and **IsCase** property to accept the values supplied to the client.

With our properties set, we're ready to begin our search.

```
mle_status.Text = 'Starting Search...'
SetPointer( HOURGLASS! )

//
// run server
//
oleGrep.fStartGrep()

SetPointer( ARROW! )
```

To start, we indicate that the search has started by updating the client status area and setting the pointer to an hourglass. The server **fStartGrep** method is called to actually kick off a search on the server. Once a search has been completed, the cursor is restored as a standard arrow shape.

With the completion of the process, we can return any messages produced by the server in the status area of the client application.

```
mle_Status.Text = oleGrep.fGetMsg

if ( oleGrep.fDone() = TRUE ) then

    //
    // get results
    //
    saFileNames = oleGrep.saFileNames
        siFileHits = oleGrep.siFileHits
        fUpdateGrid( saFileNames, siFileHits )

end if

//
// Disconnect
//
oleServer.DisconnectObject()
DESTROY oleGrep
DESTROY oleServer
```

The results of the search are returned into our two arrays, which are then used to update the client display. Our last, but perhaps most important, step is to disconnect from the object using the **DisconnectObject** function and then destroy both the **Grep** object and the server object.

The Server

Now let's take a look at the workhorse of this process: the OLE server. The OLE server doesn't provide a visual component and, in fact, can't provide a visual component due to PowerBuilder's implementation of OLE.

> When you're developing an OLE server, you must take care as to what processing is to occur and where. In an OLE server, the instantiated object in use by the client doesn't have access to any other objects defined in the server application, unless they're created by the object itself. For example, if the application object of the server were to have a global variable defined, the object instance created by the OLE client application would not have access to its values.
>
> This is due to the fact that the class is actually created in a PowerBuilder environment provided by the PowerBuilder OLE Automation server. Other objects that may have been defined in the server application and tied to the server application object aren't necessarily tied to the instantiated object, unless explicitly defined as such (i.e. by being created from within the user object being used by the client).

Our first step is to define a non-visual user object class that will be accessible to client applications. In our example, we define a class called **Grep**, which is used to process each search request made by a client.

The Variable Definitions

To start, we define a number of instance variables that are used within and external to our object.

```
//
// Public properties
//
PUBLIC:

String          saFileNames[]
Int             siFileHits[]

//
// Private Declarations
//
PRIVATE:

String          psLocation              //Where to look
String          psFilter                //File Filter
String          psSearch                //Search Value
Boolean         pbIsCase                //Case sensitive

Boolean     pbComplete = FALSE          //are we done yet
```

```
String      psMsg[]                          //current messages
Int         piLastMsg                        //Last Message

os_FileInfo    saFiles[]                     //Array of File information
Int            siHits[]                      //Array of Hit counts

CONSTANT Int  MAXFILE = 30720                //Max File size
CONSTANT String DIRDELIMIT = "\"             //Directory delimiter
```

Our first two instance variables represent the result information that will be returned to the client. As these variables are defined as **PUBLIC**, they are visible to the external client application and become a part of the classes exposed interface.

Our **PRIVATE** declarations are used internally by the object and are not visible to the client application. Here, we create variables that store the search criteria supplied by the client, along with message structures and a completion flag. Notice that we create similar file and hit arrays for internal use by the object—this avoids any possibility of presenting partial results to the client application. The file array also contains more information than simply a name, as you'll see when we take a look at the structures used in this example.

PowerBuilder uses structures to relate multiple data types to a single reference. The **Grep** example takes advantage of this facility to keep track of the files it is searching, as well as to collect specific information concerning a file that exists at the search location specified. In our case, we use the **os_FileInfo** structure that we've defined to store file information when we're working within the object itself.

```
type os_FileInfo from structure
        string      sFileName
        long        lFileSize
        boolean     bSubdirectory
        boolean     bDrive
        boolean     bHidden
        boolean     bReadOnly
end type
```

An array of data types of this structure is used to track the files found at the location specified. The additional attributes are used to determine whether or not a given name is returned to the client application. For example, if the name found is a subdirectory, its name isn't returned to the client as it's not a file that can be searched for text.

Setting the Search Location Property

So let's get started. Notice that we don't simply supply search criteria properties using public variables. We could have done this, but it would mean that we wouldn't have the opportunity to edit any of the data being supplied. To gain this editing advantage, we use public functions to collect this information.

```
// Function:  pLocation
// Syntax  :  sDirStr   -> String    'Directory
// Returns :  None
// Desc    :  Sets the Search location property
//

Int iPos      //String Pos
Int iCounter  //Loop counter
```

150

```
//
// Split dir and filter
//
iPos = Len(sDirStr)
For iCounter = iPos To 1 Step -1
    If (Mid(sDirStr, iCounter, 1) = DIRDELIMIT) Then
        psFilter = Mid(sDirStr, iCounter + 1)
        psLocation = Left(sDirStr, iCounter)
        Return
    End If
Next

Return
```

Here, the search location value provided by the client is broken down into a path value and a filter value. The path represents the location to start searching for files, while the filter represents any file selection criteria that may have been supplied by the client (i.e. ***.*** or ***.doc**).

For each method used to supply a property setting, we define a mirror method to retrieve the value.

```
// Function:  pLocation
// Syntax  :  None
// Returns :  String
// Desc    :  Returns the Search location property
//

Return ( psLocation )
```

Here, the method does nothing more then return the current value of the location property supplied. However, using this technique, you ensure that a developer using your object has the ability to retrieve any data that is supplied to the object.

Starting the Processing

With our properties defined, we can take a look at the actual processing that occurs during the search. The client application calls a function in the server, called **fStartGrep**. This is provided through a public function defined in the server object.

```
//
// set status
//
pbComplete = FALSE

//
// Tell the User What's Up
//
fStatus ("Starting Search.....")

//
// do we have a valid place to look
//
If ( psLocation + psFilter = "" Or psLocation = "") Then
    fStatus( "No Files Were Found At The Search Location Supplied. " )
    Return(FALSE)
End If
```

151

```
//
// do we have a valid property set
//
If (psSearch = "") Then
    fStatus( "The Search Property Has Not Been Supplied. " )
    Return(FALSE)
End If

//
// Call Grep Work
//
InternalGrep()
```

The **fStartGrep** function is used to edit the property values set previously and start the actual processing of the server. Our first step is to set the private **pbComplete** variable to **FALSE**, internally indicating that the process has not yet completed. This property is used in conjunction with the **fDone** method to determine the status of the search.

With the internal status value set, we check each of the property values to ensure that a value was provided. In this simplistic example, all we do is test for a value; in a real system, however, you would want to verify that the location specified existed and that the file filter derived from the location was a valid value.

If any of our edits fail, the status buffer is updated with an error message and the process ends. If the edits pass, the internal function **InternalGrep** is called to begin the actual search.

Running the Search

The **InternalGrep** function has no contact with the client application. Its purpose is to process the search, using the criteria supplied and return a result. We hide the processing logic of this object from the outside world to expose a less complex interface to the client application.

```
saFiles = saTemp
siHits  = siTemp

//
// lets take a look
//
iCounter = fDirList(psLocation + psFilter, saTemp)
If ( iCounter < 0 ) Then
        pbcomplete = TRUE
        Return
end if
```

Our first step is to set the file information array and search hits (**siHits**) array for empty values, to check that no previous search results remain. We then use the **fDirList** function to pull a list of files from the location specified by the client, filtering the returned files using the **psFilter** property. To avoid returning partial results, the resulting file information is stored in a temporary array.

```
iMaxItems = UpperBound(saTemp)
for iCounter = 1 to iMaxItems
    if (   saTemp[iCounter].bSubDirectory = False and &
           saTemp[iCounter].bDrive = False ) then
        saFiles[iCounter] = saTemp[iCounter]
```

```
           siHits[iCounter] = 0
        end if
   next


   //
   // Now lets scan them
   //
   If (fGrepScan() = False) Then
   End If

   fStatus ("Search complete.")
   pbcomplete = TRUE
```

With the file information in hand, we can now pull the data into working arrays and call the scan process. When we're moving the data from the temp array to the working arrays (**saFiles** and **siHits**), we remove any references to drives or subdirectories, as these have no meaning in this context.

The **fGrepScan** function takes the array of file information and begins searching the contents of each file. When it completes, the status buffer is again updated and the **pbCompleted** status flag is set to **TRUE**.

The scan function updates the file and search results array as it processes the search. When the **pbComplete** flag is set to **TRUE**, the client application is notified that it can retrieve the results of the search. We do this through an exposed method called **fDone**.

```
   String   saEmpty[]      //Empty array
   Int      siEmpty[]      //Empty array
   Int      iUpper         //upper bound
   Int      iCounter       //Current pos

   if ( pbComplete ) then

       saFileNames = saEmpty
       siFileHits  = siEmpty

       //
       // process
       //
       iUpper = Upperbound( saFiles )
       for iCounter = 1 to iUpper
           saFileNames[iCounter] = saFiles[icounter].sFileName
           siFileHits[iCounter]  = siHits[iCounter]
       next

       Return( TRUE )

   else

       Return ( FALSE )

   end if
```

The client application can call **fDone** at any time. However, unless a process has been completed and its status set to **TRUE**, the **fDone** function returns **FALSE** to the client application. When processing has been completed and results are ready for further processing, the **fDone** function is used to return these results to the OLE client application.

Note here that the very last step of the process is to update the public variable arrays that are visible to the client application. We do this to ensure that the client application receives the results of its query and not a partially completed result from a previous query.

With this example application, we have seen how OLE can be used to extend the capabilities of PowerBuilder by allowing PowerBuilder components to work together to produce results. The advantage of this is that these components can then be reused by other PowerBuilder applications or by other OLE compliant tools.

The Windows Registry

An OLE control provides information about itself through the registry. The registry is a key database used by the Windows operating system to keep track of internal settings, along with OLE object information, system devices and many other important items.

The registry is a system-defined database that applications and Windows system components use to store configuration data. In the past, Windows 3.1 applications stored their configuration data in **WIN.INI** or some other application-defined **.INI** file. The system stored its configuration information in **SYSTEM.INI**. This information was stored in ASCII files that a user could edit and view in any simple text editor, such as Notepad.

System registry data is now stored in binary files, so applications can no longer rely on text editors for updating the information contained in the registry. Instead, applications may either use the registry functions supplied by the Windows API or create registration files (**.REG**) that contain information to be stored in the registry. These **.REG** files are ASCII files that can be created with any text editor. The Registry Editor (**REGEDIT**) can read in these files and store the information in the appropriate places in the registry.

The Structure of the Registry

The registry stores data in a hierarchical structure. The tool that allows you to see this is called the **Registry Editor**. Each key in the tree can contain children known as **subkeys** and data entries called **values**.

Keys don't have to have values associated with them. Sometimes, all that the application needs to know is that the key exists; other times, an application may need many values to be associated with a specific key. A key can have any number of values and the values can be in any form.

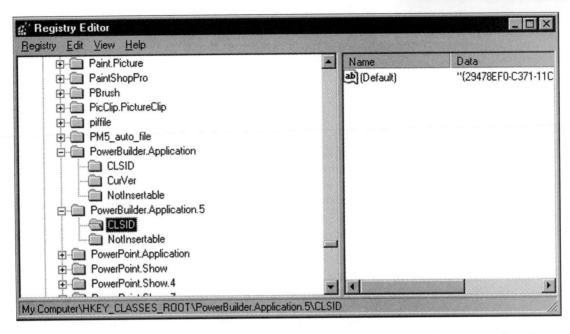

Here, we see several registry entries for the PowerBuilder development environment. In fact, these entries define the PowerBuilder OLE server object that can be accessed by OLE client applications.

The registry supports several different data types for values. Your application can use any of these data types, depending on what you want to store. The following table contains a list of the different data types supported:

Data Type	Description
REG_BINARY	Binary data in any form.
REG_DWORD	A 32-bit number.
REG_DWORD_BIG_ENDIAN	A 32-bit number in big-endian format.
REG_DWORD_LITTLE_ENDIAN	A 32-bit number in little-endian format. This is the most common format for computers running Windows NT.
REG_EXPAND_SZ	A null-terminated string that contains unexpanded references to environment variables (for example, %PATH%).
REG_LINK	A Unicode symbolic link.
REG_MULTI_SZ	An array of null-terminated strings, terminated by two null characters.
REG_NONE	No defined value type.
REG_RESOURCE_LIST	A device-driver resource list.
REG_SZ	A null-terminated string.

Predefined Keys

Predefined keys are system-defined keys that help an application navigate in the registry. They also make it possible to develop tools that allow a system administrator to change whole categories of data. The following keys are defined at the root of the registry:

- **HKEY_CLASSES_ROOT**: Entries within this key define types (or classes) of documents and the properties associated with those types. Data stored under this key is used by Windows shell applications and by OLE applications. This is where file viewers and shell extensions store their OLE CLSIDs and where in-process servers are registered. It is also the section that we're most interested in when we're dealing with OLE.

- **HKEY_CURRENT_USER**: Current user preferences are stored within this key. These preferences include items such as the settings of environment variables, data about program groups, colors, printers, network connections and application preferences. This key is included to make it easier to set the current user's settings; the key maps to the current user's branch in **HKEY_USERS**. Software vendors use this key to store the current user-specific preferences that will be used within their applications.

- **HKEY_LOCAL_MACHINE**: Entries within this key show the physical state of the computer, including data about the bus type, system memory and installed hardware and software. This key contains subkeys that contain information about network logon preferences, network security information, software-related information (server names, location of the server, and so on).

- **HKEY_USER**: This key stores information about the default user configuration and contains a branch for each user of the computer.

- **HKEY_CURRENT_CONFIG**: This key is mapped to a subkey within **HKEY_LOCAL_MACHINE**. This is where non-user-specific configuration information that pertains to hardware is stored. For example, an application may store a different server name, depending on whether the system is attached to a network.

- **HKEY_DYN_DATE**: This key is used to store dynamic registry data. The Windows 95 registry supports both static data (data stored on disk within the registry) and dynamic data (data that changes a lot, such as performance statistics). This dynamic data area is the mechanism that provides real-time data to Win32 applications that can run remotely as well as locally. This also allows the system monitor to provide performance statistics on remote Windows 95 systems.

Global Unique IDs or GUIDs appear in various places, but, as a PowerBuilder application developer, you need to deal with **.REG** files only. When you create an application, you usually create one or more **.REG** files. The **.REG** files contain the GUIDs for the OLE classes that your application exposes. These GUIDs are added to the registry when you run **REGEDIT.EXE** with the **/M** option.

Creating .REG Files

PowerBuilder provides an object to use when you're communicating with OLE objects. This object provides methods that you can use to connect to, communicate with and disconnect from external OLE servers.

However, beyond its fundamental purpose, it also helps you to generate the **.REG** file that defines the classes made available in an OLE server application. These methods (**GenerateGUID** and

GenerateRegFile) help you to define a GUID for your object and provide a mechanism to actually generate a .**REG** file for you. Let's take a look at these:

```
OLEObject    PBObject
String       GUID
Long         lResult

//
// Establish a connection to the Powerbuilder OLE Server
//
PBObject = Create OLEObject
lResult  = PBObject.ConnectToNewObject( "PowerBuilder.Application" )

If ( lResult < 0 ) Then
        MessageBox( "Connection Error", lResult )
Else

  //
  // Set Library and code type
  //
  PBObject.LibraryList = "oleserver.pbd;"    // You will need a Path here
  PBObject.MachineCode = False               // This is a pCode object

  //
  // Get a unique ID
  //
  lResult = PBObject.GenerateGUID(REF GUID)
  If ( lResult < 0 ) Then
      MessageBox( "UID Generation Error", lResult )
    Else

    //
    // Use the ID to generate a REG file
    //
        lResult = PBObject.GenerateRegFile( GUID, "Grep", &
          "pb_class.object", 1, 0, &
          "First Non Visual Object for In-Bound OLE Auto ", "Grep.reg" )
      End If
End If
```

With a connection to our server defined and a library path pointing to a library containing our non-visual class user object, we can begin the process of generating a registry file. Our first step is to call the **GenerateGUID** method to create a unique indicator for our new class.

With a GUID generated, we can create a registration file using the **GenerateRegFile** method of the **OLEObject** object. This function takes the following arguments:

Argument	Data Type	Notes
GUID	String	Globally Unique Identifier that's created by **GenerateGUID**.
ClassName	String	NVO class name that you created.
ProgID	String	OLE Programmatic Identifier. OLE clients use this name for programming.

Table continued on following page

157

Argument	Data Type	Notes
MajorVersion	Integer	Major Version.
MinorVersion	Integer	Minor Version.
Description	String	Description to be displayed by OLE.
TargetFile	String	**.REG** file name that you want to create.

The result of this processing is a file that is used to generate the actual keys within the system registry. Let's take a look at our result.

```
REGEDIT
;;;;;;;;;;;;;;;
;
; Registry entries for pb_class.object
;
; CLSID = {4626B302-D9D0-11CF-8E8D-444553540000}
;
;;;;;;;;;;;;;;;

; Version independent entries:
HKEY_CLASSES_ROOT\pb_class.object = First Non Visual Object for In-Bound OLE Auto
HKEY_CLASSES_ROOT\pb_class.object\CLSID = {4626B302-D9D0-11CF-8E8D-444553540000}
HKEY_CLASSES_ROOT\pb_class.object\CurVer = pb_class.object.1
HKEY_CLASSES_ROOT\pb_class.object\NotInsertable

; Version specific entries:
HKEY_CLASSES_ROOT\pb_class.object.1 = First Non Visual Object for In-Bound OLE
Auto
HKEY_CLASSES_ROOT\pb_class.object.1\CLSID = {4626B302-D9D0-11CF-8E8D-444553540000}
HKEY_CLASSES_ROOT\pb_class.object.1\NotInsertable

; CLSID entries:
HKEY_CLASSES_ROOT\CLSID\{4626B302-D9D0-11CF-8E8D-444553540000} = First Non Visual
Object for In-Bound OLE Auto
HKEY_CLASSES_ROOT\CLSID\{4626B302-D9D0-11CF-8E8D-444553540000}\ProgID =
pb_class.object.1
HKEY_CLASSES_ROOT\CLSID\{4626B302-D9D0-11CF-8E8D-
444553540000}\VersionIndependentProgID = pb_class.object
HKEY_CLASSES_ROOT\CLSID\{4626B302-D9D0-11CF-8E8D-444553540000}\InProcServer32 =
PBROI050.DLL
HKEY_CLASSES_ROOT\CLSID\{4626B302-D9D0-11CF-8E8D-444553540000}\NotInsertable
HKEY_CLASSES_ROOT\CLSID\{4626B302-D9D0-11CF-8E8D-444553540000}\Programmable
HKEY_CLASSES_ROOT\CLSID\{4626B302-D9D0-11CF-8E8D-
444553540000}\PowerBuilder\ClassName = Grep
HKEY_CLASSES_ROOT\CLSID\{4626B302-D9D0-11CF-8E8D-
444553540000}\PowerBuilder\LibraryList = oleserver.pbd;
HKEY_CLASSES_ROOT\CLSID\{4626B302-D9D0-11CF-8E8D-
444553540000}\PowerBuilder\BinaryType = PCODE
```

Notice that the name you supplied for the object is used to generate a key within the registry. However, the unique ID generated by the **GenerateGUID** method is what is used by the system to identify this object from all other objects. Some additional information is generated for you, such as the library list supplied to the connect object, the object types in use, in the case PCODE, and a default setting indicating the object can't be inserted.

To merge this file with the registry, run **RegEdit /M Grep.reg**. A message is displayed when the file has been successfully merged or if an error occurs.

Now that we have updated our registry with information concerning the new object, let's test to verify that the update succeeded. With the new object defined in our registry, we can use PowerBuilder's OLEObject object to connect to the class name that we've just defined.

```
OLEObject      lOLEObject
Long           lRetStatus

//
// Connect to our new Object
//
lOLEObject = create OLEObject
lRetStatus = lOLEObject.ConnectToNewObject( "pb_class.Object" )

//
// Check status, if it worked let us know
//
If lRetStatus < 0 Then
   MessageBox( "Error Info.", lRetStatus )
Else
      messagebox("Status", "Connection successful")
End If

lOLEObject.DisconnectObject()
Destroy lOLEObject
```

Summary

In this chapter, we've explored some of the real power in using OLE Automation in the PowerBuilder environment. OLE offers a number of advantages to the PowerBuilder developer. It allows for the reuse of not only code and objects, but of fully functional, independent application modules. This flexibility can greatly reduce the time required to develop applications, as well as significantly enhance applications by allowing them take advantage of prebuilt functionality and features.

Component-based Design Using Design Patterns

This chapter introduces you to designing applications using plug-and-play design patterns. We'll discuss the various types of component design, illustrating each one with examples to show its advantages and disadvantages.

An Overview of Design

Component design provides solutions for a problem domain using small, reusable, plug-and-play objects. Each object provides a specific functionality, but collectively, they provide a complete solution. For example, if you're building a desktop model of a plane from a kit, you'll find many different pieces with numbers on them, ready for assembly. The wings provide the majority of the aircraft's lift and the tail is largely for stability and control. The same wings on another aircraft will behave the same, i.e. they'll produce a similar lift. Thus, the wings can act as interchangeable components between aircraft. The ability to plug and play components is what makes a component-based design so powerful.

As such, design means planning. To provide a solution we need to take into account different types of design: structural design, usability design and layout design. For example, when you design a house, the structural design consists of the foundation, supporting beams and the framework of the house. The usability design ensures that there's enough light in the house and that the water level is maintained and provides provisions for extending the design. The layout design means good room layout and ensuring that the house follows any specific state and county construction laws.

Similarly, a software application requires a structural design, which implies that applications should have an architecture and a framework. It needs usability design to ensure acceptable performance, extendibility and flexibility to change. The application should also have an ergonomic and user-friendly graphical user interface layout, and follow the existing GUI standards and system standards for exception handling etc.

Design Considerations

Every component or pattern will satisfy some design considerations. For example, some designs have good performance but minimal flexibility, whereas others are very generic in scope but exhibit poor performance. Every application will have its own priorities for design considerations, which will affect the application's component design. Some of the main design considerations are reusability, performance, flexibility, maintainability and consistency. We'll look at each of these.

Reusability

A reusable design component provides similar functionality for many applications, minimizing development and enhancement efforts. To be reusable, a component should have a very well-defined interface, be self-contained and completely independent of other components in an application.

Reusability becomes a higher priority when the requirements need a suite of applications to provide a solution. Take Microsoft Office, for example. It provides a suite of applications which all have a graph charting functionality. The graph component was reused in every application belonging to the suite.

For a design to be reusable across applications, it should be based on common design guidelines supported by each application. For example, the OLE architecture by Microsoft supports component reuse at binary level, which allows the developer to design OCX (or ActiveX) objects to be reused for any OLE-compliant application.

Performance

Performance becomes a high priority when applications are based on real-time data. A real-time application is one that requires an immediate response to input—for example, a flight control system or financial trading application that allows traders to configure their views for the stock, bond or commodity markets from external feeds. These applications need responses within milliseconds, whereas a typical order entry application might find a one- or two-second delay acceptable.

Another scenario where high performance is needed is when there are a large number of users working on a client/server application. The server has to process requests from all the users in an appropriate time. For example, a timesheet application for a large consulting company with thousands of consultants will require adequate performance for each consultant. We would also need to keep performance in mind when we're designing an application running on a network with low bandwidth.

High performance is usually a requirement of specific applications and so components designed for such applications would tend not to be as reusable as other more generic components.

Flexibility

An application design should be scaleable and adaptive to change. In the real world, application requirements aren't always well-defined because the requirements analysis evolves iteratively during the development of the application as more facts come to light. Component-based design lends itself to providing this flexibility. For example, suppose you have an application that produces printed reports and you now need it to fax reports. You could support this new requirement with minimum effort by replacing the print component with a fax component.

You can see, then, that flexible components allow developers to meet the ever changing requirements of those who use their applications and enable them to reuse components with very little modification.

Consistency

Components designed for an application or for a suite of applications should share a consistent design with a standard way of accessing their interfaces. They should be designed with similar considerations in mind and should be based on a similar architecture. You can be consistent by prioritizing design considerations up front, making sure the requirements are understood and deciding on the application architecture and framework.

Inheritance vs. Components

When you're implementing new applications, it's helpful to be able to reuse existing solutions. One way of doing this is to reuse the components from the previous solution and assemble them as plug-and-play objects. The second method is to inherit the existing solution and then modify it. The former technique is more flexible and is easily enhanced, but is more time-consuming. The latter technique is less time-consuming, but also less flexible and can potentially cause problems for enhancements.

Components do support inheritance, which is used to provide a component hierarchy with different levels of behavioral abstraction. For example, say you need to include in an application some scanning functionality. You can build a component with an interface that will provide an external interface for other components in the application to implement scanning functionality. Within the scanner component, there can be a hierarchy of other components such as a barcode scanner, text scanner or image scanner. The application will interact with the different types of scanning components but these will use some functionality inherited from the base scanner class.

Inheritance and components work hand-in-hand to provide a solution for an application. The application should consist of many components and each component can consist of a hierarchy of objects providing a scaleable level of behavioral abstraction.

Design Patterns

You shouldn't think of reuse just in terms of reusing physical objects. You can also reuse the way objects are designed and how they interact with each other. In other words, you can reuse **design patterns**.

Design patterns are repeatable designs used in the construction of an application. An architecture for an application will consist of several design patterns. Experienced programmers reuse and revise their design patterns constantly—you should always be on the lookout for new patterns that can be reused in future design projects.

In the rest of this chapter, we'll discuss some of the design patterns that are applicable to the development of applications in PowerBuilder. These include:

 Decorators

 Global utility objects

 Object managers

Model/View/Controller

Object factory

Generator

One of the best references on design patterns is *"Design Patterns—Elements of Reusable Object-Oriented Software"* by Gamma, Helm, Johnson and Vlissides, ISBN 0-201-63361-2.

Decorators

Decorators are add-ons that provide a specific functionality to an existing component. For example, you might have a DataWindow-style decorator that provides methods for highlighting single and multiple rows using *Ctrl* or *Shift* and mouse clicks. This decorator extends the functionality of the DataWindow. Similarly, you could have decorators for DataWindows to extend the functionality for printing, sorting, etc.

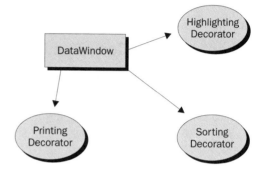

You only design decorators if a component needs to be functionally enhanced. Decorators are then referenced by the component they're enhancing. Decorators allow more flexibility than extending a component's functionality via inheritance. For example, instead of using a DataWindow-style decorator, you could inherit a DataWindow component and design a standard DataWindow user object to provide the highlighting functionality. This design would provide the functionality, but it would also make the component more inflexible. If you then wanted to extend the DataWindow functionality to allow for sorting, you would have to add another level to the inheritance hierarchy. You couldn't just use another standard DataWindow user object which has sorting functionality, as PowerBuilder doesn't support multiple inheritance.

Global Utility Objects

These are components which provide behaviors that can be accessed globally across the application. They don't enhance any other component, but they can be used by any component in the application. For example, a print utility allows printer setup, page setup and printing of any object. The data structure utility allows a component to store and access data in a linked list and dictionaries. File, string and date/time manipulation functions are all examples of global utilities.

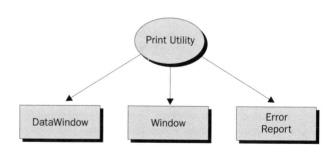

Utility objects are independent and flexible. They allow designers to reuse components with a minimum of effort. It's important to identify the scope of a component—if the scope is global to all the components in an application, you should design it as a utility object.

Object Manager

Managers implement functionality at an application level. They're components which should be included as part of your framework and can be globally accessed by any object. Managers are different from global utility objects in that a global utility object gets instantiated as and when needed; a manager gets created when the application is initialized and exists for its entire lifetime. Objects in an application can access the manager as a global object or as a member object of the global framework.

A manager allows the application to use a consistent mechanism for specific functions. For example, an exception manager allows every object to handle its messages consistently. The objects can invoke the exception manager using an exception id and the manager retrieves the information for the exception identified and displays it to the user. The user can then process the exception and the manager logs it to a log file. A help manager provides context-sensitive help consistently across the application. The help manager can be invoked with a unique keyword and will display the appropriate topic from the help file.

Every application has consistency as a major design consideration. The object manager pattern implements a consistent behavior. The managers aren't easy to maintain since a change in their interface requires changing every object that accesses them, so it's important that you design them carefully before they are implemented.

Model/View/Controller

Model/View/Controller (MVC) is probably the most commonly used design pattern in PowerBuilder applications. It relies on three major behaviors to implement a solution. The model behavior implements functionality to retrieve, validate and save data. Users interact with views which display the data and the controller navigates the request from the view to the model.

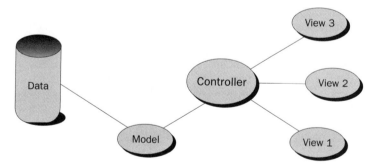

A model can have multiple views, which are kept in sync with the model.

Master/Detail Component

A common example for a MVC design is the Master/Detail implementation for a table. The Master/Detail pattern displays a master-type view (i.e. list view of data from a table) and allows users to navigate to the detail view of a selected record in the table. The model object retrieves, updates and stores the data. The two views, the master view and the detail view, display the master data and the detail data. The window is the controller and manages the interactions between the view objects and the model object.

Model Object (Non-visual User Object)

The model object contains a data store object. It's derived from a non-visual user object. The model object retrieves data and has methods to get all data, get data for a row, save data, validate and update data.

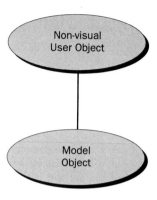

View Object (Standard DataWindow Object)

The list and detail view objects are both derived from standard DataWindow user objects. The list view object also has functionality to navigate to the detail view.

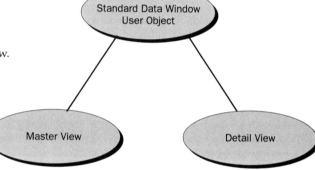

Controller Object (Window)

The controller object is a window that contains the model object by reference and the two view objects by value. The window has methods to initialize the list view, navigate to the detail view, add new data and save data to the database.

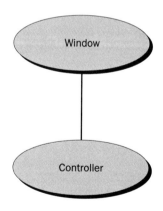

Implementation

The window creates the model object at initialization. It requests the model object to retrieve data and maps the data to the list view.

The user can either double-click on the list view or select a row and view the details by clicking on a View Details button. Either way, the controller is called to view the detail. The controller makes the detail view visible, requests the model to get the data for the selected row and maps the data to the detail view.

The user can update the data using the Save button. The **Clicked** event of the Save button will request the controller to save. The controller then maps the data from the detail view to the model and requests the model to save the data to a database. The controller also updates the list view with the updated data by requesting the model for the updated data. The model can also encapsulate functionality to validate the data.

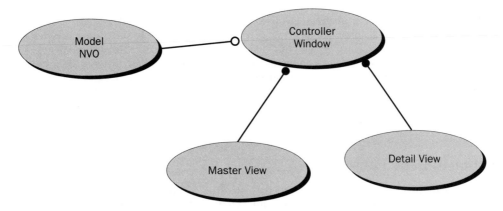

Distributed Architecture Design and the Model/View/Controller

PowerBuilder 5.0 supports distributed architecture which we'll look at in detail in Chapter 12. This allows applications to be partitioned over multiple machines. The MVC design is ideal for implementing in applications in a distributed environment. In PowerBuilder you can implement a distributed application by creating a server containing the model objects and clients containing the view objects. The controller also exists on the client. The ability to partition the model object on the server and the controller to access the model object makes this design more usable.

Let's look at implementing the same Master/ Detail component using the MVC pattern in a distributed environment.

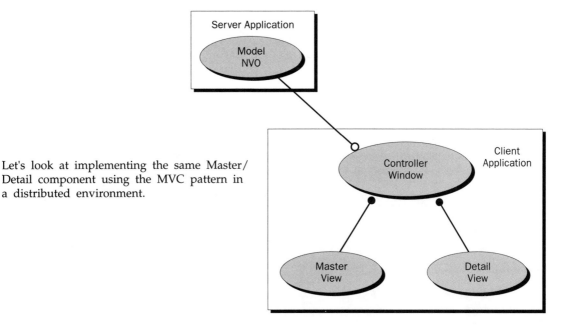

The controller window in the client application establishes a connection with the server application. The server then instantiates the model object. The controller object requests data from the model object running on the server app and displays it in the views on the client application.

Object Factory

Object factories, also known as **abstract factories**, manage objects of similar types. Earlier in the chapter, we discussed the scanner component, consisting of a hierarchy of different types of scanner objects. External objects interact with one well-defined interface to instantiate the appropriate scanner and use it. The scanner factory object can be called to get access to a scanner object. The factory will then instantiate the appropriate scanner object and hand it out to the calling object. The factory tracks the number of objects handed out to the calling objects and also makes sure that these objects are destroyed once they're no longer needed. Object factories also manage messaging from one object to another if required. Let's look at an example of an object factory in PowerBuilder.

Transaction Object Factory

This design pattern implements functionality for extending a PowerBuilder transaction object for database-specific functionality. External objects interact with the transaction object factory to instantiate and access the appropriate transaction object.

Transaction Object

This is a standard PowerBuilder transaction object.

My Transaction Object

This is derived from the standard PowerBuilder transaction object and extends the functionality of the transaction object to begin and end database units of work, signal errors and facilitate database access.

Sybase and Oracle Transaction

These are derived from **My transaction object** and implement functionality specific to the two database engines.

Implementation

The transaction factory manages the transaction objects. When an external object demands an object for a Sybase database, it instantiates the Sybase transaction object and passes it by reference to the calling object. It maintains a list of active transaction objects passed to external objects. The external object hands back the transaction object once it no longer needs it. The transaction object factory then decides to destroy it or keep it, depending on its transaction pool sharing attribute. It manages the instantiation of the appropriate database transaction object, its sharing and its destruction internally.

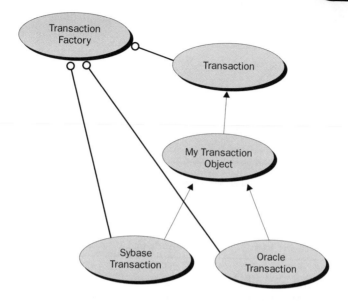

An object factory completely isolates the implementation details of different types of functionality. It's very flexible and has very little performance overhead. This layered approach to providing access to functionality makes the application scaleable and adaptive to change.

Generator

The generator design pattern implements dynamic functionality. The generator pattern will dynamically implement functionality based on soft-coded data. It has a well-defined dictionary to which users add data and an engine reads this data and dynamically generates the required behavior. For example, a browser generator implements functionality for browsing database tables. The users can browse any table by adding the table name in the browser data dictionary. The browser engine then reads the dictionary and creates browsers for the tables defined in the dictionary.

Master/Detail Maintenance Generator

The Master/Detail maintenance generator implements functionality to maintain data in database tables. Users of this component define the tables in the generator dictionary. The generator reads the dictionary and creates a selection list of tables for users to maintain. For each table in the list, the generator will create a Master/Detail component to view and update the table.

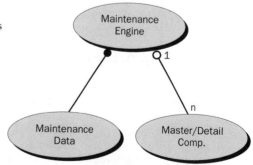

Maintenance Data

Maintenance data allows users to define data for the engine. Users can add table information and other related information to define tables they need to maintain.

For example, the data dictionary might include the following:

- Seq. Num: the sequence number for each master detail table.
- Table name: the name of the table.
- Master DW: the name of the DataObject for master view.
- Detail DW: the name of the DataObject for the detail view.
- Icon: the icon to be displayed for users to view Master/Detail.
- Editable: this flag allows editing of the detail view.

So the table might be:

Table Name	Master DW	Detail DW	Icon	Edit
Employees	d_emplist	d_empdetail	employee.bmp	1
Clients	d_clientlist	d_clientdetail	client.bmp	1

The users of this component can add as many rows as they wish. However, they need to create a master and detail DataWindow object for every table they add to the data dictionary.

Maintenance Engine

The maintenance engine is a user object which reads the data dictionary and loads the data. For each row, it dynamically creates an icon user object, assigns the icon for the row from the dictionary and displays it on its view. The user can then double-click on the icon to display the Master/Detail component.

Master/Detail Component

The Master/Detail component gets the master and detail object information from the engine and then implements the Master/Detail functionality as described earlier.

Pros and Cons

The generator pattern supports consistency and flexible design considerations. It allows the users of the components to extend the functionality dynamically. However, there's a performance overhead in maintaining the data dictionary and implementing generic functionality.

Design Standards

Design standards make for a consistent design approach for the application. Design considerations help identify the design patterns to be implemented for the application and design standards define the rules for interaction between objects, as well as standards for data and message exchange. For example, PowerBuilder has chosen a standard way of overriding the default behavior of events using the **SetActionCode** function. We can use this function in a DataWindow's **itemchanged** event to override the validation of a DataWindow column.

Standards for Object Interactions

In a PowerBuilder application, objects can send messages and data to each other using the PowerBuilder message object which is a global structure that has a number, string and a

PowerObject element. However, the message structure isn't sufficient in most applications for inter-object messaging. There are different ways of defining standards for your message interactions. The following example discusses a generic inter-object messaging method.

Message Interaction via Communication Manager

The communication manager allows two PowerObjects to send messages and data to each other. It has a data dictionary which defines:

- The message name
- Input data
- The data types of the input data
- The message sequence of the input data
- The output data
- The data types of the output data
- The message sequence of output data.

The object that wants to send a message to another object will start a message stream using the communication object. The calling object will then register the data as the PowerBuilder Any data type in the communication object. The communication object will check for the appropriate type and store it. Once the input data has been registered, the calling object will send the message to the recipient object. The recipient object will get the registered data from the communication object, process it and register the output data to the communication object. The calling object then retrieves the registered output data from the communication object and closes the message stream.

Summary

This chapter has introduced component-based design using design patterns. Component-based design implements a flexible and maintainable solution.

Designing reusable components requires planning. As a designer, you have to prioritize your design considerations. You should ensure that the component design implements reusability, has an acceptable performance and is flexible and consistent. Component design doesn't mean that we don't need inheritance—inheritance is used within the component.

Design patterns establish a consistent way to manage the state of objects and for objects to interact. Good designers reuse their design patterns. To summarise, the design patterns that we've looked at and the issues we've explored in this chapter were:

- Decorators and extending functionality for a component.
- Global utility objects and providing global functionality.
- Object managers and implementing a function at global level.
- Model/View/Controller and achieving flexibility and support for the distributed model.
- Object factories and managing objects of similar types.
- Generators and implementing dynamic functionality based on soft-coded data.

Object-oriented Analysis and Design

PowerBuilder provides a 4GL object-oriented development environment. Unfortunately, formal object-oriented methodologies are focused towards languages such as C++ or Smalltalk and there's no formal object-oriented analysis and design methodology geared towards developing object-oriented applications using PowerBuilder.

This chapter will introduce you to object-oriented analysis and design concepts as applied to PowerBuilder. We'll cover:

- The requirements analysis
- The role of prototyping
- Domain analysis
- Identifying use cases
- Designing domain classes
- Defining class categories
- Class interaction diagrams
- Designing implementation classes

The Analysis Process

Suppose you have just been given the task to develop an application, using PowerBuilder, to solve a particular business requirement. Where do you start?

Requirements Analysis

The first step is to analyze the requirements and define the boundaries of the system that you're to build. The analysis process will help you understand the nature of the problem and what the solution must provide. The key players at this stage are the people who are very familiar with the business processes that the application addresses, because they define the functional requirements of the system. Getting this right is the first step to success. Wherever possible, you should try to apply your experiences in designing similar systems. By the end of the process, you should have defined the 'charter' of the system and the problem domain of the application.

PowerBuilder is a rapid application development tool and you should use this benefit at the requirements analysis stage. You should build a prototype to give users an indication of what the system will look like and to help you understand the users' expectations and requirements. A screen layout on paper isn't as powerful as a 'working' prototype of that screen.

Use case models also help validate the requirements. In the context of a prototype, a use case model consists of a sequence of specific function invocations in the GUI by users to perform certain operations in the system. The prototype should allow all use case models which the users are likely to require to be performed.

You should build the prototype using standard controls, such as radio buttons, list boxes, DataWindows etc. Don't get too adventurous and start building user objects and custom classes. Many developers get carried away at this stage and start designing classes and their interactions, only to have the prototype change drastically the next day. Try not to access the database to display data—instead, store the required data in DataWindows. Remember, the main purpose of the prototype is to perform all the use case models, help design the GUI and get feedback from the users. It should only serve as a tool to help you firm the system requirements.

You should also conduct **JAD** (joint application development) sessions with a wide audience of users to help refine the system requirements. A JAD session consists of potential users of a system getting together with a moderator to discuss requirements of the system.

Remember that the requirements aren't cast in stone, even once you've built the prototype and you think that they're finalized! Software design is an iterative process. The prototype, however, provides a good starting point for designing and building the application.

Let's review an example problem that we'll use throughout this chapter. Users require a database application to allow them to order parts and manage inventory more efficiently. The requirements analysis states that the application should allow a user to order a part from a vendor and manage the inventory. We should develop a prototype that consists of screens which allow users to maintain information on parts and vendors, set up a purchase order, review the inventory and reduce it as parts are used.

The prototype allows the users to simulate the use cases and validate the interface and functionality of the system. These are the different use cases which encompass the complete functionality of the system:

- Retrieve a part record from the database and save it after editing.
- Retrieve a vendor record from the database and save it after editing.
- Set up a new vendor and save the new record in the database.
- Set up a new part and save the new record in the database.
- Order a part from a vendor.
- Edit an order, i.e. add comments, change the status to received or canceled etc. and save the edited order in the database.
- View inventory of all parts or a particular part and deplete inventory as parts are used.

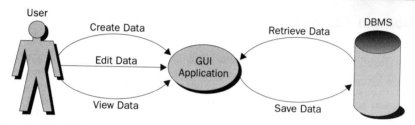

Domain Analysis

Domain analysis involves identifying the key abstractions in the problem domain identified during the requirements analysis.

In a 'pure' domain analysis, you should completely ignore implementation level details and only think in terms of logical or conceptual classes. Unfortunately, the prototype could force you to also think in terms of the physical structure, because it provides access to screens. In this context, the domain represents the boundaries of the issues that a system will deal with. You should use the prototype to simulate the interaction between the user and the system.

Identifying Domain Classes

A good starting point is to first identify all the functional modules in the system, as these will give you an idea of the different operations that the application will have to perform. The modules will depend on many different classes to carry out their responsibilities.

In an object-oriented GUI application, developed using PowerBuilder, windows invariably serve as classes which contain many other classes. These classes interact and collaborate with each other to provide the required functionality. The design should allow classes to be reused in different screens and to interact with and integrate with other classes.

Classifying the prototype screens into functional modules helps identify the responsibilities and roles of each class, the different classes that interact with each other and the mechanics of interaction between them.

So, if we go back to our order and inventory management system, we can see that the requirements analysis states that the application should allow a user to order a part from a vendor and manage the inventory. As determined from the prototype, the functional modules in the application are **order management**, **inventory management** and **part and vendor maintenance**. We can determine the major classes by analyzing the system requirements and identifying the nouns. If we do this, we can see that the key abstractions in the system are **order**, **vendor**, **part** and **inventory**.

The prototype and the functional requirements indicate the relationships that exist between the main abstractions in the system. A part is ordered from a vendor and the delivered parts are added to the inventory. The inventory gets depleted as parts are used up. So, as you can see, the prototype not only helps the users define the requirements but also helps the system architects identify the main abstractions and understand their relationship with each other.

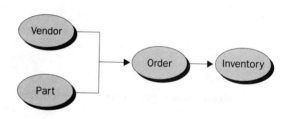

Designing Domain Classes

Now that we've identified the main abstractions in the system, let's define their functions and operations. The functions and operations enable each abstraction to carry out its responsibilities, as well as enabling the classes to interact with one another. Examining each use case model at the atomic level reveals all the abstractions involved and all the operations required. The class interaction diagram for each use case model illustrates the interaction between all the abstractions for that use case. The superset of these operations will identify all the operations of the main abstractions and their interaction with each other.

Let's identify the operations of the main abstractions in the inventory and order management system example.

```
Class Name:      Vendor
Operations:      Add( )
                 Delete( )
                 Modify( )
                 View( )
```

```
Class Name:      Part
Operations:      Add( )
                 Delete( )
                 Modify( )
                 View( )
```

```
Class Name:      Order
Operations:      Add( )
                 Modify( )
                 View( )
```

```
Class Name:      Inventory
Operations:      Modify( )
                 View( )
```

Once we've distinguished the operations of a class, we can identify its properties. We can derive certain properties in a class from other properties of the same class. We can either provide an operation that derives the value of this property or make it persistent. We should then analyze the superset of properties of all the classes in the system and their general data types to derive a list of logical data types in the system. This also helps to maintain consistency when properties are referenced in the systems.

If we list the properties of the classes identified in the order and inventory management system, listing their data types in terms of logical data types, we'll end up with the following:

```
Class Name:      Vendor
Properties:      Name             VendorName
                 Address          Address
                 ContactPerson    Name
                 TelephoneNumber  TelephoneNumber
                 Status           Status
                 Comments         Comments
```

```
Class Name:      Part
Properties:      PartName         PartName
                 PartNumber       PartNumber
                 Description      Description
                 Price            Money
```

Class Name:	Order	
Properties:	OrderNumber	OrderNumber
	Part	Part
	Vendor	VendorName
	Quantity	Quantity
	Tax	Money
	ShippingCost	Money
	TotalCost	Money
	OrderDate	Date
	DeliveryDate	Date
	Status	Status
	Comments	Comments

Class Name:	Inventory	
Properties:	Part	Part
	Quantity	Quantity

Now that we've identified the properties and operations of all the classes, we can establish similarities between them. Instances of different classes may be very similar in certain functionality and properties, in which case we can develop a superclass and derive more specialized subclasses from it. This is called an **inheritance relationship**.

Identifying inheritance relationships, superclasses and subclasses is an iterative process. Superclasses are based on the lowest common denominator approach—they are defined by the operations and properties common to a number of classes. Before you define the superclass, you should make sure you understand the difference between subtyping and subclassing.

In our example, vendor, part, order and inventory (the main abstractions) don't share any common features, so don't require superclassing and subclassing.

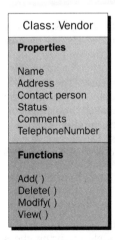
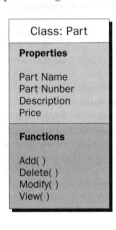

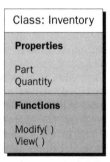

The Design Process

The analysis phase established the requirements and identified the domain classes. The goal of the design phase is to design and build an effective system which provides the functionality outlined in the requirements analysis.

The Design Model

It's very important to design a sound architecture (i.e. internal design, external interfaces, infrastructure etc.) for the system, making it scaleable, maintainable and reusable. You're far more likely to reuse the implementation classes than the domain classes across the domains. To allow the physical classes to be portable and at the same time remain unaffected by a change in the domain model, the architecture shouldn't provide a very close mapping and coupling between the domain and physical classes.

The design process involves mapping the logical classes identified in the domain analysis to physical classes and objects. Each domain class will map to a collection of physical classes which collaborate to provide the behavior identified with the domain class.

Good object-oriented design involves designing well-encapsulated objects. Every object should have a well-defined interface to its behaviors and properties. An object can have its behaviors invoked by another object or it can invoke another object's behavior. However, if all objects randomly invoked behavior on other objects or had their behaviors invoked, the entire system would be a tightly entwined collection of objects and determining the impact on the system of a change in an object would be an onerous task.

We therefore advise you to design a layered architecture for the system, grouping together objects that provide a certain service in a layer or class category. For example, in a GUI application, you might have a GUI layer, a business/application logic layer and a controller objects and frameworks services layer. The class categories (layers) should be hierarchical, with the higher level categories using the services provided by those on the lower level. Interaction between the different class categories should be as loosely coupled as possible. A layered architecture allows the application components to be more adaptable to change because a change will only have a direct affect on objects in the higher layers.

Classifying objects into categories provides an easy way of organizing all the classes into logical groups, based on their responsibilities. Class categories also help encapsulate classes because they allow you to selectively make classes available to other categories.

As we mentioned earlier, object-oriented system design is an iterative process. The initial superclasses, classes and relationships are derived from the domain model. The design model requires a higher level of detail than the domain model. Preparing a detailed implementation model from the abstract domain model leads you to identify new classes, modify existing classes and inheritance hierarchies and change the relationships between classes. Developing a prototype provides a bridge between the domain model and the design model and so helps you understand the requirements of the design model.

Designing for Reuse

Reuse should be the cornerstone of any design model. Remember that there are different levels of reuse. You could use parts of the domain model in different domain models requiring the same business processes, or reuse the entire design architecture in another system. Reuse isn't automatic—you have to design for reusability, which isn't a trivial task. You have to keep the implementation model separate from the domain model to avoid reducing its reusability.

You could reuse a generic application framework which provides low-level system services, or port and reuse other generic classes in a number of applications. It's very important that you have a firm grasp on the level of reuse, though. You shouldn't try to design every class so that the whole world can reuse it, but rather define and optimize the scope of the implementation model to solving the problem at hand.

By reuse, we don't just mean using classes in other applications. You can also reuse design solutions. When you're developing applications, you'll very often come across many similar design problems that have similar solutions. However, the solutions may not involve the same design implementation. Experienced designers can leverage their design experience by providing abstract solutions to design problems they have encountered while building different applications. These abstract solutions consist of descriptions and responsibilities of classes collaborating with each other to solve a particular object-oriented design problem. The implementation of each solution is only valid in the context of an application.

You should make the implementation model consistent in its entirety—the GUI look and feel should be consistent throughout the application and consistency should also extend to the architecture. You should also standardize messaging between components, error handling and database interaction and create lower level objects to provide these services.

There are many factors affecting the system design process. For example, designing generic classes will adversely affect the performance of the system. On the other hand, designing classes that are tuned and customized for use in a particular application will render them non-reusable by other systems. You should, then optimize the implementation model for performance, reuse and scalability.

Designing the Order and Inventory Management System

The goal of the design process is to implement a system that satisfies the system requirements. Before we start designing an implementation model for our example system, let's just review the information that we have about the system:

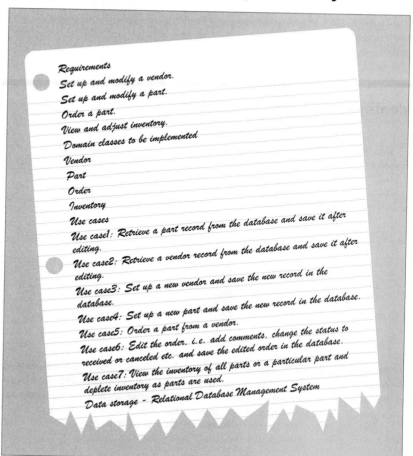

Requirements
Set up and modify a vendor.
Set up and modify a part.
Order a part.
View and adjust inventory.
Domain classes to be implemented
Vendor
Part
Order
Inventory
Use cases
Use case1: Retrieve a part record from the database and save it after editing.
Use case2: Retrieve a vendor record from the database and save it after editing.
Use case3: Set up a new vendor and save the new record in the database.
Use case4: Set up a new part and save the new record in the database.
Use case5: Order a part from a vendor.
Use case6: Edit the order. i.e. add comments. change the status to received or canceled etc. and save the edited order in the database.
Use case7: View the inventory of all parts or a particular part and deplete inventory as parts are used.
Data storage - Relational Database Management System

Classifying the Objects

The next step is to group the objects that provide a certain service into layers or class categories. The implementation class categories for our system are as follows.

- GUI objects: used to develop the graphical user interface.
- Interface objects: used to implement interface logic in the GUI objects.
- Factory objects: provide the interface to different functional modules in the system.
- Framework objects: provide low-level system services.
- Business/application objects: implement the domain-specific business logic and functionality.
- Control objects: integrate objects in the different class categories.

GUI objects are specific to the platform on which the system is to be deployed and provide a uniform look and feel. They consist of controls on windows and menus. The different behaviors of the GUI objects are implemented by **interface objects**. This category consists of class user objects which encapsulate different behaviors of different GUI classes. The **factory objects** class category consists of class user objects which define the interface to the different functional modules. This ensures a simplified and standard interface to all modules in the application. **Framework objects** are class user objects which provide low-level system services e.g. database access, error handling and access to utility classes. The **business/application objects** class category consists of class user objects which encapsulate domain-specific functionality. **Control objects** integrate all the different class categories to provide a functioning application. In a typical PowerBuilder application, MDI sheets and the MDI Frame fall into this class category.

Identifying the Relationships

We have to organize the class categories that we've defined above into a hierarchy. This figure identifies therelationships between the different class categories:

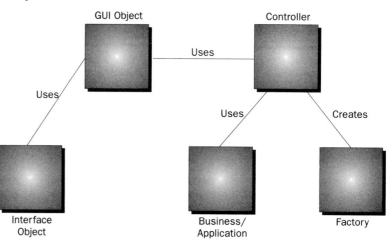

The figure identifies two basic relationships: **uses** and **creates**. A **uses** relationship implies that there's an interface between the two classes. A class category can have classes exported to be used by other class categories and classes in a higher level class category can use classes exported by lower level class categories to implement their functionality. A **creates** relationship implies that objects in one class category have the ability to instantiate classes in another class category.

Framework objects are global in scope and can be accessed by any class requiring their services. Factory objects create controller objects for different modules. Controller objects integrate GUI objects and business objects to provide the desired functionality. GUI objects use interface objects to implement their different behaviors.

Class Interaction Diagrams

When we were analyzing the requirements, we identified certain use cases that helped us understand the system requirements. We can extend the use case diagrams to create what are known as **class interaction diagrams**, which show which objects participate in each case and provide information about the roles and responsibilities of the different objects in each use case. Class interaction diagrams also shed light on the responsibilities and relationships of all the objects in the application.

Let's review the use cases and construct a class interaction diagram for each one.

Use Case 1: Retrieve a Part Record and Save it after Editing

The first use case starts as a user retrieves a part record from the database and saves it after editing. The user has to select the appropriate menu item to open the parts screen. This action initiates the parts factory object, which invokes the parts controller class to retrieve data from the database. The controller class also invokes the class to validate and save the edited parts with the updated information in the database. Here's the class interaction diagram for this use case:

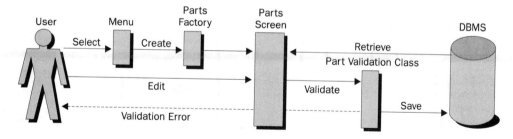

Use Case 2: Retrieve a Vendor Record and Save it after Editing

The second use case is very similar to the first. This case starts as a user retrieves a vendor record from the database and saves it after editing. The user first has to select the appropriate menu1item to open the screen which displays vendor information. This action initiates the vendor factory object, which invokes the controller class to retrieve vendor data from the database. This controller class also invokes the class to validate and save the edited vendor information in the database.

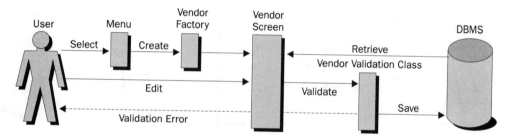

Use Case 3: Set up a New Part and Save the Record

The third use case starts when a user selects a menu item to set up a new part. This initiates the parts factory object, which initiates the controller object to provide a template to enter information about the part. The controller object also invokes a validation object to validate the information entered by the user before it's saved in the database. The class interaction diagram for this use case is shown in the figure below:

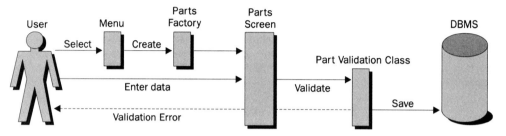

Use Case 4: Set up a New Vendor and Save the Record

The fourth use case is similar to the third. It starts when a user selects a menu item to set up a new vendor. This initiates the vendor factory object, which initiates the controller object to provide a template to enter information about the vendor. This controller object also invokes a validation object to validate the information entered by the user before it's saved in the database.

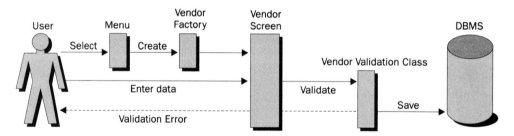

Use Case 5: Order a Part from a Vendor

The fifth use case starts when a user selects the menu item to order a part. This action initiates the order factory object. The order factory object invokes the controller object which provides a template to select a part, selects the vendor and enters order information. The controller object also invokes a validation object to validate the data before it's saved to the database. Here's the class interaction diagram for this use case:

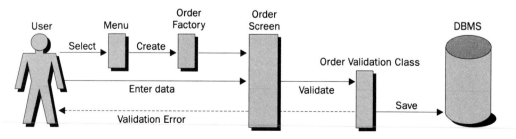

Use Case 6: Edit and Save an Order

The sixth use case starts when a user selects the menu item to review orders. The order factory object is invoked and initiates a controller object which retrieves order information from the database. The edited order information is validated by another object before it's saved. This is the class interaction diagram for this use case:

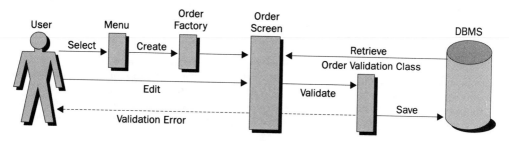

Use Case 7: View Inventory and Deplete it as Parts are Used

The seventh use case starts when a user selects the menu item to view the current inventory. This action invokes the inventory factory object which, in turn, initiates a controller object which retrieves inventory information from the database. The user can edit inventory information and save the modified data in the database. The controller object invokes an object to validate the inventory data before it's applied to the database.

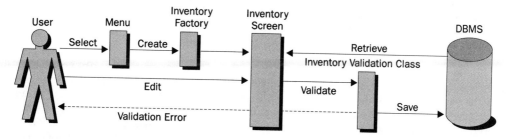

Implementing the Design

The prototype helped you design the graphical user interface and standardize the look and feel of the application. Designing the internals of the application is a more complex process. However, domain analysis, use cases and class interaction diagrams all help you to design the implementation classes and their relationships. We're going to look now at designing the major classes of the order and inventory management system.

Designing Framework Objects

Framework objects provide low-level system services. Though this class category is global in scope, members need not have all their functionality exported.

The order and inventory management application requires these framework classes: database transaction manager, exception handler, style manager and menu generator. We can export the functionality provided by these classes to other class categories by using two techniques. We can either give other class categories a direct reference to each of these framework classes or we can give them access to just their functions.

With the first technique, other class categories directly access functions and behaviors of the framework classes. This requires them to have complete knowledge about the concrete framework classes. This may be disadvantageous in the long run, because other classes would have tight coupling with the framework classes.

The second technique requires a level of indirection between the framework classes and classes that access them. We can construct a class user object that serves as a wrapper for the framework classes. It provides an interface to the public functions of all the framework classes. This insulates other classes from the exact implementation of the framework classes.

PowerBuilder provides certain global variables (such as **SQLCA**, **message**, **error** etc.) defined at the application level and allows designers to declare the class category of each global variable. In the example application, we've defined the global variable **SQLCA** to be of the type **nvo_transaction** and **error** to be of the type **nvo_error**. Therefore, these classes are declared as global variables and aren't provided with a wrapper to provide a level of indirection.

We'll use the second technique for our example. The first step is to design a class user object, named **nvo_framework**, to encapsulate the framework classes. This user object should be instantiated globally in the application. Let's review each of the framework classes.

Transaction Manager

The first is a class user object named **nvo_transManager**. This user object provides a public interface which allows the application to establish and manage one or multiple connections to the database. This user object manages a pool of transaction objects, each connected to a database. It also provides an interface enabling other classes to access a transaction object connected to a particular database.

The function **f_connect** is overloaded and has an optional parameter **ps_dbProfile**. If this parameter isn't supplied, the transaction manager reads the profiles from the **INI** file and connects to all of them. The function **f_disconnect** is also overloaded and has an optional parameter **ps_dbProfile**. If this parameter isn't supplied, the application disconnects all the connections; otherwise it only disconnects the transaction indicated by **ps_dbProfile**. The function **f_getTransaction** accepts a parameter **ps_dbProfile** and returns the corresponding transaction object.

```
Class Name:          nvo_transManager
SuperClass:          custom non visual user object
Public Functions:    f_connect
                     f_disconnect
                     f_getTransaction


Public Function f_connect
     Parameters:     ps_dbProfile (optional)
     Returns:        boolean

Public Function f_disconnect
     Parameters:     ps_dbProfile (optional)
     Returns:        boolean

Public Function f_getTransaction
     Parameters:     ps_dbProfile
     Returns:        sqlca
```

Exception Handler

The exception handler, **error**, is a global variable of the type **nvo_error**. **nvo_error** is implemented as a standard non-visual user object of the type **error**. It extends the functionality of the standard PowerBuilder error class and provides the capability to report and process application-specific errors and pop-up message boxes. **nvo_error** has an overloaded function, **f_reportError**, and a function, **f_messageBox**. **f_reportError** has one required parameter, **ps_errorMsg**, and an optional parameter, **pl_errorNum**. The function **f_messageBox** has parameters which include **ps_msg**, **pi_bmpStyle** and **pi_buttonStyle**.

```
Class Name:              nvo_error
SuperClass:              error
Public Functions:        f_reportError
                         f_messageBox

Public Function f_reportError
     Parameters:         ps_errorMsg
                         pl_errorNum (optional)
     Returns:            boolean

Public Function f_messageBox
     Parameters:         ps_msg
                         pi_bmpStyle
                         pi_buttonStyle
     Returns:            pi_buttonSelected
```

Style Manager

The style manager, **nvo_styleManager**, is a non-visual object. It has two functions: **f_saveDesktop** and **f_restoreDesktop**. Both these functions accept a parameter **pw_sheet**. The parameter **pw_sheet** provides a reference to the window or MDI sheet that requires its style properties saved or restored. The design of this class is described below:

```
Class Name:              nvo_styleManager
SuperClass:              non visual user object
Public Functions:        f_saveDesktop
                         f_restoreDesktop

Public Function f_saveDesktop
     Parameters:         pw_sheet
     Returns:            boolean

Public Function f_restoreDesktop
     Parameters:         pw_sheet
     Returns:            boolean
```

Menu Generator

The menu generator, **nvo_menuGenerator**, is derived from a non-visual user object. It has one function, **f_generateMenu**, which accepts one parameter, **pw_sheet**. The parameter **pw_sheet** provides a reference to the window or MDI sheet that requires its menu generated and initialized. The design of this class is described here:

```
Class Name:              nvo_menuGenerator
SuperClass:              non visual user object
```

```
Public Functions:        f_gnerateMenu

Public Function f_generateMenu
     Parameters:         pw_sheet
     Returns:            boolean
```

The design of the class user object, named **nvo_framework**, which provides an interface to all the functions of the different framework category objects is shown below. This class can selectively export functionality provided by the framework category objects. The object, **nvo_framework**, also has a function, **f_createFramework**, which initializes all the framework classes. This function should be called when the application starts up.

```
Class Name:              nvo_framework
SuperClass:              non visual user object
Public Functions:        f_createFramework
                         f_saveDesktop
                         f_restoreDesktop
                         f_connect
                         f_disconnect
                         f_getTransaction
                         f_reportError
                         f_messageBox
                         f_saveDesktop
                         f_restoreDesktop
                         f_generateMenu
                         f_getFactory

Public Function f_createFramework
     Parameters:         NONE
     Returns:            boolean

Public Function f_saveDesktop
     Parameters:         pw_sheet
     Returns:            boolean

Public Function f_restoreDesktop
     Parameters:         pw_sheet
     Returns:            boolean

Public Function f_connect
     Parameters:         ps_dbProfile (optional)
     Returns:            boolean

Public Function f_disconnect
     Parameters:         ps_dbProfile (optional)
     Returns:            boolean

Public Function f_getTransaction
     Parameters:         ps_dbProfile
     Returns:            qlca

Public Function f_reportError
     Parameters:         ps_errorMsg
                         pl_errorNum (optional)
     Returns:            boolean

Public Function f_messageBox
     Parameters:         ps_msg
                         pi_bmpStyle
```

```
                        pi_buttonStyle
        Returns:        pi_buttonSelected

Public Function f_saveDesktop
        Parameters:     pw_sheet
        Returns:        boolean

Public Function f_restoreDesktop
        Parameters:     pw_sheet
        Returns:        boolean

Public Function f_generateMenu
        Parameters:     pw_sheet
        Returns:        boolean

Public Function f_getFactory
        Parameters:     ps_moduleName
        Returns:        nvo_factory
```

The framework class category can also include classes providing general utility functions, etc.

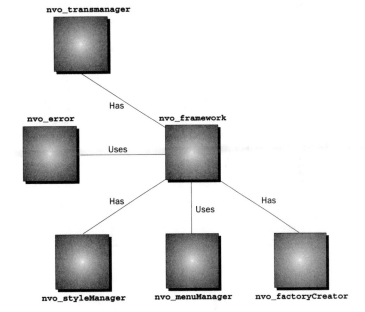

Designing Factory Objects

Applications have many functional modules. Each module is composed of different objects which collaborate to provide a certain functionality. The external interface to create windows and objects in different modules must be the same at the framework level. Objects which help create and initialize objects in different modules in the application belong to the class category, **factory objects**. The class which encapsulates functionality to 'create' or instantiate a module at run time is called a **factory**. The superclass from which all factory objects for the different modules are subclassed is called an **abstract factory**.

The factory for each module in the application is implemented at the subclass level, but the interface is defined in the abstract class. The framework classes are coupled with the factory classes using the interface defined in the factory abstract class and they need not have any knowledge about the concrete factory classes in an application.

187

How does the framework know which factory subclass is to be used for a functional module? Obviously, an object class must create the appropriate factory subclass for a functional module in the application.

Keeping with the practice of not embedding any application-specific logic in the framework, we have to create a **factoryCreator** abstract class that will help define the interface between the framework and subclasses of the **factoryCreator** class. There should be one subclass of the **factoryCreator** class in an application, where the logic that relates subclasses of the abstract factory with modules in the application is defined.

Before you design the interface of the abstract factory, you should carefully analyze how you will create and initialize all functional modules. Analysis of the order and inventory management application shows that we have to create the modules in two modes: one that only allows editing and another that allows creation of new records.

The **factoryCreator** class is implemented by creating a class user object named **nvo_factoryCreator**. We define a parameterized virtual function in this user object, named **f_getFactory**, which returns a factory object for a specified module. This class is further encapsulated by the wrapper object, **nvo_framework**, that we discussed above.

We can then subclass **nvo_factoryCreator** to create a class user object: the application level **factoryCreator** object. This implements the function **f_getFactory**.

We implement the abstract factory class by creating a class user object. Call this user object **nvo_factory**. Then define two virtual functions: **f_createNew** and **f_create**. **f_createNew** initializes a module in a mode that allows the user to create a new record. **f_create** initializes a module in a mode that allows the user to only edit a record. Subclass **nvo_factory** to create the factory objects for the different modules in the application. You should implement the functions, **f_createNew** and **f_create** in each subclass.

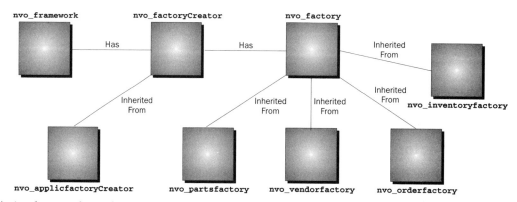

Let's implement the architecture that we've described in the order and inventory management system. This system has four functional modules: part management, vendor management, order management and inventory management.

Inventory Management Functional Modules

Create four factory objects, **nvo_partsFactory**, **nvo_vendorFactory**, **nvo_orderFactory** and **nvo_inventoryFactory** inherited from **nvo_factory**. Implement the functions **f_create** and **f_createNew** in each of these four objects. These objects interact with the controller objects in each module.

We need an application-specific object to help the framework object **nvo_framework** access the application's factory objects. Create a new class user object, called **nvo_applicFactoryCreator**, inherited from **nvo_factoryCreator** and implement the parameterized function **f_getFactory**. This function accepts the module name as a parameter and returns a reference to the factory object for it.

nvo_factory is also referred to as the abstract factory. This is its design:

```
Class Name:          nvo_factory
SuperClass:          non visual user object
Public Functions:    f_create
                     f_createNew

Public Function f_create
     Parameters:     NONE
     Returns:        boolean
Public Function f_createNew
     Parameters:     NONE
     Returns:        boolean
```

The design of the four application-specific subclasses of the abstract factory, one for each module, is described below:

```
Class Name:          nvo_partsFactory
SuperClass:          nvo_factory
Public Functions:    f_create
                     f_createNew

Public Function f_create
     Parameters:     NONE
     Returns:        boolean
Public Function f_createNew
     Parameters:     NONE
     Returns:        boolean
```

```
Class Name:          nvo_vendorFactory
SuperClass:          nvo_factory
Public Functions:    f_create
                     f_createNew

Public Function f_create
     Parameters:     NONE
     Returns:        boolean
Public Function f_createNew
     Parameters:     NONE
     Returns:        boolean
```

```
Class Name:          nvo_orderFactory
SuperClass:          nvo_factory
Public Functions:    f_create
                     f_createNew

Public Function f_create
     Parameters:     NONE
     Returns:        boolean
Public Function f_createNew
     Parameters:     NONE
     Returns:        boolean
```

189

```
Class Name:              nvo_inventoryFactory
SuperClass:              nvo_factory
Public Functions:        f_create
                         f_createNew


Public Function f_create
      Parameters:        NONE
      Returns:           boolean
Public Function f_createNew
      Parameters:        NONE
      Returns:           boolean
```

Here's the design of the abstract class **nvo_factoryCreator**:

```
Class Name:              nvo_factoryCreator
SuperClass:              non visual object
Public Functions:        f_getFactory


Public Function f_getFactory
      Parameters:        ps_moduleName
      Returns:           nvo_factory
```

This class is subclassed and the description of this class, **nvo_applicFactoryCreator**, is provided below:

```
Class Name:              nvo_applicFactoryCreator
SuperClass:              non visual object
Public Functions:        f_getFactory


Public Function f_getFactory
      Parameters:        ps_moduleName
      Returns:           nvo_factory
```

You're probably wondering why we created the two abstract classes, **nvo_factory** and **nvo_factoryCreator**, and created an inheritance hierarchy. We basically did this to insulate the framework from the knowledge of any application-specific classes and to make the application scaleable. For example, the function **f_getFactory** in the object **nvo_applicFactoryGenerator** returns a reference to the appropriate factory object. We can now safely declare the return type as **nvo_factory** and not worry about the exact subclass. Also, none of the return data types from functions or function parameters have to be changed if a new module is added to the application, because the factory object for this module will also be inherited from **nvo_factory**.

The framework wrapper object **nvo_framework** has a function, **f_getFactory**, which in turn calls the function, **f_getFactory**, defined in the object **nvo_applicFactoryCreator**. This interaction is implemented in such a manner that **nvo_framework** has access to an object of the type **nvo_factoryCreator** and invokes the function **f_getFactory** in that object. There is no hard-coded reference to **nvo_applicFactoryCreator**; the reference is made at run time. This ensures that the framework you design and implement is very portable and scaleable.

Designing GUI and Interface Objects

GUI objects are used to display and enter data into the system and invoke functionality in the application by clicking on buttons, menus etc. There's also a category of objects which help implement the behavior of GUI objects. This class category is often referred to as **interface objects**.

For example, the logic to highlight the clicked row in a spreadsheet control need not be implemented in the control itself, but can be implemented in an interface object. Many spreadsheet controls can then use the interface object to implement its clicked behavior.

The order and inventory management application allows users to enter and edit new parts, vendors and orders and edit inventory data.

All the modules need a GUI class that can retrieve data from the database and validate and save the edited data. This class should also be able to report and recover from database errors. This GUI class can be implemented by designing a standard DataWindow user object which satisfies these requirements.

Construct a standard DataWindow user object named **udw_dataDisplay**. Subclasses of **udw_dataDisplay** will implement the specific behavior required in each module.

Now let's design the interface classes that **udw_dataDisplay** will use. The main interface classes that we have to design include a database error handler, a class to report data type validation errors and a class that checks whether the data violates any business requirements before it's applied to the database.

The design should account for the fact that the validation behavior is going to be polymorphic in the different subclasses of **udw_dataDisplay**.

We should design an abstract class for each of the three interface classes, where we define the functions of these classes as virtual functions. This DataWindow will use functions of the interface classes to implement its behavior. We should establish the relationships between the DataWindow and the interface classes at the abstract class level.

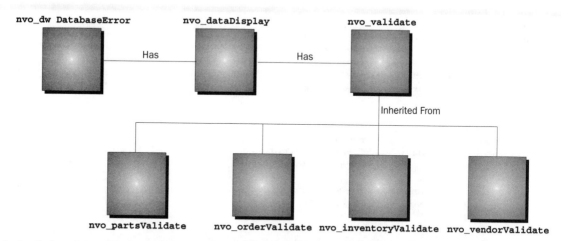

Let's design the validation abstract class. We can construct this class as a custom class user object, named **nvo_validate**, with two virtual functions **f_datatypeValidate** and **f_dataRulesValidate**. Four subclasses have to be derived from this abstract class—one for each module. The two functions **f_datatypeValidate** and **f_dataRulesValidate** are implemented in each subclass. You'll see the design of this class hierachy on the next page:

```
Class Name:              nvo_validate
SuperClass:              non visual object
Public Functions:        f_datatypeValidate
                         f_dataRulesValidate


Public Function f_datatypeValidate
     Parameters:         pw_datawindow
     Returns:            boolean

Public Function f_dataRulesValidate
     Parameters:         pw_datawindow
     Returns:            boolean
```

```
Class Name:              nvo_partsValidate
SuperClass:              nvo_validate
Public Functions:        f_datatypeValidate
                         f_dataRulesValidate


Public Function f_datatypeValidate
     Parameters:         pw_datawindow
     Returns:            boolean

Public Function f_dataRulesValidate
     Parameters:         pw_datawindow
     Returns:            boolean
```

```
Class Name:              nvo_orderValidate
SuperClass:              nvo_validate
Public Functions:        f_datatypeValidate
                         f_dataRulesValidate


Public Function f_datatypeValidate
     Parameters:         pw_datawindow
     Returns:            boolean

Public Function f_dataRulesValidate
     Parameters:         pw_datawindow
     Returns:            boolean
```

```
Class Name:              nvo_inventoryValidate
SuperClass:              nvo_validate
Public Functions:        f_datatypeValidate
                         f_dataRulesValidate


Public Function f_datatypeValidate
     Parameters:         pw_datawindow
     Returns:            boolean

Public Function f_dataRulesValidate
     Parameters:         pw_datawindow
     Returns:            boolean
```

```
Class Name:              nvo_vendorValidate
SuperClass:              nvo_validate
Public Functions:        f_datatypeValidate
                         f_dataRulesValidate
```

```
Public Function f_datatypeValidate
     Parameters:        pw_datawindow
     Returns:           boolean

Public Function f_dataRulesValidate
     Parameters:        w_datawindow
     Returns:           boolean
```

We also require an interface class that reports database errors encountered by the subclasses of **udw_dataDisplay** as they retrieve or save data. We don't have to design this class for polymorphic behavior because the functionality that it provides is standard for all subclasses of **udw_dataDisplay**.

Let's build a class user object named **nvo_dwDatabaseError**. Implement a function, **f_dbError**, which includes the logic to report and recover from database errors. The design of this metaclass is shown below:

```
Class Name:          nvo_dwDatabaseError
SuperClass:          non visual object
Public Functions:    f_dbError

Public Function f_dbError
     Parameters:        pw_datawindow
     Returns:           boolean
```

At this stage, you're probably wondering how these classes are coupled. As we mentioned earlier, we should identify the relationships between them at the abstract class level.

In the abstract class, **udw_dataDisplay**, create two private instance variables **invo_validate** and **invo_dwError** of the type **nvo_validate** and **nvo_dwError** respectively. Create two functions, **f_setValidateClass** and **f_setDwErrorClass**, which initialize the two instance variables, **invo_validate** and **invo_dwError**, respectively. You also have to add script in the **itemerror** and **dberror** events of the abstract class **udw_dataDisplay**. The script in the **itemerror** event should call the function **f_datatypeValidate** in the class to which the variable **invo_validate** provides a reference at run time in order to validate the data types of the edited data.

```
invo_validate.f_datatypeValidate(this)
```

The script in the **dberror** event should call the function in **f_dbError** in the metaclass **nvo_dwError**, to which the variable **invo_dwError** provides a reference at run time.

```
invo_dwError.f_dbError(this)
```

We can validate the data for business requirements by overloading the DataWindow **update** function. This overloaded function should first call the function **f_dataRulesValidate** in the class to which the variable **invo_validate** provides a reference at run time. This function should call the function **update** in its superclass if the data passes validation.

```
if invo_validate .f_datatypeValidate(this) then
    super::update()
else
    //some processing
end if
```

The design of the abstract class **udw_dataDisplay** is shown below:

```
Class Name:              udw_dataDisplay
SuperClass:              datawindow
Public Functions:        f_setValidateClass

Private Variables invo_validate
     Type:               nvo_validate

Private Variable invo_dbError
     Type:               nvo_dbError

Public Function f_setValidateClass
     Parameters:         pnvo_validate
     Returns:            boolean

Public Function f_serDwErrorClass
     Parameters:         pnvo_dwError
     Returns:            boolean

Public Function update
     Parameters:         NONE
     Returns:            integer
```

We have to build four subclasses of **udw_dataDisplay**, named **udw_partsDisplay**, **udw_vendorDisplay**, **udw_orderDisplay** and **udw_inventoryDisplay**, for each module in the application. Each of these subclasses uses the appropriate interface subclass to implement their behavior. The **update** function is implemented in each subclass, based on the functionality required in that domain or functional module.

Menus also belong to the GUI class category. Menus attached to all the windows in the order and inventory management application are constructed dynamically by the framework object **nvo_menuGenerator**. We'll discuss the mechanism to generate menus dynamically in detail in Chapter 5. There, you'll see that dynamic menus require a menu template class and a menu class that's instantiated at run time to create a menu item. By default, all windows in the application are assigned the template menu class. We generate dynamic menus by creating instances of a menu class at run time to create menu items and attaching the dynamically constructed menu items to a window's menu.

Let's design the menu class, **m_generator**, which is instantiated at run time to generate menu items. This class requires a function to set the menu items behavior mode when it's clicked and to define the callback message to the menus parent window. This is the design of the class **m_generator**:

```
Class Name:              m_generator
SuperClass:              menu
Public Functions:        f_setCallbackMode

Private Variables ib_callBackMode
     Type:               boolean

Private Variable is_callbackMsg
     Type:               string

Public Function f_setCallbackMode
     Parameters:         pb_callEvent
                         ps_callbackMsg
     Returns:            boolean
```

Designing Business/Application Objects

Objects which belong to this class category encapsulate functionality to perform application-specific logic. They implement the functionality described by the domain classes. They should have a flexible design to allow other applications that have similar domain classes to use them.

The application object designed for a domain class should support that domain's operations. You can design an object hierarchy for the application objects. You can also design one or more abstract classes and implement their behaviors as virtual functions.

Earlier, we identified the four main domain classes in the order and inventory management system. If we look at their operations, we'll see that a single abstract application class is sufficient, as the four domain classes have similar operations.

The abstract class is implemented as a custom class user object named **nvo_abstractDomain**. This class has four virtual functions, **f_delete**, **f_add**, **f_modify** and **f_view**, which is the superset of the operations of the domain classes. Each of these functions has to, in turn, perform operations on the DataWindow used to display data. For example, the function **f_save** in the vendor domain subclass has to save vendor data displayed in the DataWindow **udw_vendorDisplay**.

In the section on GUI class category objects, we designed an abstract class, **udw_datawindow**, of the type DataWindow, from which all DataWindows used to display domain data were subclassed. All the virtual functions in **nvo_abstractDomain** accept a parameter of the type **udw_datawindow** as a parameter. Coupling the two classes at the abstract class level makes the implementation and integration of the subclasses much easier.

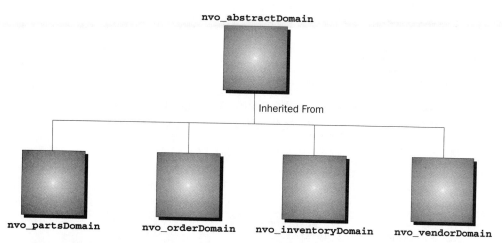

The design of the application class hierarchy is shown below. The first class described is the abstract application class, **nvo_absractDomain**.

Class Name:	nvo_abstractDomain
SuperClass:	non visual object
Public Functions:	f_delete
	f_add
	f_modify
	f_view

```
Public Function f_delete
       Parameters:           pudw_dataDisplay
       Returns:              boolean


Public Function f_add
       Parameters:           pudw_dataDisplay
       Returns:              boolean


Public Function f_modify
       Parameters:           pudw_dataDisplay
       Returns:              boolean


Public Function f_view
       Parameters:           pudw_dataDisplay
       Returns:              boolean
```

The abstract application class, **nvo_abstractDomain**, is subclassed into the four domain application classes and the operations are implemented in them. Four non-visual objects inherited from **nvo_abstractDomain** are created. The design of each subclass is shown below. Only the required functionality is implemented in each subclass.

```
Class Name:              nvo_partsDomain
SuperClass:              nvo_abstractDomain
Public Functions:        f_delete
                         f_add
                         f_modify
                         f_view


Public Function f_save
       Parameters:           pudw_dataDisplay
       Returns:              boolean

Public Function f_add
       Parameters:           pudw_dataDisplay
       Returns:              boolean

Public Function f_modify
       Parameters:           pudw_dataDisplay
       Returns:              boolean

Public Function f_view
       Parameters:           pudw_dataDisplay
       Returns:              boolean
```

```
Class Name:              nvo_vendorDomain
SuperClass:              nvo_abstractDomain
Public Functions:        f_delete
                         f_add
                         f_modify
                         f_view


Public Function f_delete
       Parameters:           pudw_dataDisplay
       Returns:              boolean

Public Function f_add
       Parameters:           pudw_dataDisplay
       Returns:              boolean
```

196

```
Public Function f_modify
        Parameters:      pudw_dataDisplay
        Returns:         boolean

Public Function f_view
        Parameters:      pudw_dataDisplay
        Returns:         boolean


Class Name:              nvo_orderDomain
SuperClass:              nvo_abstractDomain
Public Functions:        f_add
                         f_modify
                         f_view

Public Function f_add
        Parameters:      pudw_dataDisplay
        Returns:         boolean

Public Function f_modify
        Parameters:      pudw_dataDisplay
        Returns:         boolean

Public Function f_view
        Parameters:      pudw_dataDisplay
        Returns:         boolean


Class Name:              nvo_inventoryDomain
SuperClass:              nvo_abstractDomain
Public Functions:        f_modify
                         f_view

Public Function f_modify
        Parameters:      pudw_dataDisplay
        Returns:         boolean

Public Function f_view
        Parameters:      pudw_dataDisplay
        Returns:         boolean
```

Designing Control Objects

Objects in this class category serve as the 'glue' which integrates the different classes to provide a working application. A window is an ideal candidate for a control object in a GUI-based application. This GUI class serves as a 'container' for different controls with which users interact to trigger and access the application's functionality.

In a typical PowerBuilder application, you can use windows as controller objects. These windows shouldn't embed any application-specific logic, but should only serve to integrate different controls and application classes.

We can design a hierarchy of control objects in the order and inventory management application. The control abstract class is of the type window and has to be coupled with the framework and the other abstract classes it integrates. Coupling with the abstract classes ensures that the relationship allows polymorphic behavior to be implemented and integrated easily in the concrete classes.

Coupling the control abstract class with the framework ensures that concrete classes don't reference global variables and remain portable.

197

You implement the abstract controller class by creating a window named
w_abstractController. You should create an instance of the framework in the **Open** event of
this window. This ensures that all subclasses will automatically have access to the framework.

You should couple the abstract controller class, **w_abstractController,** with the abstract
domain class **nvo_abstractDomain** and the abstract DataWindow class **udw_dataDisplay**.
Declare protected instance variables **invo_domain** of type **nvo_abstractDomain** and
iudw_dataDisplay of the type **udw_dataDisplay**. You'll have to initialize these two instance
variables with the appropriate subclass of **nvo_domain** and **udw_dataDisplay** in each domain's
control subclass.

You should declare four custom events, **ue_domainDelete, ue_domainAdd, ue_domainModify**
and **ue_domainView**, in **w_abstractControl**. In turn, these user events call the functions
f_delete, f_add, f_modify and **f_view**, respectively, in the abstract domain class
(**invo_Domain**).

A domain's control subclass gets created by that module's factory subclass. The abstract control
class should provide an interface that will be used by the abstract factory class to instantiate the
concrete control classes in the desired mode. You should set up two functions, **f_create** and
f_createNew, in **w_abstractControl** for this purpose. The framework function to configure the
menu should also be invoked as this window is created.

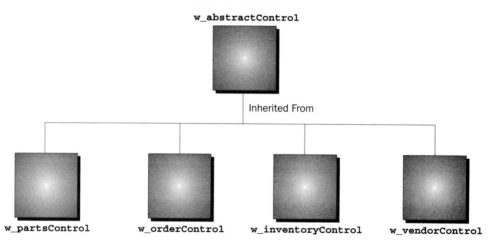

w_abstractControl

Inherited From

w_partsControl   w_orderControl   w_inventoryControl   w_vendorControl

The design of the abstract control class is shown below:

```
        Class Name:            w_abstractControl
        SuperClass:            window
        Public Functions:      f_create
                               f_createNew

        Events:                ue_domainAdd
                               ue_domainDelete
                               ue_domainModify
                               ue_domainView

    Public Function f_create
            Parameters:        NONE
            Returns:           boolean
```

198

```
Public Function f_createNew
      Parameters:        NONE
      Returns:           boolean
```

You should create four subclasses of the abstract control class, one for each module/domain:

```
Class Name:                w_partsControl
SuperClass:                w_abstractControl
Public Functions:          f_create
                           f_createNew
Events:                    ue_domainAdd
                           ue_domainDelete
                           ue_domainModify
                           ue_domainView


Public Function f_create
      Parameters:          NONE
      Returns:             boolean

Public Function f_createNew
      Parameters:          NONE
      Returns:             boolean

Class Name:                w_vendorControl
SuperClass:                w_abstractControl
Public Functions:          f_create
                           f_createNew
Events:                    ue_domainAdd
                           ue_domainDelete
                           ue_domainModify
                           ue_domainView


Public Function f_create
      Parameters:          NONE
      Returns:             boolean

Public Function f_createNew
      Parameters:          NONE
      Returns:             boolean

Class Name:                w_orderControl
SuperClass:                w_abstractControl
Public Functions:          f_create
                           f_createNew
Events:                    ue_domainAdd
                           ue_domainDelete
                           ue_domainModify
                           ue_domainView


Public Function f_create
      Parameters:          NONE
      Returns:             boolean

Public Function f_createNew
      Parameters:          NONE
      Returns:             boolean
```

199

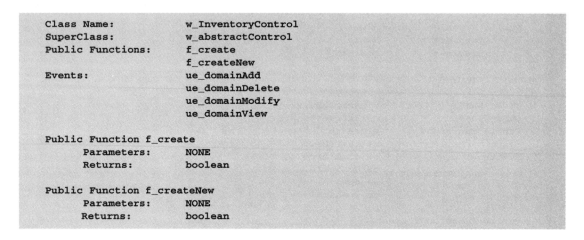

```
Class Name:              w_InventoryControl
SuperClass:              w_abstractControl
Public Functions:        f_create
                         f_createNew
Events:                  ue_domainAdd
                         ue_domainDelete
                         ue_domainModify
                         ue_domainView

Public Function f_create
      Parameters:        NONE
      Returns:           boolean

Public Function f_createNew
      Parameters:        NONE
      Returns:           boolean
```

Putting It All Together

Now that we've looked at all the various objects it's helpful to see how they all fit together. The following figure illustrates how the control classes interact with the other classes we've described.

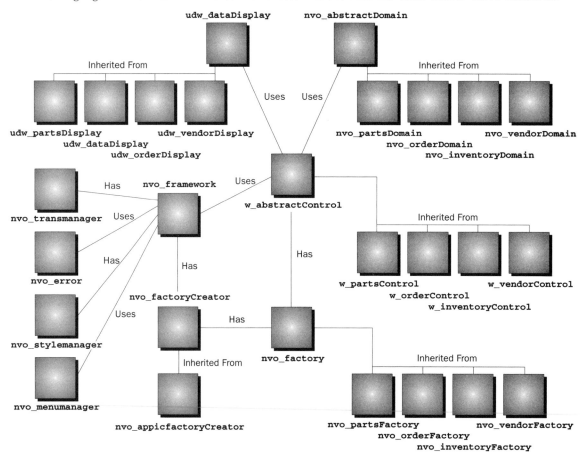

Summary

By taking you through an example application, this chapter has introduced you to object-oriented analysis and design concepts applied to developing PowerBuilder applications. Amongst other things, we've covered formalizing system requirements, setting up use cases, domain analysis, class interaction diagrams, defining class categories and designing implementation classes.

This chapter proposed a technique for integrating different PowerBuilder objects by using abstract classes coupled through virtual functions.

In the next chapter, we'll look in detail at application frameworks.

Chapter

10

Designing Frameworks and Object Libraries

Designing, constructing and deploying an application are all tedious jobs. And the task doesn't end there; once you've done all this, you then have to worry about maintenance and all the tasks that go with it—fixing bugs, enhancing an application's functionality, etc. Just imagine the number of tasks that would have to be duplicated if a development team was responsible for a number of applications.

In the last chapter, we looked at how you can reduce the effort that you need to put into development by reusing design patterns. You can also reuse code, which, I should add, means building reusable classes, not cutting and pasting code! We're talking about building reusable application frameworks and object libraries.

Reusing code allows you to focus on designing application-specific functionality instead of reinventing common objects such as error handlers, database transaction managers etc. It also gives you access to tested and debugged code which reduces the maintenance effort.

In this chapter, we'll discuss how to build application frameworks and reusable class libraries using PowerBuilder.

Application Frameworks

A framework provides an application with components which are already tested and debugged and have a proven design.

As a PowerBuilder developer, you'll no doubt be familiar with the fact that certain components and objects provide services that are required in almost all applications that you deploy. These objects include MDI frames, menus, error handlers, database transaction handlers, message managers, etc. At some point, you may well have rebuilt some or, in certain cases, *all* of these objects in every application that you have deployed. If you have, you'll not only have spent a lot of time designing similar objects, but you'll also have spent time testing and debugging them.

This is where **application frameworks** come into the picture. You can abstract all the system services type of functionality that your applications usually require and design a standard for implementing them. The implementation of this design will result in a number of classes and objects that collaborate to provide the basic system level functionality required by your applications and can be termed an application framework.

Application frameworks are not only limited to providing system level services such as error handling, database transaction management etc. You can also incorporate into them certain functional modules. For example, many organizations have a requirement for ad hoc reporting applications. You can abstract this functionality into a soft-coded (dynamic) 'reporting engine' and include it in the framework. Applications which use this framework would have to include soft-coded rules for this reporting engine to get a working reporting application.

Designing Application Frameworks

Like any other software development project, the first thing you have to do when you're designing an application framework is to decide on the requirements and the scope of the development effort. Designing an application framework for use in a particular suite of applications is very different to designing a framework to sell commercially.

Two of the key considerations to keep in mind when you're designing frameworks are **encapsulation** and **scalability**. The implementation of the functionality provided by the framework should be well hidden, because applications that use it shouldn't be affected if some of the implementation logic gets modified. The applications should also be able to modify the behavior of any framework component if they need to. The design of the framework should allow you to easily integrate a new release into an application without having to redesign the framework functionality that has been extended in the application.

Let's review the requirements of a framework in a typical database application built using PowerBuilder. The application requires an MDI frame, a hierarchy of menus, database access and a transaction manager which allows users to log into the database and manages database transactions, an error handler which reports errors in a standard manner and a class which provides access to utility functions.

Let's evaluate these requirements in detail. The error handler and database transaction manager will be used by all the windows in the application. The MDI frame will serve as the vehicle for initializing the framework. The menu hierarchy will be used by the different windows in the application to trigger functionality on the active sheet or to initialize different application modules.

The framework should also enforce a messaging standard between windows and a standard interface for creating and initializing application modules. It should provide a utility function class which is accessible by all windows in the application. The utility class provides access to often used functions, such as string manipulation functions, color functions etc. There's also the need for a class framework controller which will integrate all the framework classes.

We could summarize a few basic requirements for a framework as:

- Framework controller
- Database transaction manager
- Error handler
- Module factory
- Messaging services
- Utility functions
- Menu hierarchy
- MDI frame and windows

Let's design a framework which provides this functionality.

Framework Controller

The first framework component that we should discuss is the framework controller. As the name itself suggests, this class is responsible for creating and initializing the various framework components.

All logic pertaining to creating, initializing and destroying framework classes should be embedded in this class. This also ensures that the framework remains portable and easy to integrate.

As it's a non GUI object, we should construct the framework controller as a custom class user object, called **nvo_frameworkController**. This object will be used by various application classes, so we should instantiate it as a global object. We should declare the different framework components that it creates as private instance variables:

```
private:
nvo_tranManager invo_tranManager
nvo_strUtilityManager invo_strUtilityManager
nvo_abstractFactoryController invo_abstractFactoryController
nvo_osApi invo_osApi
```

It should have a function, **f_initFramework**, to create the different framework components and initialize the instance variables. Of course, this assumes 'heavy' usage of all the framework classes. If some of the classes aren't frequently referenced, you can instantiate them on an 'as needed' basis. This object should also have code in its **destructor** event to destroy the objects that it creates.

The framework controller class should have an interface which application objects utilize to access framework services. This class provides access to framework components in two ways: it either completely encapsulates a framework component or it provides the framework component itself to application classes. For example, it should have a function, **f_getTranManager**, which provides access to **invo_tranManager**. This will become clearer as you read about the different framework components in this chapter.

There are instances where the framework only provides an abstract class. The application then has to implement the concrete class that the framework will use. The module factory framework object (explained later in this section) is an example of such an object. In such a situation, how does the framework controller know which object to instantiate?

It would be bad design practice to force all applications to give the module factory a particular name. Other solutions include having developers add code in the framework controller, provide an extended interface to **nvo_frameworkController**, allowing applications to provide it with concrete class names etc. The more elegant solutions involve setting up an **INI** file or having a configuration database provide **nvo_frameworkController** with concrete class names. These solutions are deemed to be more elegant, because configuration issues shouldn't involve adding code to core framework classes or having an extensive API to initialize the framework.

This is the design for **nvo_frameworkController**:

```
Class Name:       nvo_frameworkController
Parent Class:     non visual object
Instance Variables:
```

```
        nvo_tranManager invo_tranManager (Private)
        nvo_strUtilityManager invo_strUtilityManager (Private)
        nvo_abstractFactoryController invo_abstractFactoryController (Private)
        nvo_osApi invo_osApi (Private)

Functions:
        f_getTranManager( ) returns nvo_tranManager
        f_getStrUtilityManager( ) returns nvo_strUtilityManager
        f_getFactoryController( ) returns nvo_abstractFactoryController
        f_getOsApi( ) returns nvo_osApi
```

Database Transaction Manager

We've discussed implementations of a database transaction manager in other chapters in this book. In this section, we'll discuss transaction managers within the scope of frameworks.

The database transaction manager should allow an application to establish and manage one or more transactions to one or more databases. It should also be sophisticated enough to connect to different DBMS engines.

The basic design of the transaction manager consists of a custom class user object, **nvo_tranManager,** and standard class user object, **ntran_base,** of the type transaction.

ntran_base

ntran_base implements the interface to this class through virtual functions. You can inherit from this abstract class to build concrete classes which implement functionality to connect to specific DBMS engines. The interface implemented in **ntran_base** includes the functions **f_init,** **f_beginTran, f_commitTran** and **f_rollbackTran.** The function **f_init** initializes the attributes of a transaction object from the **INI** file, which is passed as a parameter to this function. The functions **f_beginTran, f_commitTran** and **f_rollbackTran** begin a database unit of work, commit a unit of work and rollback a unit of work respectively. You can inherit from **ntran_base** to create an object specific to a particular database, e.g. **ntran_sybase** to implement functionality specific to Sybase.

This is the design of the abstract class **ntran_base:**

```
Class Name:      ntran_base
Parent Class:    transaction
Instance Variable:
        NONE
Functions:
        f_init (ps_iniFile, ps_profile) returns boolean
        f_beginTran( ) returns boolean
        f_commitTran( ) returns boolean
        f_rollbackTran( ) returns boolean
```

The design of the concrete class **ntran_sybase** is shown here:

```
Class Name:      ntran_base
Parent Class:    ntran_base
Instance Variable:
        NONE
Functions:
```

```
f_init(ps_iniFile, ps_profile) returns boolean
f_beginTran( ) returns boolean
f_commitTran( ) returns boolean
f_rollbackTran( ) returns boolean
```

nvo_tranManager

nvo_tranManager serves as a class which encapsulates functionality to create and manage instances of the correct descendant of **ntran_base**, depending on the DBMS engines that the application has to connect to. It also shields the application classes from concrete classes derived from **ntran_base**.

The functions implemented in this class include **f_create**, **f_getTransObject** and **f_promptLogin.** The function **f_create** accepts parameters specifying the **INI** filename and an array of section names which provide the transaction connection parameters. This function creates instances of the appropriate descendants of **ntran_base** and initializes an instance variable **itran_transactions[ ]** with them and another instance variable **is_dbProfiles[ ]** with their respective profiles. The function **f_getTransObject** returns a pointer to an object of the type **ntran_base** which is 'connected' to a specified database profile, passed as a parameter to this function.

Here's the design of the class **nvo_tranManager**:

```
Class Name:      nvo_tranManager
Parent Class:    non visual object
Instance Variable:
                 ntran_base itran_transactions[ ] (private)
string           is_profile[ ] (private)
Functions:
                 f_create(ps_iniFile, ps_profile[]) returns boolean
                 f_getTransObject(ps_profile) returns ntran_base
                 f_promptLogin( )    returns boolean
```

The figure shows the relationship between **nvo_tranManager, ntran_base** and **nvo_frameworkController**.

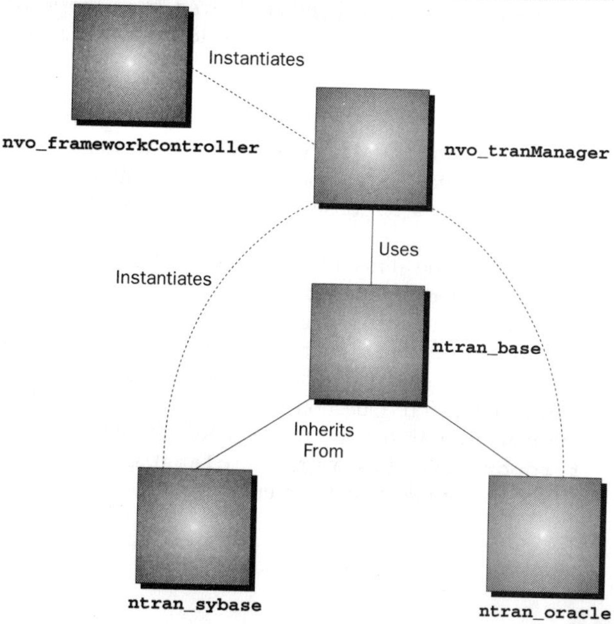

You might wonder why we went to the trouble of hiding the concrete transaction classes from the application classes? Well, let's see what happens when we have to provide connectivity to an Oracle database. All we have to do is build an object, **ntran_oracle**, inherited from **ntran_base** and implement the four virtual functions. We have to modify the function **f_create** in **nvo_tranManager** to introduce logic to create an instance of the class **ntran_oracle** when an application requires to connect to an Oracle database. The outside world would remain unaffected by the addition of this new concrete class, because all the application classes care about is the interface defined in **ntran_base**, which remains unchanged!

Error Handler

In a database application, errors can basically be grouped into three categories: PowerBuilder run-time and programming errors, database errors and business logic and data validation errors. You should design an error handler to report these errors and solicit a response from the user. It should provide a standard interface to classes in the application for reporting errors and, to enforce a standard look and feel, all messages in the application should be reported by a single GUI class.

> When you're designing a framework, you should always remember to separate GUI classes from non-GUI classes. Why? Well, what if users of another application using the framework don't appreciate your GUI design skills!?

There are a couple of ways of interfacing an error handler with application classes. The framework controller can 'hide' the error handler completely, in which case other classes won't directly interface with the error handler. They will use an API provided by a framework controller to address attributes of the error object.

Another technique, which, in my opinion, is simpler, involves all application classes directly addressing the error object. Examine the way PowerBuilder itself treats the error object. It natively provides a global error object with public attributes. So why over-engineer when a simpler solution will suffice?

So let's build an error handler derived from the standard PowerBuilder error object. Name this object **nerror_error**. You'll have to declare the global error object in your application to be of this class.

The application classes will have to set the properties of the global error object. Provide a set of overloaded functions, **f_reportError**, to make this task easier. You should design each function to report a specific category of error—database, business logic or run-time. This function should return the user's response to the error prompt.

Let's review the different variations of the function **f_reportError**. This function should be called from the **systemError** event. No parameters are necessary because PowerBuilder sets the attributes of the error object internally when a run-time error occurs. The function **f_reportError(ls_Msg, ls_bmpType, ls_btnType)** should be called when a business logic error is to be reported. The parameters **ls_bmpType** and **ls_btnType** are used to indicate the bitmap (StopSign, Question etc.) and the buttons (OK, Cancel, Yes No etc.) that get displayed in the window which pops up to report the error. You should use the function **f_reportError(ls_msg, ls_className, ls_method, ls_lineNum)** to report database errors and application logic errors.

The error object uses a response window to display error messages. Create an abstract class, **w_abstract_error**, and implement the interface and behavior of this class. Every application which uses this framework should inherit from this window and create a window as per its look and feel standards.

This error object should provide a function, **f_initAppVar**, to set its application level variables—namely the window class to display the error message and the name of the application. Functionality can also be provided to log errors to an error log.

The design of the class **nerror_error** is shown below:

```
Class Name:        nerror_error
Parent Class:      error
Instance Variables:
        w_abstract_error iw_error
        string ls_appName
Functions:
        f_initAppvar(ps_appName, pw_error) return boolean
        f_reportError() returns int
        f_reportError(ls_Msg, ls_bmpType, ls_btnType)  returns int
        f_reportError(ls_Msg, ls_className,  ls_method, ls_lineNum)  returns int
```

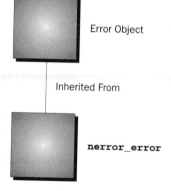

Error Object

This figure shows the design of the error handler:

Inherited From

nerror_error

Module Factory

A module factory provides a standard interface to all the functional modules in an application. For example, a trading system user is viewing a list of orders and then selects a menu item to open a trade entry window. The menu item should have no knowledge of the implementation of the trade entry module. By common design techniques, the menu item will trigger an event on the MDI frame or the active sheet, which in this case will be the order display window. Should the MDI frame and other application windows have knowledge of classes used in the implementation of the various modules? What happens when modules have to be modified or new modules added? How easy is it to share functional modules between applications?

We can design an architecture to provide a solution to these problems and integrate it within the framework. To provide a packaged solution, we can integrate the module factory with the menu or window hierarchy provided by the framework.

One way of doing this is to abstract the interaction between different functional modules in an application and create an application abstract factory class. This class implements the interface to create and interact with a module and can be implemented as a custom class user object, **nvo_abstractFactory**. We can derive concrete classes from this abstract class to build concrete factories for each functional module.

As you will have realized, we need another controller class to instantiate the appropriate factory. This abstract controller class enforces the interface and should also be implemented as a custom class user object, **nvo_abstractFactoryController**. The concrete class, **nvo_factoryController**, developed at the application level, derived from **nvo_abstractFactoryController**, implements the logic to create the different factory classes. This is the class with which the menu would indirectly interact when a user selects a menu item to open a particular window. A window initiated with framework components will be able to act as the class which receives the message from the menu and dispatches it to **nvo_factoryController**.

The interface that the abstract module factory provides depends on the type of applications and domains that the framework is to be used with. The controller class provides an interface which allows menus and other application classes to communicate messages to concrete module factories.

Let's apply these concepts to an example problem. Your application requires screens in different modules to be opened in a mode to add new records, so you can define a virtual function **f_addNewRecord** in the abstract module factory class. The functionality for this will be implemented in each module's concrete module factory class. The code in these objects can reference classes and objects specific to each module. The 'outside world' will be well insulated from this logic and won't need to be aware of the different classes that constitute a module. All that classes external to this module (e.g. menus, sheets/windows) have to do is to invoke a function in **nvo_factoryController** and pass it a parameter indicating the logical name of the module in which we want to create new record. This function should return a pointer to the appropriate class in a variable of the type **nvo_abstractFactory**. We can then invoke the function **f_addNewRecord** in that object because we used an abstract class to define the interface. The next snippet of code illustrates this example:

```
nvo_abstractFactory l_moduleFactory
nvo_AbstractFactoryController l_factoryController
string ls_moduleName
int li_rc

//instantiate l_factoryController
----

----
l_moduleFactory = l_factoryController.f_getFactory(ls_moduleName)
if IsValid(l_moduleFactory) then
    li_rc  = l_moduleFactory.f_addNewRecord( )
    //error checking
else
    //error reporting
end if
```

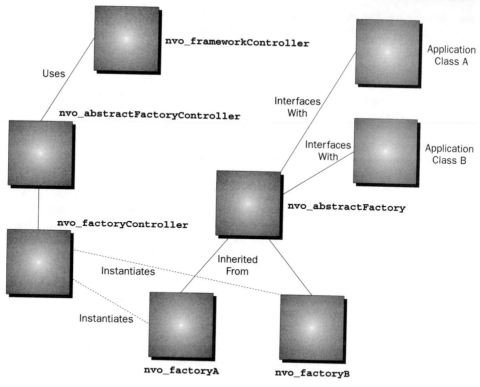

Diagram labels:

nvo_frameworkController

Uses

nvo_abstractFactoryController

Application Class A

Interfaces With

Interfaces With

Application Class B

nvo_factoryController

nvo_abstractFactory

Instantiates

Inherited From

Instantiates

nvo_factoryA

nvo_factoryB

Messaging Services

A framework requires a standard mechanism for messaging between different classes. PowerBuilder allows parameters to be passed to objects as they're 'opened'. The parameters can be of the type string, numeric or PowerObject. We use structures because, usually, we have to pass more than one parameter between objects.

One technique that we can adopt to provide a solution to messaging involves setting up a custom class object and creating structures specifically designed for each parameter set to be passed between objects. We have to declare an instance variable for each structure created in this object.

Let's consider the example where we have to pass two types of message—**employee_id**, **dept_id** and **vendor_id**, **part_id**—between classes. Create a user object **nvo_msgStruct**, of the custom non-visual object type and set up two structures—**MsgA** and **MsgB**—in this object.

Structure:	MsgA	
Elements:	employee_id	long
	dept_id	long

Structure:	MsgB	
Elements:	vendor_id	long
	part_id	long

Declare two instance variables, one for each structure:

MsgA	iMsgA
MsgB	iMsgB

211

The base window (or any class for that matter) should have an instance variable declared of the type **nvo_msgStruct**. It should also have code to create an instance of this object.

```
nvo_msgStruct i_msgStruct
```

The calling object should initialize the appropriate structure in the object **i_msgStruct** and open the called object passing the object **i_msgStruct** as a parameter. The **PowerObjectParm** property of the **message** structure provides a reference to the object **i_msgStruct**. The called object has to create an instance of **nvo_msgStruct** and initialize it with **message.PowerObjectParm**. The parameters are available to the called object by dereferencing the appropriate structure in its instance variable **i_msgStruct**.

In Version 5.0, a structure itself can be passed as a parameter when an object is created. We can also declare the structures as global structures. The design becomes more contained if a class is constructed to serve as a structure container and an instance of this class is passed as a parameter.

This approach requires a custom structure for each interaction and would become restrictive if the application was large with a lot of interaction between different classes. We need a more generic design for larger applications.

Extending the Design

We can extend this design to be more generic. PowerBuilder provides a data type called Any which can point to any supported data type in PowerBuilder. Let's use this data type and the PowerObject class from which all PowerBuilder classes are derived. We'll be able to support all data types and classes if we design a messaging architecture based on the Any data type and the PowerObject class.

Design a standard class user object derived from the message object and name it **nmsg_msg**. You'll have to set up the global error object in your application to be of the type **nmsg_msg.**

Create three public instance variables in this object: an unbound array **variable[]** of the type Any, an unbound array **class[]** of the type PowerObject and an unbound array **msgType** of the type string.

```
Public:
any        variable[]
powerobject    class[]
string        msgType[]
```

Each variable is an unbound array because, as we mentioned earlier, we have to pass multiple parameters from one class to another. The variable **msgType** stores the parameter tag, which identifies the parameter that the variable represents. The following example explains this design.

Suppose a window opens another window and has to pass the following parameters: a DataWindow **dw_EmpDetail** tagged as **EmpDetail**, the variable **ll_employee_id** of the type long, tagged as **empId** and the variable **ll_dept_id** of the type long, tagged as **deptId** (the tags are used to determine the significance of the data—without them, all we would be able to determine from the class variable is string, int etc.).

The calling window will have to set up the message object like this:

```
Message.variable[1]=NULL
Message.class[1]= dw_EmpDetail
Message.msgType[1]="EmpDetail"

Message.variable[2]= ll_employee_id
Message.class[2]= NULL
Message.msgType[2]="empId"

Message.variable[3]= ll_dept_id
Message.class[3]= NULL
Message.msgType[3]="deptId"
```

This message object is automatically available to the called window. The called window will then have to loop through the variables to derive the parameters. You'll also have to implement a function in **nmsg_msg** to reset the arrays, which will be invoked by the called object once it has processed the message.

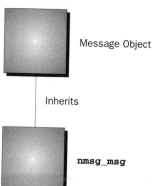

Message Object

Inherits

nmsg_msg

This technique requires a repository where messages have to be defined. Defining a message involves defining the parameters and the data types for an object pair. Each object can then validate a message (or parameter set) for both content and data type accuracy.

Utility Functions

We can package commonly used utility functions in custom class user objects, grouping the functions based on the functionality they provide. For example, we can build a custom class user object, **nvo_strUtilityManager**, to serve as a container for string manipulation functions. All application classes which require string manipulation functions should use an instance of this object and access the library of functions that it provides.

You can also create an object to encapsulate operating system calls, designing the class to provide cross-platform portability to your application—API calls in the 16-bit Windows environment are different to those in the 32-bit Windows environment. It's highly inadvisable to have a **CASE** statement construct wherever an operating system call has to be made in the application, i.e.:

```
string ls_OSName
//determine the OS Name
—

—

CHOOSE CASE ls_OSName
   CASE "win31"
      //call a 16 bit external OS function
      functionXYZ( )
   CASE "NT"
      //call a 32 bit external OS function
      functionABC( )
END CHOOSE
```

Instead, an abstract class, **nvo_osAPI**, should be created to define the interface. Concrete classes should be inherited from this abstract class to implement operating system specific functionality, for example **nvo_31API** and **nvo_NTAPI** addressing Windows 3.x and Windows NT, respectively. The framework controller should detect the operating system at run time and instantiate the appropriate concrete class. The framework would then provide all application classes access to this object.

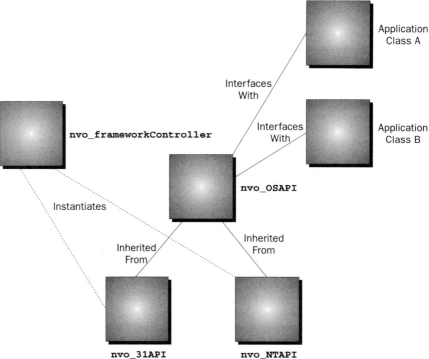

Menu Hierarchy

Implementing menus in large applications isn't one of the easier tasks, because PowerBuilder poses a number of limitations on designing menu hierarchies. For example, you can't introduce menu items in descendant menus in between menu items defined in the ancestor menu. Neither can you clone menu items, i.e. you have to embed logic in the **clicked** event of all menu items which interact with the module factory.

One of the ways to overcome this limitation is to design an architecture for generating menus at run time. We covered this in detail in Chapter 5. Please refer to it for an explanation of topics in this section.

The ideal approach is to have a menu architecture which consists of static and dynamic menus. The static menu should serve as a template which gets extended at run time by the dynamic menu engine to provide windows in the application with functional menus.

This architecture requires developers to define each window's menu layout and menu item properties in tables in a configuration database. A menu consisting of one menu item with logic to interact with the parent window and module factory is also required. This menu item is cloned at run time by the menu engine as per the definition in the configuration database to generate and configure menus for windows.

The scope of the menu engine could be extended to include application security. This class should implement functionality to retrieve menu configuration details from the database and generate the menu for a window.

The menu engine can be encapsulated by the framework controller. The framework controller should provide an interface, **f_generateMenu(pw_window)**, which all windows in the application can call to get their menus configured.

MDI Frames and Windows

The framework should provide a base window and a base MDI frame. The base MDI frame should initiate the framework controller. The application's MDI frame should be derived from the base MDI frame, which would mean you wouldn't have to add framework-related code at the MDI frame—it would come packaged in the base MDI frame.

Let's design an MDI frame base class, **w_MDIBase**, in the context of the framework architecture provided in this chapter. This window will require a custom event **ue_initFramework**, which should have functionality to initiate the framework controller as a global variable. This event should be triggered from the **open** event.

```
g_frameworkController = create nvo_frameworkController
if not isValid(g_frameworkController) then
    //error processing
end if
```

This window should also destroy **g_frameworkController** in the **close** event. Applications usually have functionality to initiate database connectivity in the MDI frame. The functionality to connect to various databases can also be implemented in the base MDI frame.

Create a protected instance variable **invo_tranManager** of the type **nvo_tranManager** in **w_MDIBase**.

```
nvo_tranManager invo_tranManager
```

Create a custom event, named **ue_databaseLogin** in **w_MDIBase**. Code in the **ue_initFramework** event should also initialize the instance variable **invo_tranManager**.

```
If isValid(g_frameworkController) then
    invo_tranManager = g_frameworkController.f_getTranManager()
        if isValid(invo_tranManager) then
            triggerEvent("ue_databaseLogin")
        end if
else
    //error processing
end if
```

The application MDI frame should implement code in the event **ue_databaseLogin** to use functions in **invo_tranManager** to log in to the database.

```
string ls_iniFile, ls_profile[]

//set the database profiles
    ls_profile[1] = "xyz"
    ls_profile[2] = "abc"
```

215

```
//code to initialize these variables with the appropriate values
if invo_tranManager.f_create(ls_iniFile, ls_profile) = 0 then
    if invo_tranManager.f_promptLogin() = -1 then
        //error processing
    end if
else
    //error processing
end if
```

This demonstrates that you can make the MDI frame in the application connect to the database just by adding a couple of lines of code, because the base MDI frame and framework controller did most of the preparatory work.

Similarly, you can initiate the base class window with certain framework components to eliminate framework interaction. Earlier, we mentioned that certain framework components are encapsulated by the framework controller and other components (e.g. transaction manager, utility classes etc.) can be directly accessed by the application classes. In other words, application classes can get a reference to these framework classes and directly access the functions they provide. The base class window has to be initiated with these objects. Let's design a base class window in the context of the framework described in this chapter.

Create a window, **w_base**, and declare protected instance variables representing the framework components that the application classes can directly reference:

```
protected:
nvo_tranManager invo_tranManager
nvo_strUtilityManager invo_strUtilityManager
nvo_abstractFactoryController invo_abstractFactoryController
nvo_osApi invo_osApi
```

Create a custom event, **ue_initWindow**, and trigger it from the **open** event of the window. The code in this event should set the instance variables and have the menu engine generate the menu.

```
if isValid(g_frameworkController) then
    invo_tranManager = g_frameworkController.f_getTranManager( )
    invo_strUtilityManager = g_frameworkController.f_getStrUtilityManager( )
    invo_abstractFactoryController = g_frameworkController.f_getFactoryController( )
    invo_osApi = g_frameworkController.f_getOSApi( ) &
                        g_frameworkController.f_generateMenu(this)

else
    //error handling
end if
```

All application windows will then automatically have access to all framework components.

Object Libraries

Say you need a DataWindow which provides the functionality to highlight a selected row and you need this object in several applications. You could develop a generic object which provides this highlighting functionality and use it wherever required. A collection of reusable and generic objects such as this constitute an **object library**.

Reusable objects can be domain or business-related objects and non-domain objects. The latter have a larger scope of applicability. For example, a class which has the functionality to highlight a selected row in a DataWindow will have more reusability than a class encapsulating logic to validate an options trade.

There are a number of commercially available PowerBuilder object libraries which address functionality such as application security, database access, DataWindow-related functionality, etc. PowerSoft has also introduced a class library with Version 5.0 of PowerBuider: the Powersoft Foundation Class (PFC) library. We'll look at this in the next chapter.

Design Considerations

What are the characteristics of a good object library? Well, firstly, it should be very easy to integrate the object library into your application, without having to alter your basic application design.

The library should ideally consist of low level components which you can use to create higher level classes in the application fairly easily. For example, all applications use objects to model master-detail.data relationships. How many of these objects look the same?

The class library that would add the most value in the above Master/Detail example would be one that provides components which you could easily use to assemble a Master/Detail class tailored to a particular requirement. Class libraries providing high level classes usually prove to be very inflexible and hard to use.

The design of the class library components should easily allow implementation of polymorphic and custom behavior. This requirement is necessary because it's very hard for a class library to provide behaviors which satisfy every application's requirement.

The design of components in a class library should allow you to easily integrate a new release of the class library into an application. The custom and polymorphic behaviors implemented in various framework components used in that application should not be lost.

Designing Class Libraries

Let's discuss class library design using DataWindows as an example. We can use DataWindows in many different ways in any application and certain behaviors are also often repeated, so how do we architect a reusable DataWindow?

A DataWindow which implements all the behaviors isn't the correct solution. This approach provides a non-optimal solution in a situation where only a subset of functionality is required. The design proves to be very inflexible as it's very hard to extend and adapt it to diverse requirements.

A design which provides the different behaviors encapsulated in 'plug-and-play' components provides a more practical solution. This design approach allows developers to assemble higher level classes from components. Developers aren't forced to inherit from a class which provides diverse functionality. This approach also ensures that inheritance hierarchies are specific to the situation.

Chapter 9 explained this design style with a few examples. This section provides an insight into designing reusable components by examining two design styles that can be used to design a class library of components which enhance the functionality of DataWindows.

Let's assume that, in an application, the required DataWindow functionality includes the ability to select a row when clicked, trap database errors and to pop up a menu when the user clicks the right mouse button. Remember that this is the superset of functionality and not all DataWindows will have to implement all the behaviors. As we mentioned earlier, it wouldn't be practical to implement all the behavior in a single object. What if one of the objects derived from this DataWindow doesn't require a pop-up menu to appear when the user clicks the right mouse button, but requires a modification in the **clicked** behavior?

Let's design two component architectures to illustrate different design techniques which address these requirements. These components can be classified as **decorator** objects, and should be used to add functionality to objects dynamically. They help reduce the proliferation of subclasses to support the different combinations of behaviors.

PowerBuilder 5.0 supports dynamic functions, which permits developers to design a weakly typed solution. Prior versions of PowerBuilder didn't support this feature and type mismatch errors were detected at compile time.

Providing the Required DataWindow Functionality

The first solution we'll look at is based on dynamic function calls. It involves setting up an abstract class for the DataWindow that uses the decorator objects.

Construct an abstract class from which all components enhancing the functionality of DataWindows will be derived. Build a custom class user object named **nvo_dwDecoratorBase**. Declare a private instance variable, **idw_parentDW**, in this object of the type DataWindow to store a reference to the DataWindow it enhances. Then declare a function **f_setParentDW** which initializes this variable and a custom event named **ue_init** which should be used by descendants of **nvo_dwDecoratorBase** to embed logic to initialize them.

Both design techniques provided in this section use classes derived from **nvo_dwDecoratorBase**. This is the design of **nvo_dwDecoratorBase**:

```
Class Name:        nvo_dwDecoratorBase
Parent Class:      non visual object
Instance Variables:
                   idw_parentDW datawindow
Functions:
                   f_setParentDW(pdw_dataWindow)
```

Derive three objects from **nvo_dwDecoratorBase** for implementing functionality to select a row, report database errors and to display a pop-up menu when the user clicks the right mouse button. Name these objects **nvo_clkDecor**, **nvo_errDecor** and **nvo_rgtClkDecor**, respectively.

Solution 1

The first design relies on a function-based interaction between the decorators and the DataWindow. Create a function **f_click** in the class **nvo_clkDecor** which implements the functionality to select the clicked row in the DataWindow that uses it. Similarly, implement the functions **f_dbError** and **f_rgtClick** in the objects **nvo_errDecor** and **nvo_rgtClkDecor** respectively to report database errors and display a pop-up menu when the user clicks the right mouse button.

Here's the design of these three decorator objects:

```
Class Name:        nvo_clkDecor
Parent Class:      nvo_dwDecoratorBase
Functions:

                   f_click()
```

```
Class Name:        nvo_errDecor
Parent Class:      nvo_dwDecoratorBase
Functions:

                   f_dbError()
```

```
Class Name:        nvo_rgtClkDecor
Parent Class:      nvo_dwDecoratorBase
Functions:

                   f_rgtClick()
```

Now that we've created these decorator objects, how do we integrate them with the DataWindow object?

Create a standard DataWindow user object, named **udw_exampleAbstract**. Create an array of protected instance variables of the type **nvo_dwDecoratorBase** in this user object to store references to **nvo_clkDecor**, **nvo_errDecor** and **nvo_rgtClkDecor**. Also create two associative arrays of the type string to store class names and tags identifying the utility of the class.

```
protected:
nvo_dwdecoratorBase    invo_decor[]
string                 is_className[], is_classTag[]
```

Create a protected function, named **f_setDecorator**, which initializes these instance variables. This function should also initialize the decorator objects that it creates. This function has to be invoked from a custom event **ue_createDecorators** in the DataWindow. This event, in turn, should be triggered from the **open** event of the window in which the DataWindow is used as a control (we use a user event because the event assigns to a protected variable).

```
/******************************************************************
Function Name:     f_setDecorator
Parameters:        ps_className[]     string
                   ps_classTag[]      string
ReturnValue        NONE
******************************************************************/
int li_numClasses, i
li_numClasses = upperBound(ls_className)
for I = li_numClasses to 1 step -1
   invo_decor[i] = create nvo_dwDecoratorBase using ps_className[i]
         invo_decor[i].f_setParentDW(this)
         invo_decor[i].triggerEvent("ue_init")
   is_className[i] = ps_className[i]
   is_classTag[i] = ps_classTag[i]
next
```

We'll also need a function, **f_getDecorator**, that will return a decorator object for a particular class tag. This tag identifies the utility that the object provides. For example, the tag associated with the object **nvo_clkDecor** is **clicked**. This function can be called in events of the DataWindow to access the decorator for a particular utility.

```
/*********************************************************
Function Name:    f_getDecorator
Parameters:       ps_classTag string
ReturnValue       nvo_dwDecoratorBase
*********************************************************/
int li_numClasses, I
nvo_dwDecoratorBase lnvo_dwDecoratorBase
li_numClasses = upperBound(ls_classTag)
for I = 1 to li_numClasses
   if is_classTag[i] = ps_classTag then
     lnvo_dwDecoratorBase = invo_decor[i]
     exit
   end if
next
return lnvo_dwDecoratorBase
```

Now let's add code in the appropriate events to call functions in the decorator objects. We can gain access to the appropriate decorator object by calling the function **f_getDecorator** and passing it a tag value.

Here's the code in the **clicked** event:

```
nvo_dwDecoratorBase lnvo_dwDecoratorBase
lnvo_dwDecoratorBase = f_getDecorator("clicked")
    If isValid(lnvo_dwDecoratorBase) then
       lnvo_dwDecoratorBase.FUNCTION DYNAMIC f_click()
    end if
```

This is the code in the **dberror** event:

```
nvo_dwDecoratorBase lnvo_dwDecoratorBase
lnvo_dwDecoratorBase = f_getDecorator("dbError")
    If isValid(lnvo_dwDecoratorBase) then
       lnvo_dwDecoratorBase.FUNCTION DYNAMIC f_dbError()
    end if
```

The code in the right mouse click event is shown here:

```
nvo_dwDecoratorBase lnvo_dwDecoratorBase
lnvo_dwDecoratorBase = f_getDecorator("rightClick")
    If isValid(lnvo_dwDecoratorBase) then
       lnvo_dwDecoratorBase.FUNCTION DYNAMIC f_rgtClick()
    end if
```

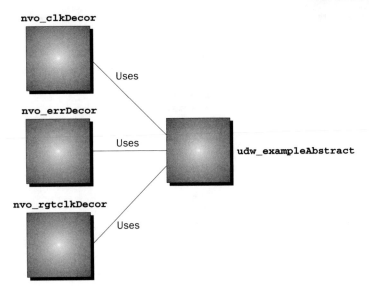

nvo_clkDecor

Uses

nvo_errDecor

Uses

udw_exampleAbstract

nvo_rgtclkDecor

Uses

When this DataWindow user object gets created in a window or custom user object, the function **f_setDecorator** gets invoked in the **ue_createDecorators** event to instantiate the decorators. The code that has to be implemented in the **ue_createDecorators** event in a window or custom user object which uses this DataWindow as a control is shown below:

```
string ls_className[], ls_tagName[]

ls_classname[1]="nvo_clkDecor"
ls_tagName[1]="clicked"

ls_classname[2]="nvo_errDecor"
ls_tagName[2]="dbError"

ls_classname[3]="nvo_rgtClkDecor"
ls_tagName[3]="rightClick"

    f_setDecorator(ls_className, ls_tagName)
```

If there's a setup or initialization error, you'll get a run-time error because the interaction between the decorators and the DataWindow is based on dynamic function calls.

Solution 2

Let's review a variation of this design in which the interaction between the decorator objects and the DataWindow is based on triggering events. With this approach, each decorator registers the message that it responds to as the class tag with the DataWindow. If an event needs to invoke a decorator, it invokes a function, **f_sendMessage**, in the DataWindow and passes it the class tag. This function is similar to and replaces the function **f_getDecorator**. It provides logic to determine the correct object to pass this message to. The function **f_setDecorator** has to be modified to ensure that the class tag array **is_classTag[]** has unique values, otherwise two objects could respond to the same message. Let's review the function **f_sendMessage**.

```
/********************************************************
 Function Name:   f_sendMessage
 Parameters:      ps_classTag   string
 ReturnValue      0 Success, -1 error int
 ********************************************************/
int li_numClasses, I, li_rc
nvo_dwDecoratorBase lnvo_dwDecoratorBase
li_numClasses = upperBound(ls_classTag)
for I = 1 to li_numClasses
    if is_classTag[i] = ps_classTag then
      lnvo_dwDecoratorBase = invo_decor[i]
      exit
    end if
next
if isValid(lnvo_dwDecoratorBase) then
      lnvo_dwDecoratorBase.triggerEvent(ps_classTag)
      li_rc = 0
else
      li_rc = -1
end if
return li_rc
```

We'll have to modify code in the three events that we showed earlier to only invoke the function **f_sendMessage**.

This is code in the **clicked** event:

```
if f_sendMessage("clicked") = -1 then
//error processing
end if
```

This is the code in the **dberror** event:

```
if f_sendMessage("dbError") = -1 then
//error processing
end if
```

The code in the right mouse click event is shown below:

```
if f_sendMessage("rightClicked") = -1 then
//error processing
end if
```

We have to create the decorators in the DataWindow control in the **ue_createDecorators** event using the function **f_setDecorator**, which we have modified to ensure that the tag names are unique.

We've also modified the decorator objects. The functions that we created in the three decorator objects **nvo_clkDecor**, **nvo_errDecor** and **nvo_rgtClkDecor** have to be implemented as events. Create events in these three objects with the same name as their class tags—create the events **clicked**, **dbError** and **rightClick** in the objects **nvo_clkDecor**, **nvo_errDecor** and **nvo_rgtClkDecor**. The modified design of these three objects is shown below:

```
Class Name:      nvo_clkDecor
Parent Class:    nvo_dwDecoratorBase
Events:
                 clicked
```

Class Name:	nvo_errDecor
Parent Class:	nvo_dwDecoratorBase
Events:	
	dbError

Class Name:	nvo_rgtClkDecor
Parent Class:	nvo_dwDecoratorBase
Events:	
	rightClick

So, you've set up the functionality in the three decorator objects and implemented this solution in a number of screens, but what if one screen requires a Windows file manager type clicked behavior in the DataWindow instead of the clicked behavior implemented in **nvo_clkDecor**? Let's review how both the solutions adapt this polymorphic behavior.

Modifying a DataWindow's Clicked Behavior for One Screen

In the first design, the decorators and the DataWindow interface with each other using functions. The code in the **clicked** event of the DataWindow invokes the function **f_click** in the appropriate decorator. This design enforces the decorator to implement the clicked behavior in a function named **f_click**. The design is, however, flexible enough in that it doesn't enforce an inheritance hierarchy—both subclassing and subtyping are supported. If the new clicked behavior is independent of the functionality implemented in **nvo_clkDecor**, we can build a completely new decorator object (inherited from **nvo_dwDecoratorBase**). Obviously, the only constraint is that the functionality has to be implemented in a function **f_click**.

On the other hand, an object inherited from **nvo_clkDecor** should implement it in an overloaded function, **f_click**, if the required functionality is an extension of the clicked behavior implemented in **nvo_clkDecor**. In either situation the DataWindow control has to be initialized with the appropriate decorator objects, using the function **f_setDecorator**.

In the second design, the decorators and the DataWindow are loosely coupled. The interaction is based on the **triggerEvent** function which is available as a method in the object **nvo_dwDecoratorBase**, hence there are no class constraints.

If the new clicked behavior is independent of the functionality implemented in **nvo_clkDecor**, a completely new decorator object (inherited from **nvo_dwDecoratorBase**) can be built. The only requirement is that the behavior has to be implemented in a custom event, **clicked**. An object inherited from **nvo_clkDecor** should extend the functionality implemented in the **clicked** event if the required functionality is an extension of the clicked behavior implemented in **nvo_clkDecor**.

Avoiding Constraints on Event Names

The above solution forces us to hard code the tag values of decorators in the DataWindow object, which means that we have to standardize events names. We can implement a solution that provides independence from the event name constraint by providing a level of indirection between the tag name of a decorator and the message parameter provided to the function **f_sendMessage** by the code in each event. This would require a change in the function **f_setDecorator** and the function **f_sendMessage**.

The function **f_setDecorator** would require another parameter indicating the message which maps to the class tag. Another instance variable, **is_message[]**, of the type string would have to be declared in the object **udw_exampleAbstract**. The modified function **f_setDecorator** is shown on the next page.

```
/*************************************************************
Function Name:    f_setDecorator
Parameters:       ps_className[]      string
                  ps_classTag[]       string
                  ps_message[]        string
ReturnValue       NONE
*************************************************************/
int li_numClasses, i
li_numClasses = upperBound(ls_className)
for I = li_numClasses to 1 step -1
    invo_decor[i] = create nvo_dwDecoratorBase using ps_className[i]
    invo_decor[i].f_setParentDW(this)
    invo_decor[i].triggerEvent("ue_init")
    is_className[i] = ps_className[i]
    is_classTag[i] = ps_classTag[i]
    is_message[i] = ps_Message[i]
next
```

We would have to modify the function **f_sendMessage** to map a message to a class tag and then invoke the appropriate event in a decorator object. The modified **f_sendMessage** function is shown here:

```
/*************************************************************
Function Name:    f_sendMessage
Parameters:       ps_message          string
ReturnValue       1 Success, -1 error int
*************************************************************/
int li_numClasses, I, li_rc
nvo_dwDecoratorBase lnvo_dwDecoratorBase
string ls_classTag
li_numClasses = upperBound(is_message)
for I = 1 to li_numClasses step -1
    if is_message[i] = ps_message then
    lnvo_dwDecoratorBase = invo_decor[i]
     ls_classTag = is_classTag[i]
     exit
    end if
next
if isValid(lnvo_dwDecoratorBase) then
    li_rc = lnvo_dwDecoratorBase.triggerEvent(ls_classTag)
else
    li_rc = -1
end if
return li_rc
```

Summary

Frameworks and object libraries are powerful concepts. They provide easy to use, proven designs and quality debugged code.

This chapter has provided an introduction to designing frameworks and object libraries. We've discussed a sample framework architecture that provides a high level design of some of the main components required in a framework.

We should build object libraries as a collection of reusable components which can be assembled to build more complex objects. We've discussed some of the design styles for building reusable components and provided a design that uses these styles for some reusable components which could be integrated into a DataWindow component library. Remember, though, that component libraries are of no use to developers if they're not documented—it's very important to document the use and description of each component.

PowerBuilder
Foundation Class Library

In previous versions of PowerBuilder, Powersoft introduced the concepts of window, menu and class object inheritance for developing applications. Even though PowerBuilder helped speed Windows GUI development, it still required a lot of work and a lot of code. Alternative approaches included writing your own class library or using a third party class library, such as PowerFrame or PowerTool. As we described in the previous chapter, building frameworks and object libraries requires a large amount of effort and can be a complex task to undertake. If your company is just getting started with PowerBuilder, creating a framework on your own would be challenging. An alternative solution would be to bring in outside consultants who have the technical expertise to assist you in developing your framework. This could be just as costly and you may or may not end up with a well-designed framework that fits your corporation's development needs, and you would still have to invest in the time to develop it. Typically, you could save yourself the development time and buy a third-party product, but you'll still need to do some sort of analysis. If you're just getting started with PowerBuilder, you probably don't know what features to look for in a framework.

Powersoft has responded to user demand by including a service-based Foundation Class library (PFC) architecture in the Enterprise Edition of PowerBuilder 5.0. You now have a foundation class library which is supported by the vendor, similar to what Microsoft has done with the Microsoft Foundation Class (MFC).

Having a foundation class library in the primary tool itself reduces the need for relying on third-party class libraries, but it's only intended to provide a consistent framework and foundation which future third party libraries are expected to build on.

This chapter introduces PFC, its features and merits and discusses the service-based architecture used by PFC. We'll also look at how you can extend PFC and use it to create your own frameworks and class libraries.

What is a Class Library?

As we described in the previous chapter, an application framework is a set of interdependent, reusable base classes that form the basis for an application. A class library can be defined as a set of reusable objects that we can use within the context of a framework, but also as stand-alone objects. PFC is both a framework and a class library. It has services that support a framework and utility services that can be used as stand-alone objects.

How is PFC Different from Third-party Class Libraries?

It's important to understand the differences between the architectures of the various third-party products available on the market today. Framework architectures can be classified into three major categories: general purpose classes, nested generalization classes and service-oriented classes. Each category has its pros and cons.

General Purpose Classes

General purpose classes usually place all of the required functionality into one ancestor class, which includes anything that an application might need. This typically leads to 'fat' ancestor classes being defined with unnecessary functionality. The functionality is turned on by setting Boolean instance variables in the **Constructor** event of the object. For example, take the user object **u_dw**:

```
// Super Class: u_dw
// Instance Variables:
        Boolean ib_sort
        Boolean ib_filter
        Boolean ib_rowselect
        Boolean ib_resize
        Boolean ib_undo

// Functions:
        of_sort()
        of_filter()
        of_rowselect()
        of_resize()
        of_undo()
```

```
// Constructor event of u_dw:

        this.ib_sort = true
        this.ib_filter = true
        this.ib_rowselect = true
        this.ib_resize = true
        this.ib_undo = true
```

When you inherit your DataWindow from **u_dw**, you automatically get all of the functions included from the ancestor class. If you were creating a simple DataWindow, you may not need all of the included functionality, but unfortunately you get it whether you want it or not. Imagine all of the additional overhead added to the application if you inherited 100 DataWindows with functionality you didn't even need.

Nested Generalization Classes

Nested generalization classes attempt to eliminate the 'fat' ancestor design of the general purpose classes. Base ancestor classes are created with the most basic functionality and objects are progressively inherited until all required combinations of functionality have been defined.

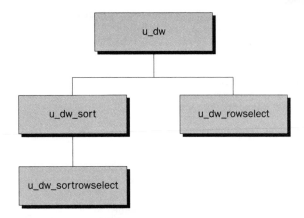

First, we would create the base ancestor class, **u_dw**, with basic functions and then create individual objects with specific functionality, like **u_dw_rowselection** and **u_dw_sort** inherited from **u_dw**. If we needed to create a DataWindow with functionality from both user objects, we would create a new DataWindow, called **u_dw_sortrowselection**, and inherit from either **u_dw_rowselection** or **u_dw_sort**. Since PowerBuilder doesn't support multiple inheritance, we can only inherit from one object, so we need to duplicate the functionality required from the object that we didn't inherit from.

The disadvantages of this architecture should be obvious at this point. We can't reuse objects or code, we now have multiple copies of the same code which translates to higher maintainability and, more importantly, poor programming practices.

Service-oriented Classes

PFC is based on the final category, service-oriented classes. The service-based architecture follows true object-oriented programming methodologies, since its foundation is based on encapsulation. This architecture encapsulates functionality in reusable custom classes called **services**, which perform the work delegated to them. Since the functionality isn't embedded in the user object (requester), these services are not instantiated until you request them

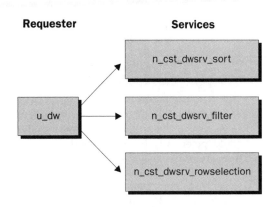

With service-based classes, **u_dw** contains only methods that it must have. All other functionality is separated into service classes. What we end up with is a visual user object (**u_dw**) and custom class user objects with specific functionality, such as **n_cst_dwsrv_sort, n_cst_dwsrv_filter** and **n_cst_rowselection**. If **u_dw** needs to sort, filter or provide **rowselection** functionality, it simply requests the service from one of these custom class user objects.

```
// Class: u_dw

// Instance Variables:
        n_cst_dwsrv_sort              inv_sort
        n_cst_dwsrv_filter            inv_filter
```

```
         n_cst_dwsrv_rowselection        inv_rowselection

// Constructor event of u_dw:
    of_setsort(TRUE)
    of_setfilter(TRUE)
    of_setrowselection(TRUE)

// Function:    of_setsort(Boolean)

If IsNull(ab_switch) Then
    Return -1
End If

If ab_Switch Then
    If Not IsValid (inv_Sort) Then
        inv_Sort = Create n_cst_dwsrv_sort
        inv_Sort.of_SetRequestor (this)
        Return 1
    End If
Else
    If IsValid (inv_Sort) Then
        Destroy inv_Sort
        Return 1
    End If
End If

Return 0
```

Another important feature of this architecture is **event redirection**, which basically allows you to call specific events of an active service from the requester. This provides any additional processing that might be required if a service has been activated.

```
// Clicked event of u_dw:

If IsValid(inv_rowselect) Then
    inv_rowselect.event pfc_clicked(xpos, ypos, row, dwo)
End If
```

The disadvantage of this architecture is that there's some minimal overhead in the requester class, since they provide hooks for non-visuals via instance variables. Multiple instances of each service could potentially be instantiated, thus causing the additional overhead. However, the advantages to the service-based architecture far outweigh the disadvantages. Ancestor classes are 'thinner', since functionality is provided only when requested. The object hierarchy is much easier to maintain, since we're not creating duplication of code due to lack of multiple inheritance. In fact, we can use this technique to simulate multiple inheritance.

PFC Architecture

PFC is a set of reusable and extendible classes that work together to serve as a base for building object-oriented PowerBuilder applications and class libraries. We can use it to enforce corporate, departmental and application consistency. It includes a base class of framework objects and utility objects that can be used 'as is'. PFC also contains extension layers for all classes from which you inherit your application-specific objects. It replaces the application library that was included with PowerBuilder 4.0 and has been completely redesigned to take advantage of Version 5.0 features.

This includes function overloading, parameterized events and new controls (Tabs, TreeView and ListView) as well as taking advantage of Version 5.0 syntax improvements. It doesn't, however, carry any old techniques from **applib**, such as obsolete functions or hierarchical overloading.

In a client/server environment, the server performs services in response to the client requests. You have different types of servers, such as database server, file server, printer server, etc. The database server performs database-related services. It responds to client's SQL requests, such as **select**, **insert**, **delete** and **update**. The file server performs network-file related functions. The print server performs printing services.

PFC uses this familiar concept of clients (or requesters) and services. In simple terms, requesters talk to services and services talk back to requesters.

Requesters

Requesters are service-aware by having **instance variables** assigned to them. The instance variables, or **reference variables** (pointers) as they are sometimes called, are declared for specific services that relate to a particular object. For example, **u_dw** has services you would normally associate with DataWindow functionality.

```
Class Name:        pfc_u_dw
Parent Class:      non visual object
Instance Variables:
        n_cst_dwsrv_sort               inv_sort
        n_cst_dwsrv_filter             inv_filter
        n_cst_dwsrv_rowselection       inv_rowselection
```

Setting **Requester.of_setservice(TRUE)** populates the pointer to the service instance and setting **Requester.of_setservice(FALSE)** destroys the pointer. These services are automatically destroyed in the **Destructor** event of each non-visual user object, thus cleaning up after themselves and eliminating any memory leaks.

Requester events are redirected to a service object if necessary. Looking at our **u_dw** example, let's say that a user clicks on a specific row. In the **Clicked** event of **u_dw**, we would want to check any services that may need to be notified that this event has occurred. If the DataWindow had the **rowselection** services activated, it would call the user-defined event **pfc_clicked** of **n_cst_dwsrv_rowselection**. The **pfc_clicked** event would in turn validate the request and process the clicked behavior, depending on the selection option, by calling the **of_rowselect** function of **n_cst_dwsrv_rowslection**.

Services

Services are classified as a group of related types of processing that provide specific functionality to requesters. The services are inherited from a base class service as shown opposite:

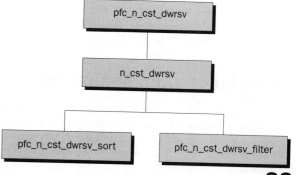

In the same way that requesters have pointers to services, base service classes have a pointer to a requester and a method to set it. Most services set their properties access to protected. However, when necessary, public functions provide access to get and set properties.

Using services brings numerous encapsulation benefits. First of all, objects are notified when a property changes and an object can verify whether a property is changeable. This ensures that there is no unexpected behavior from sudden changes to properties.

PFC provides the following services:

- Application
- Window
- DataWindow
- File
- Date/Time
- String
- Platform

Let's take a brief look at the two main ones.

Application Services

Application services include transaction object, error handling, security and debugging. They are controlled through the application manager, **n_cst_appmanager**. This maintains application-related information, including **INI** filename, help filename, version, company name, user ID, the current window and the frame window. It's a customized replacement for the application object.

The **n_cst_appmanager** user object also includes instance variables for each of the application services includes functions to control creating and destroying these service objects.

DataWindow Services

DataWindow services include reporting, printing, searching, sorting, filtering, selection and query mode services. The DataWindow services are implemented through the **u_dw** DataWindow control user object. This user object includes instance variables for each of the DataWindow services and also includes functions to control creating and destroying these service objects.

> For a full listing of the various services provided by all the service objects, see Chapter 8 of the PFC User's Guide in the Advanced Developer Toolkit collection in the PowerBuilder Online Books.

Inter-object Communication

PFC's objects communicate using events, function calls and a **message router**, which passes messages between a window and any PowerBuilder object, typically a menu. The message router uses a search algorithm to determine the appropriate object to receive a message and includes built-in debugging. Your script only needs to know the event to trigger, not the current window or associated control name.

Object-orientation in PFC

We already mentioned that PFC uses PowerBuilder's object-oriented capabilities. What we haven't discussed is how these concepts are implemented and shown specific examples. Let's start with encapsulation.

Encapsulation

As we said, the services offered by PFC are fully encapsulated. Let's look at the implementation details. PFC implements encapsulation in its objects by defining object functions and instance variables as either protected or public, depending on the level of outside access that other objects are to have. You can get access to the protected instance variables by using **of_getvariablename** and **of_setvariablename**. For example, if you wanted to modify the style of the filter DataWindow service, you would call **of_setstyle(1)** and provide the type of style you wanted to set. Likewise, if you wanted to see what style is currently active, you would call **of_getstyle()** and this would return the protected instance variable **ii_style**.

```
Class:        n_cst_dwsrv_filter

Instance Variables:
        Protected:
        integer              ii_style

Function: of_setstyle(integer ai_style)  returns integer

// Check the dw reference.
If Not IsValid(idw_Requestor) Then Return -1

// Check to see if the passed style number is valid.
If IsNull (ai_style) or (ai_style > 2 or ai_style < 0) Then      Return -1

ii_style = ai_style
Return 1

Function: of_getstyle()  returns integer

Return ii_style
```

PFC also defines instance variables as public, usually when you're using custom class user objects. This allows you direct access to these user objects from anywhere in your application by referencing their instance names.

```
Class:        pfc_n_cst_appmanager

Instance Variables:
        Public:
        application          iapp_object
        environment          ienv_object
        n_cst_trregistration inv_trregistration
        n_cst_dwcache        inv_dwcache
        n_cst_debug          inv_debug
        n_cst_error          inv_error
```

Polymorphism

PFC uses polymorphism in the sense that it lets functions with the same name behave differently. The functions can reside within one object, an inheritance hierarchy, and among multiple objects. PFC uses two types of polymorphism.

Operational Polymorphism

This allows two separate objects to define a function with the same name. For example, in **pfc_n_cst_winsrv** and **pfc_n_cst_dwsrv**, you can find the function called **of_setrequester**. This function performs different tasks, depending on the referenced object. In the DataWindow services, **of_setrequester** sets the active DataWindow whereas in the window services, it sets the active window.

Inclusional Polymorphism

This lets various objects in an inheritance chain define a function with the same name but with different arguments. It is accomplished by function overriding and function overloading, which we've discussed in earlier chapters.

Delegation

PFC's service-orientation architecture can be defined along the lines of the object-oriented concept of delegation, which divides the main object and its implementation into separate object hierarchies. PFC is implemented with two types of delegation relationships.

An **aggregate relationship** means that a service object can't function apart from its ancestor object. For example, **u_dw** uses numerous DataWindow services, but these services can't be used outside of **u_dw**.

An **associative relationship** means just the opposite. Most of the utility services fall into this category, since you can turn them on or use them from anywhere in your application. The string services provided by the **n_cst_string** user object are a good example of this.

Inheritance Hierarchy

The inheritance hierarchy of PFC is very extensive and sometimes quite complicated. These figures illustrate the hierarchy of windows and menus:

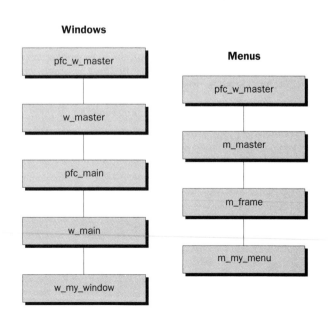

As you can see, this can be very confusing when you're trying to debug a problem in your application. You've probably also noticed that the naming conventions seem a little confusing. The inheritance hierarchy adds to this confusion, since the objects are spread out across several **.pbl**s. All of this confusion can be cleared up by explaining PFC extensions.

The Extension Level

You could use PFC right out of the box, but it's more than likely that you'll want to customize it to integrate application-wide functions and objects that fit your specific needs. PowerBuilder has supplied an extension level for all of its PFC inheritance hierarchies and these extension objects are contained in separate PowerBuilder libraries.

Contents	Ancestor PBL	Extension PBL
Application/global services	**Pfcapsrv.pbl**	**Pfeapsrv.pbl**
DataWindow services	**Pfcdwsrv.pbl**	**Pfedwsrv.pbl**
Visual/standard class user objects	**Pfcmain.pbl**	**Pfemain.pbl**
Window services	**Pfcwnsrv.pbl**	**Pfewnsrv.pbl**

Objects in the ancestor libraries contain all instance variables, events and functions, while objects in the extension libraries are unmodified descendants of corresponding objects in the ancestor library and have access to the ancestor's instance variables, events and functions.

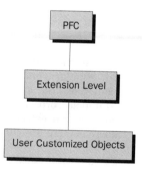

PowerBuilder has included an extension level to PFC so that we can modify and inherit objects from the extension level and customize them accordingly. You should never make changes directly to the ancestor level, because in future versions of PowerBuilder there may be upgrades to PFC. If you have modified objects in PFC, applying the new version would overwrite any changes you had made. This can seriously affect the operation of all your applications. The extension level is in effect a security layer between PFC and your user-defined objects.

You can put any corporate, department, or application-level behavior directly into the extension layer without affecting the base classes. You can now extend ancestor classes directly or change their behavior by overloading functions and overriding events. These changes won't affect other descendants that may not need to be changed. All of this makes your applications easier to maintain, since all of your customized code is isolated in the extension layers.

PFC ancestor objects all use the **pfc_** prefix. For example, the ancestor for the DataWindow selection service object is **pfc_n_cst_dwsrv** and the extension level descendent is **n_cst_dwsrv**. PFC-defined user events also use the **pfc_** prefix. This makes it easy for you to distinguish your application's user events from PFC. To reiterate our warning, you should never make changes to an object with a **pfc_** prefix.

Adding Extra Extension Levels

You can use PFC as a base class library and extend it to support your corporate or department functional needs. You could establish a corporate layer to customize the framework so that additional logic is made available to every application in the corporation. Below that, you could add a department or project layer and provide a more specific set of functionality to their applications. Look at the following example:

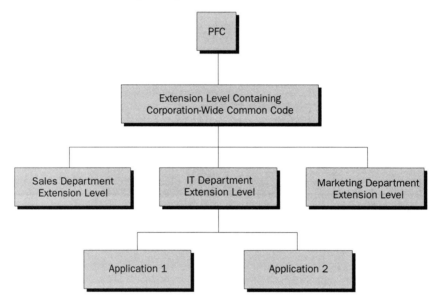

Here we've made corporation-wide common code changes to the extension level provided by PowerBuilder. Before we get down to the application level, we have a departmental layer of extensions. The applications would still use objects in PFC's libraries, but they now have access to additional corporate or departmental ancestors that we have created. This is just one example of how we can extend PFC. The actual implementation will differ between companies, depending on how they are structured.

To summarize then, these are the main advantages of using extension levels:

- Since extension level objects are placed in a separate `.pbl`, none of the modifications you make affect the ancestor PFC objects. This means that upgrading to a new release of PFC is very easy.

- You can create as many extension level objects as you need. This helps you build a library of extension level objects and is of considerable assistance when developing vertical market applications. If you're developing commercial products, you can use the PFC and extension level objects to develop both a common base library and a specific library for each of your applications.

- Extension level objects encourage object-oriented programming and the reuse of code.

PFC Tips and Techniques

Listed below are a few tips and techniques that you should keep in mind when you're using PFC to deploy your next PowerBuilder application:

- Before you begin coding, outline a strategy of how you're going to use the PFC. Prepare a list of the services that your application does or doesn't need and enable only those services required.

- Take advantage of PFC's inheritance and reusability. It saves you a tremendous amount of time and effort. You need not create every class user object from scratch.

- Take advantage of the extension level objects. Use them as the sole foundation for your application or to create your own customized class library.

- Make a commitment to maintaining and updating your class library on a regular basis. Obviously, you should also document your class library.

- Follow standard naming conventions when naming your class user objects, attributes and methods. Adopt a good and consistent naming convention, preferably the one that PFC already uses so that you aren't mixing coding standards within your applications.

- Create good, efficient and well-tested class libraries. We can't stress enough the importance of testing.

- Include good error processing logic in your user object code.

Although PFC is a new and complex feature of PowerBuilder, it's worth spending some time getting to know how it works and the various services and features that it contains. A good starting point in learning how to use PFC is to run through the PFC tutorials that are contained on the online books. This is Part 2 of the PFC User's Guide in the Advanced Developer Toolkit collection.

Summary

Powersoft has introduced the Foundation Class Library in the Enterprise Edition of PowerBuilder 5.0. This chapter introduced PFC, its features and merits. We looked at the different types of class library available, the PFC architecture, how to use extension levels and tips and techniques for using PFC.

In the next chapter, we'll look at another new feature to PowerBuilder, one that experienced PowerBuilder developers have been yearning for: distributed objects.

Distributed Computing

Powersoft have leveraged off their non-visual object technology to make distributed computing with PowerBuilder a reality in Version 5.0. This new technology has made it possible to partition PowerBuilder applications across multiple hosts. In this chapter, we'll look at what distributed computing means and see how PowerBuilder deals with it. We'll also walk through a detailed example of creating a distributed application in PowerBuilder.

The Client/Server and Distributed Models

Application architecture paradigms have evolved over the years. A monolithic architecture which made no distinction between user interface logic, business logic and data management logic developed into the Client/Server model.

The Client/Server model distinctly separates the presentation logic from the data management logic. Business logic can either exist on the client or the server or be distributed between both, resulting in fat clients or server-centric applications. In many cases, this increases application complexity.

> The client application usually takes care of the GUI and data presentation logic. The database (server) usually takes care of data management logic. I've rarely come across an application with an SQL query optimizer programmed into the client or data entry validation routines programmed into a database server. There's nothing stopping anyone from building an application that way, but it just doesn't make sense to do it.

The distributed application architecture model allows developers to distinctly organize their code into three tiers or extend it to n tiers. Data management, business logic and user interface logic are implemented in distinct layers. Application architects can also provide additional layers which provide access to specialized resources and heterogeneous data repositories. For example, a data access layer can provide a GUI application access to different diverse databases without the GUI being aware of it. The GUI would set up a connection to this layer and invoke methods to retrieve data without actually knowing where the data was.

Let's review another example that illustrates specialized services. Many trading applications in a brokerage house have to access information on financial instruments. This information is specialized and assimilated from various sources, which makes it impractical to embed this functionality in every trading application. Instead, we should partition the functionality to run on a server which handles requests for information about financial instruments from various applications.

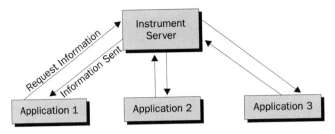

Online transaction monitors and open servers allow developers to rely on RPC technology to implement their business rules in separate components. An **online transaction monitor** is a messaging mechanism used in a networked environment. An **open server** is an extension to the Sybase SQL server product that allows for the development of specialized servers. An RPC or **remote procedure call** is a technique by which an application can call a procedure in a remote server from a local server. In some cases, an RPC can be used to call an application program that resides on the server but isn't part of the database server. The specifics of this depend upon the particular vendors implementation of the concept.

These components reside neither on the server nor the client, but on any networked hardware. Developing a distributed application using different tools and programming languages leads to increased development and maintenance costs by introducing another code base to maintain and presents integration problems. Using PowerBuilder 5.0 means that you have a single tool that you can use to develop all the components in the application.

Distributed Computing and PowerBuilder

PowerBuilder 5.0's distributed computing features are based on **non-visual objects** (NVOs). These were first seen in PowerBuilder Version 3.0 and allowed application architects to distinctly separate presentation logic from business and other non-presentation logic. In Version 5.0, architects can partition their PowerBuilder application with NVOs across multiple hardware platforms running any operating system and networking protocol supported by PowerBuilder.

The different communication protocols and operating systems supported by distributed PowerBuilder are shown in the following table:

Platform	Driver	Client	Server
Windows 3.x	Sockets	Yes	No
	OpenClientServer	Yes	No
Windows 95	Sockets	Yes	Yes
	OpenClientServer	Yes	No
	Named Pipes	Yes	No
Windows NT	Sockets	Yes	Yes
	OpenClientServer	Yes	Yes
	Named Pipes	Yes	Yes

The Winsock driver provides a socket interface which is used for interprocess communication in a TCP/IP networking environment. You can use the named pipes driver where named pipes are used for interprocess communication and the open client server driver in various environments where processes/peers communicate via TDS packets.

The distributed computing architecture implemented in PowerBuilder 5.0 doesn't comply with any established distributed computing model, such as CORBA or DCE, nor does it provide a proprietary object broker.

CORBA (Common Object Request Broker Architecture) is a standard for distributed objects being developed by the Object Management Group (OMG). It provides the mechanisms by which objects transparently make requests and receive responses, as defined by OMG's Object Request Broker (ORB). The CORBA ORB provides interoperability between applications built in (possibly) different languages, running on (possibly) different machines in heterogeneous distributed environments. It's the cornerstone of OMG's CORBA architecture.

DCE is the Distributed Computing Environment from the Open Software Foundation. It consists of multiple components, such as Remote Procedure Call (RPC), the Cell and Global Directory Services (CDS and GDS), the Security Service, DCE Threads, Distributed Time Service (DTS) and Distributed File Service (DFS), which have been integrated to work closely together.

PowerBuilder 5.0 doesn't yet provide sophisticated distributed capabilities. Application architects have to design standards for object interaction, exception handling, load balancing, monitoring, etc. in their distributed applications.

PowerBuilder have introduced some new non-visual object types which are critical to building distributed applications: **the transport object**, **the connection object** and **proxy objects**. Let's review these new objects before we go on to build a distributed application.

Transport Object

The transport object provides functionality for PowerBuilder applications to behave as server applications and process requests from client applications. This object is used by servers to listen for requests from clients, to instantiate objects, invoke their methods and access their properties.

Properties

The properties of this object include **Application, ErrText, ErrCode, Driver, Location, Trace String** and **Options**.

- Application stores the identity of the application which is listening for requests. The value of this variable is dependent on the communications driver used. For example, if the protocol used is TCP/IP, this attribute identifies the service name from the services file or the raw port number which the server will be listening on.

- ErrCode indicates success or failure. A value of zero denotes the success of an operation. A non-zero value shows that it has failed, with the number indicating the cause.

- ErrText contains the error message.

- Driver identifies the protocol used to communicate between the server and client.

- Location is available but not used by the transport object because it can identify the local host.

Trace String is used for debugging purposes.

 Options is used to specify the transport protocol specific parameters. For example, if the transport protocol is TCP/IP, you can use this variable to set the values for attributes such as **RawData**, **BufSize**, **NoDelay**, etc.

Events

By default, the transport object processes the **Constructor** and **Destructor** events, but you can also define custom events for it.

Functions

The transport object has two functions: **Listen** and **stopListening**. The **Listen** function initiates the server to start listening for requests from clients. It returns zero if it's successful and a non-zero value if an error occurs. Again, the number that is returned indicates the error. The **stopListening** function terminates this behavior. This function also returns zero if no error occurred and a non-zero value otherwise.

Connection Object

The connection object is used by applications to connect to server applications. It's 'network-aware' and encapsulates behaviors to instantiate objects remotely.

Properties

This object has properties similar to the transport object, with the following exceptions:

 Application stores the identity of the application to which the client is connecting. As before with the transport object, the value of this variable is dependent on the communications driver used.

 Location identifies the server application host name to which the client wants to establish a connection.

Events

The connection object responds to the **constructor**, **destructor** and **error** messages. The **Error** event is triggered when a connection error occurs. This allows designers to program error handling and recovery into the connection object.

Functions

The connection object has five functions:

 ConnectToServer connects the client application to the server application using the values set in its various properties.

 DisconnectServer disconnects the client application from the server application.

 RemoteStopConnection allows a connected client application with administrative privileges to disconnect a specified client connection from the server application.

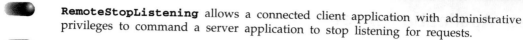

- **RemoteStopListening** allows a connected client application with administrative privileges to command a server application to stop listening for requests.

- **GetServerInfo** allows a client to retrieve information about its connection to the server into a structure of the type **connectionInfo**. It also allows a client with administrative privileges to retrieve information about all client connections to a server in a structure array of the type **connectionInfo**. The **connectionInfo** structure has the following properties:

Property	Data Type	Description
Busy	Boolean	Indicates whether the client connection is currently making a request.
CallCount	Long	Indicates the total number of requests made by that client connection.
ClientID	String	Indicates the ID of the client connection.
ConnectTime	DateTime	Indicates the date and time the client initiated the connection.
LastCallTime	DateTime	Indicates the date and time of the last request made by this client connection.
Location	String	Indicates the location of the client.
UserID	String	Indicates the user ID of the client that made the connection.

Proxy Object

The proxy object is generated internally by PowerBuilder as a wrapping layer for the remote object. It defines the remote object's interface and instance variables and exists only on the client side to represent the remote object and redirects messages and calls to it.

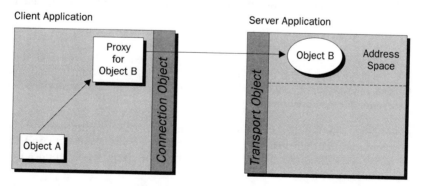

You specify the name of the proxy object for a user object in the User Object painter by selecting from the right-click menu option. The client application only requires access to an object's proxy object, not to the physical object itself.

We'll take a detailed look at how these objects are used when we come to create our distributed application.

New Application Object Events

The application object has two new events: **ConnectionBegin** and **ConnectionEnd**.

ConnectionBegin is triggered in the server application when it receives a request for a connection from a client application. You can use it to authenticate the connection request and grant connection privileges to the requesting client application. You can also use the **ConnectionBegin** event to regulate the number of active connections based on the resources available to the server application.

ConnectionEnd is triggered in a server application when a client application disconnects from it.

We'll see how these events come into play when we create our application.

Building a Distributed PowerBuilder Application

At the end of the analysis and design phase of your PowerBuilder application, you should have your objects classified as GUI objects, data management objects or business logic objects. The first step in building a distributed system is to identify the objects as client and server objects.

The server or distributed objects get instantiated remotely, so objects which are good candidates for 'remoting' include:

- Objects that encapsulate changing or security-sensitive business logic.
- Objects that require hardware with higher processing capacity to implement their functionality.
- Objects that connect to heterogeneous data sources.
- Objects that need to be instantiated for the entire client session.

Let's review the example where a PowerBuilder application wants to retrieve data from a database and perform analytical calculations to derive a financial risk model. To improve performance, we can implement this behavior in an NVO and 'remote' it on a host with more processing capacity.

The server objects have to be constructed as well-encapsulated objects with well-defined interfaces. They require a proxy object on the client side which behaves as a 'wrapper' and interface to the remote NVO. The remote object, on the other hand, resides on the server application, is a real object and has script for its functions.

A PowerBuilder distributed application physically consists of two applications—a client and a server—with communication between the connection object on the client side and the transport object on the server side. Multiple clients can connect to the same server application.

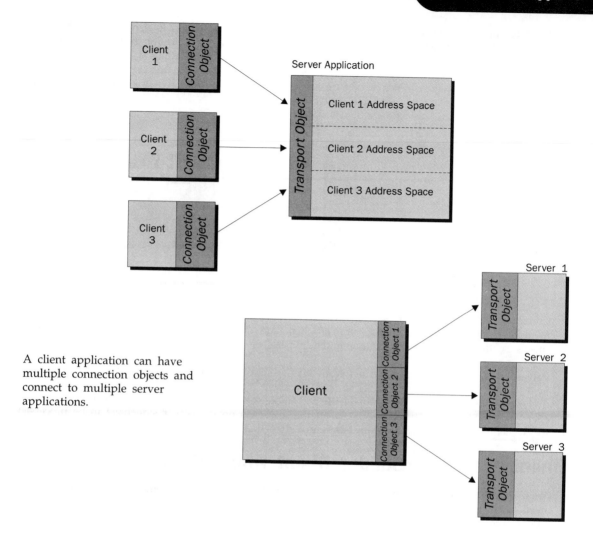

A client application can have multiple connection objects and connect to multiple server applications.

You can also design an application so that it can exist both as a server and a client.

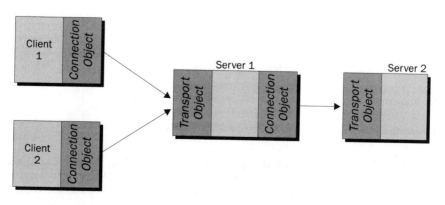

A server application allocates memory space for each connected client. It also creates a thread for each connected client application to process requests. Each client connection has a footprint of about 80K–90K of memory on the server. The server application maintains a 'pool' of client connections and reuses resources when it accepts new ones. However, the server application doesn't share code pages. When you're designing and evaluating the dynamics of the system, you should be careful not to overload the server application.

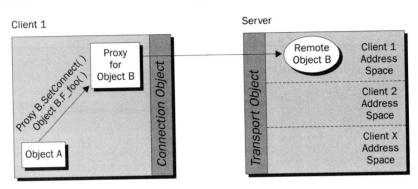

Connected clients on the server side can't exchange messages because each one has its own private memory space allocated on the server. The client and the server obviously have their own address spaces, so the remote object can't manipulate objects on the client side by reference.

PowerBuilder allows objects inherited from NVOs, simple data types and structures to be passed by value between objects on the server and the client. You should keep this in mind when you design the interface of an object that will be remotely instantiated. The communication between a client and the server is synchronous, so all the messages on the server side have to be processed for a client application before control is returned to that client.

Building a PowerBuilder Client Application

We'll test our example locally, so, because PowerBuilder emulates the remoter server, we won't need to create a transport object. We will, however, look at how you would move this example into a true client/server situation, using one of the standard communications drivers.

Before we begin building a client application, it's useful to lay out exactly what we'll have to do. The steps are:

1 Set up a client application.

2 Build a non-visual object to be 'remoted' and its proxy.

3 Create a connection object to communicate with the server.

4 Configure the client application to communicate with the server.

Create a client application, named **clnt_app**, and save it in a PBL, named **Clnt_app.pbl**. Now design a custom class user object, named **nvo_compoundInterestCalc**, and save this object in a library, called **Remote.pbl**. This will provide the functionality to calculate the compound interest due on a long term deposit at maturity.

Declare a user object function, **f_calculateinterest**, in **nvo_compoundInterestCalc** like this:

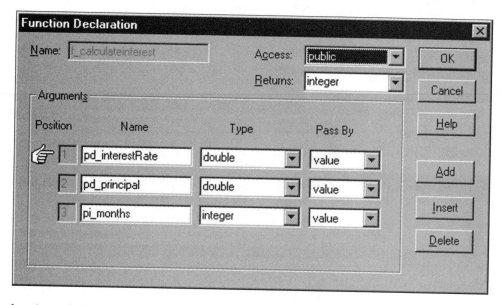

This function calculates the compound interest on any amount for a specified time period. This is the code:

```
/*****************************************************************
Function Name:    f_calculateInterest
Parameters:       pd_interestRate    double
                  pd_principal       double
                  pi_months          int
ReturnValue    ld_interest           double
*****************************************************************/
double ld_interest, ld_total, ld_years
    ld_years = pi_months / 12
    ld_total = pd_principal * ((1 + (pd_interestRate /100))^ld_years)
    ld_interest = (ld_total - pd_principal)
return ld_interest
```

Save this function and set the proxy name for the user object by selecting from the right-click pop-up menu.

Name the proxy object **pnvo_compundInterstCacl** and move it from **Remote.pbl** into **Clnt_app.pbl**. By default, the proxy is saved in the same PBL as the actual object, so you have to manually move it to the required PBL in the Library painter.

Now we'll build the user interface for the interest calculator. The window w_interestcalculator, as shown below, has a DataWindow with the three input fields, principal, interest_rate and months, and a field to display the calculated interest.

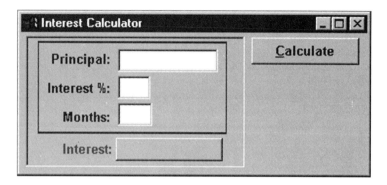

The **Clicked** event on the Calculate button triggers a custom event called **ue_interest_calc** on the window. The script in this event retrieves the interest parameters from the DataWindow, instantiates **nvo_compoundinterestcalc** locally and calls the function **f_calculateinterest** to calculate the interest. Here's the script for **ue_interest_calc**:

```
/*************************************************************
Event Name:        ue_interest_calc
Parameters:        wParam    long
                   lParm     long
ReturnValue        <NONE>
*************************************************************/

nvo_compoundInterestCalc l_compoundInterestCalc
double ld_interestRate, ld_principal, ld_interest
int li_months, li_rowNum

li_rowNum = dw_IntRateCalc.getRow()
if li_rowNum > 0 then
   dw_IntRateCalc.acceptText()
   ld_principal = dw_IntRateCalc.getItemNumber(li_rowNum, "principal")
   ld_interestRate = dw_IntRateCalc.getItemNumber(li_rowNum, "interest_rate")
   li_months = dw_IntRateCalc.getItemNumber(li_rowNum, "months")
   if ld_principal > 0 and ld_interestRate > 0 and li_months > 0 then
      l_compoundInterestCalc = create nvo_compoundInterestCalc
      ld_interest = l_compoundInterestCalc.f_calculateInterest(ld_interestRate, &
ld_principal, li_months)
      destroy l_compoundInterestCalc
      dw_IntRateCalc.setItem (li_rowNum, "interest", ld_interest)
   else
       MessageBox("Interest Calc Error", "Please enter valid data")
   end if
else
   MessageBox("Interest Calc Error", "Cannot access data")
end if
```

This instantiates the object locally and calls the method **f_calculateInterest**, passing it parameters by value to calculate the interest. Add script in the **Open** event of the application clnt_app to open the window w_interestcalculator. Run this application and test the compound interest rate calculator.

If it works, we're ready to modify it to function as a distributed application. We have to modify the client application to connect to a server, remotely instantiate **nvo_compoundInterestCalc** and call the function **f_calculateInterest**.

The first step is to set up the connection object in the client application. Like the transaction object, the connection object maintains the connection to a PowerBuilder server application. You have to set up a variable, scoped correctly, for the connection object yourself, because PowerBuilder doesn't provide a default global connection object.

We recommend that you inherit from the standard connection object and build your own connection object with exception handling capabilities. We'll look at this in detail later in the chapter, but for now we'll create a simplified version.

> **If your application has to connect to multiple PowerBuilder server applications, you have many design options. To keep the design scaleable and robust, you could create a server connection manager to encapsulate the physical connections. The design of such an object is similar to the transaction object manager described in Chapter 3. This object should provide functionality to maintain a pool of connection objects and also provide application objects access to connection objects to access server applications.**

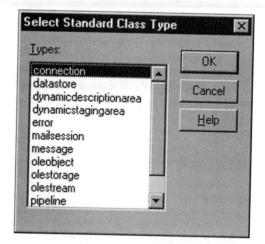

Create a standard class user object derived from the PowerBuilder connection object and save it as **nvo_connection**.

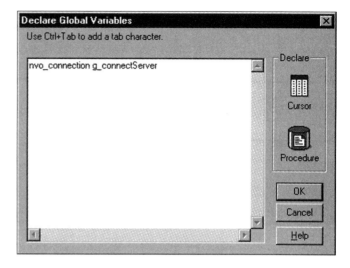

Now declare a global variable, **g_connectServer**, of the type **nvo_connection**:

In the **Open** event of the application, instantiate the object **g_connectServer** and specify its connection parameters. Set the Driver property of the connection object to **"local"**.

```
/*****************************************************************
Event Name:        open
Parameters:        CommandLine string
ReturnValue        <NONE>
*****************************************************************/
setPointer(hourGlass!)
g_connectServer = create nvo_connection
if IsValid(g_connectServer) then
    g_connectServer.driver = "local"
    g_connectServer.application = ""
    g_connectServer.location = ""
    g_connectServer.options = ""
    if g_connectServer.ConnectToServer( ) <> 0 then
        messageBox("Application Error", "Cannot connect to server")
    end if
end if
```

The parameters specified in the Options property of the connection object are transport protocol specific. None of them are relevant in this example because we've specified the driver as **"local"**. PowerBuilder uses the DLL, **Pbdpb050.dll**, to create a pseudo server which exists in the same address space as the client application. Though this permits debugging of server objects, it can cause conflicts if the remote object and client application use globals with the same name. The **ConnectionBegin** and **ConnectionEnd** events, which are triggered in the server application, are triggered in the client application when the remote object is tested locally. The function **ConnectToServer** initiates the connection to the server application using the parameters specified.

In a true distributed environment, you would have to address the following considerations.

Named Pipes

If the protocol is named pipes, you have to set the Driver property of the connection object to 'NamedPipes'. The pipe name is a combination of the location and application names and should be unique The pipe name is derived as \\location\PIPE\application, so the values of the Location and Application properties can be derived from the pipe name. The Options property isn't currently supported for this protocol.

TCP/IP

If the protocol is TCP/IP, you have to set the Driver property of the connection object to 'WinSock'. You have to set the Application property to either the raw port number that the client application will try to connect to or the service name from the services file. The location of the services file differs for each TCP/IP stack vendor. The Location property can be set to either the IP address in dot notation or the name of the host as specified in the **hosts** file. The location of the **hosts** file again depends on the vendor of the TCP/IP stack. The different options supported include rawData, bufSize, npDelay and maxRetry.

OpenClientServer

You can use the OpenClientServer driver in various network environments. You need to set the Application property to the query service entry from the **Sql.ini** file which will be used to connect to a server. The only other property that can be set is the Options property, which can be initialized to indicate the TDS packet size.

Now let's get back to the interest rate calculator example. Modify the script in the event **ue_interest_calc** on the window **w_interestCalculator** to reference the proxy object and 'remote' the object **nvo_compoundInterestCalc**.

The modifications include instantiating the proxy object, removing any references to the real object and calling the **setConnect** function. This function links the proxy object to the connection object and instantiates the object on the server. Here's the modified script for the event **ue_interest_calc**:

```
/***************************************************************
Event Name:      ue_interest_calc
Parameters:      wParam    long
                 lParm     ong
ReturnValue      <NONE>
**************************************************************/
/*****Use this script when using the proxy object******/
pnvo_compoundInterestCalc l_compoundInterestCalc
double ld_interestRate, ld_principal, ld_interest
int li_months, li_rowNum

li_rowNum = dw_IntRateCalc.getRow()
if li_rowNum > 0 then
    dw_IntRateCalc.acceptText()
    ld_principal = dw_IntRateCalc.getItemDecimal(li_rowNum, "principal")
    ld_interestRate = dw_IntRateCalc.getItemDecimal(li_rowNum, "interest_rate")
    li_months = dw_IntRateCalc.getItemNumber(li_rowNum, "months")
    if ld_principal > 0 and ld_interestRate > 0 and li_months > 0 then
        l_compoundInterestCalc = create pnvo_compoundInterestCalc
```

```
        if isValid(l_compoundInterestCalc) then
            l_compoundInterestCalc.setConnect(g_connectServer)
            ld_interest  = &
            l_compoundInterestCalc.f_calculateInterest(&
                ld_interestRate, ld_principal, li_months)
            destroy l_compoundInterestCalc
            dw_IntRateCalc.setItem (li_rowNum, "interest", ld_interest)
        else
            MessageBox("Interest Calc Error", "Cannot create proxy")
        end if
    else
        MessageBox("Interest Calc Error", "Please enter valid data")
    end if
else
    MessageBox("Interest Calc Error", "Cannot access data")
end if
```

We've highlighted the important differences in the script. You can see that we create the proxy object rather than the true object and then use the **setConnect** function to connect to the connection object

Make sure that the **Remote.pbl** library is in the application library list and run the application as before. Although there's no reference to the **nvo_compoundInterestCalc** object in any of the scripts run by the application, it functions exactly as before.

Building a PowerBuilder Server Application

A PowerBuilder server application services requests from multiple client applications. As we described earlier, it uses the transport object to 'listen' for messages from client applications. The steps for setting up a server are:

1 Create a server application.

2 Create a transport object.

3 Program the application to set the properties of the transport object and 'listen' to requests from client applications.

You won't be able to run this example as it stands because communication protocols vary between machines and we have no way of knowing how your machine is set up, but we'll explain the various options and hopefully put you on the right path to developing your own distributed applications.

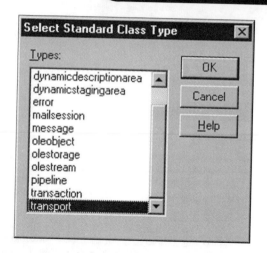

Create a new application, name it **Server_app** and save it in the **.pbl** file named **Serv_app.pbl**. Now, create a standard class user object based on the transport object.

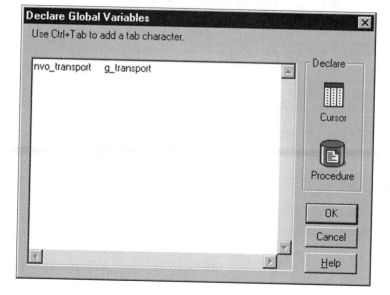

Save this as **nvo_transport** and declare a global variable **g_transport** of the type **nvo_transport**:

Create an instance of this object in the application **Open** event and instantiate the application to listen for requests from client applications. You need to configure the properties of the transport object depending on the transport protocol.

If the transport protocol was named pipes, the driver has to be set to 'NamedPipes' and the Application property has to be set to the pipe name on which the server listens. If the protocol is Winsock, the Driver property has to be set to 'WinSock' and the Application property has to be set to the raw port number on which the server or the service name from the services file of the port the server listens on. You'll have to check the documentation provided by your TCP/IP stack vendor for the location of the services file.

The open script of the application **server_app** is shown on the following page. This code snippet demonstrates how the properties of the transport object would have to be set up if the protocol is TCP/IP. We make the assumption that the server application listens on raw port number 6052 for requests. The **listen** function invokes the server to 'listen' on port number 6052 for requests from client applications. You'll have to initialize the properties of the transport object in the sample code based on the driver that you use.

```
/****************************************************************
Event Name:      open
Parameters:      CommandLine string
ReturnValue      <NONE>
****************************************************************/
int li_errCode
string ls_errText

g_transport = create nvo_transport

if isValid(g_transport) then
    g_transport.driver = "winsock"
    g_transport.application = "6052"
    g_transport.options = "RawData=1, BufSize=8192, NoDelay=1"
    li_errCode = g_transport.Listen( )

    if li_errCode <>  0 then
        ls_errText = "Error number: " + string(li_errCode) + &
            "encountered while starting server"
        destroy g_transport
        MessageBox("ServerError", ls_errText)
    else
        //open the monitor window - see paragraph below for explanation
        open(w_server_monitor)
    end if

end if
```

That is all you need to program to set up a very basic PowerBuilder server application. The server application that we've created starts 'listening' in the **Open** event. We can't put the code to 'stop listening' in the **Close** event, because this event will be triggered automatically as the application doesn't open a window. So, we would create a window, named w_server_monitor, and open it from the **Open** event of the server application. We can the program logic in the window w_server_monitor to shutdown the server application.

The window should look something like this:

The required code would be something like this:

```
/***************************************************************
Event Name:        ue_stop_listening
Parameters:        wParam   long
                   lParm    long
ReturnValue        <NONE>
***************************************************************/
setPointer(hourGlass!)
long ll_errCode
int li_errCode
string ls_errText

if MessageBox("ServerAdmin", "Are you sure you want to shut down the server?", &
StopSign!, OKCancel!) = 1 then
    ll_errCode = g_transport.stopListening()
    destroy g_transport
    if li_errCode <>  0 then
        ls_errText = "Error number " + string(li_errCode) + &
                     " encountered while bringing down server"
        MessageBox("ServerError", ls_errText)
    end if
    close(this)
end if
```

To test this application, you would need to create an executable for the server so that it can run in the background and then run the client application from the development environment.

The server application would need to have the **Remote.pbl** library in its library list. The most important thing to remember is that the server application requires access to the remote object, while the client application only needs access to the proxy.

Exception Handling and Monitoring

The code snippets that we've seen have helped you set up very basic client and server applications. Server applications have to be stable and have a very high level of reliability, because numerous client applications depend on them for their functionality. Client applications, on the other hand, should be sophisticated enough to recover from disruptions in their connections to server applications.

Client Application Error Handling

Errors in the connection object could occur for various reasons:

- The server application could shut down.
- The server could be busy or reach its connection threshold.
- The connection between the client machine and the application server could terminate abnormally.
- The client's request could be incomplete or get terminated abnormally.
- The server may not be able to create an instance of the object.

255

In any of these situations, the **Error** event on the connection object is triggered. It has the following parameters:

Parameter	Description
ErrorNumber	The error number generated by the erroneous operation.
ErrorText	The error description.
ErrorObject	The name of the object whose script caused the error.
ErrorScript	The text of the script which caused the error.
ErrorLine	The line number in the script which caused the error.
Action	Enumerated data type which controls the applications course of action. This variable is passed by reference.
ReturnValue	The value returned. This value is used only if the action specified is **ExceptionSubstituteReturnValue**!

Depending on the severity and type of error, the action variable in the **Error** event should be set as one of the following:

- **ExceptionFail!** This triggers the applications **SystemError** event.
- **ExceptionIgnore!** This results in the error being ignored.
- **ExceptionRetry!** This executes the operation that caused the error.

You should use **ExceptionIgnore!** with caution because it could cause another operation to fail later.

Trace flags can also be set in the Trace attribute of the connection object to report errors. The trace flags **ObjectCalls**, **ObjectLife**, **ThreadLife**, **Console**, **Level** and **Log** allow different levels of information to be logged. The information can be reported to a log file (by setting the LogFlag attribute to the log file name) or, in Windows 95 and Windows NT, to a console window.

Server Application Error Handling

The server application calls for a high level of reliability, because it services numerous client applications. The server application should be able to regulate the number of connections that it accepts and report its status on a console. You can use the application object's **ConnectionBegin** event to regulate the number of connections that the server application is handling. This event is triggered when the server gets a connection request. It accepts three parameters—**userId**, **password** and **connectString**—and returns the **ConnectPrivlege** enumerated variable. Based on the **userId** parameter and the number of connections that the server application has accepted, it can return one of the following:

- **ConnectPrivilege!** Accept an incoming connection.
- **NoConnectPrivilege!** Refuse an incoming connection.
- **ConnectWithAdminPrivilege!** Accept a connection with administrative privileges.

256

A server can be monitored by a client application which has administrative privileges. A server application can be designed so that it connects to itself as a client application with administrative privileges.

Summary

PowerBuilder have extended their non-visual object technology to application partitioning and distribution, which means that we can now create both client and server applications and set up three tier and *n*-tier applications. The client and server application paradigm is fairly loose, so that an application can function as a server as well as be a client of another server application.

In this chapter, we've looked at a simple example of a distributed application and discussed some of the more complex options and possibilities.

In future versions of PowerBuilder it's likely that there will be a generic object broker that will conform to the CORBA object model.

Index

Index

Go for the end zone *with full-contact* PowerBuilder 5.0 training.

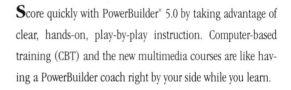

Interactive courses let you train right at your desktop!

Score quickly with PowerBuilder® 5.0 by taking advantage of clear, hands-on, play-by-play instruction. Computer-based training (CBT) and the new multimedia courses are like having a PowerBuilder coach right by your side while you learn.

Each CBT lesson includes interactive, graphical exercises that walk you through the application development process. Multimedia courses combine sight and sound in "video" demos and instruction for a highly effective training program.

Best of all, you learn at your own pace — anytime, anywhere.

So before you tackle your next development project, order these self-paced training courses and take 15% off with this ad! See reverse for course topics and order form or call **800-395-3525** today.

Discount is valid only on purchases made through Powersoft from Jan. 1 - Dec. 31, 1996.

Save 15% on any PowerBuilder 5.0 self-paced training course.

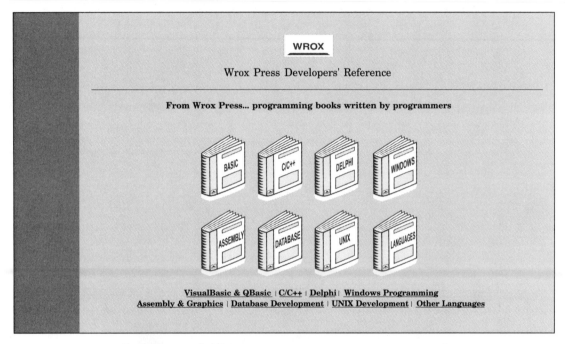

Revolutionary Guide to Visual Basic 4 Professional

This book focuses on the four key areas for developers using VB4: the Win32 API, Objects and OLE, Databases and the VB development cycle. Each of the areas receives in-depth coverage, and techniques are illustrated using rich and complex example projects that bring out the real issues involved in commercial VB development. It examines the Win32 API from a VB perspective and gives a complete run-down of developing multimedia apps. The OLE section includes a help file creator that uses the Word OLE object, and we OLE automate Netscape Navigator 2. The database section offers complete coverage of DAO, SQL and ODBC, finishing with a detailed analysis of client/server database systems. The final section shows how to design, code, optimize and distribute a complete application. The book has a CD including all source code and a hypertext version of the book.

Author: Larry Roof   ISBN: 1874416370

Price: $44.95 C$62.95 £49.99

Instant SQL Programming

This is the fastest guide for developers to the most common database management language. If you want to get the most out of your database design, you will need to master Structured Query Language. SQL is the standard database language supported by almost every database management system on the market. This book takes you into the concepts and implementation of this key language quickly and painlessly, covering the complete ANSI standard SQL '92 from basic database design through to some of the more complex topics such as NULLS and 3-valued logic. We take you through the theory step-by-step, as you put into practice what you learn at each stage, gradually building up an example database while mastering essential techniques.

Author: Joe Celko   ISBN: 1874416508

Price: $29.95 C$41.95 £27.99

Revolutionary Guide to MFC 4 with Visual C++

Written by one of Microsoft's leading MFC developers, this is the book for professionals who want to get under the cover of the Microsoft class library. It starts by putting the application architecture under the microscope, explaining the classes used in AppWizard generated code and examining their base classes. The use of threads is given special consideration, before the Document/View architecture is explained. Advanced user interface programming is also detailed. The book covers utility and exception classes, dealing with exception handling at both the MFC level and at the compiler level. It then describes how to write particular types of application: DLLs, console, database-enabled and OLE-enabled applications. The OLE coverage extends to writing OLE servers, containers, controls and control containers. The book also offers some great insights into writing applications specifically for Windows 95.

Author: Mike Blaszczak   ISBN: 1874416923

Price: $49.95 C$69.95 £46.99

Revolutionary Guide to Office 95 Development

The book initially has primers for WordBasic and Visual Basic for Applications (VBA), and gives details of DDE and OLE technology which is the 'glue' which holds the Office 95 applications together. Stand-alone applications in Word, Excel and Access are developed to complete the readers understanding of these applications. The book then goes into detail of client/server design, before developing applications hosted in, again, Word, Excel and Access, that show how it is possible to combine functionality of the host application with the other applications in Office 95. Information on mail-enabling applications is also provided, using Exchange as well as the built-in mail capabilities. A detailed explanation of the workflow paradigm is given, before showing a complete office system built from the components so far discussed. The book finishes off with how to extend Word's capabilities by writing a WLL (using C), and finally considers what is required to make an application ready for distribution.

Author: Steve Wynkoop   ISBN: 1874416699

Price: $49.95 C$69.95 £46.99

OX

What's black and white and red all over?

Have you ever thought to yourself "I could do better than that"? Well here's your chance to prove it! Wrox Press are continually looking for new authors and contributors and it doesn't matter if you've never been published before.

Interested?

contact John Franklin at Wrox Press, 30 Lincoln Road, Birmingham, B27 6PA, UK.

from US call:800 814 3461
or
e-mail johnf@wrox.com
compuserve: 100063,2152

Register Instant PowerBuilder Objects and sign up for a free subscription to The Developer's Journal.

A bi-monthly magazine for software developers, The Wrox Press Developer's Journal features in-depth articles, news and help for everyone in the software development industry. Each issue includes extracts from our latest titles and is crammed full of practical insights into coding techniques, tricks and research.

Fill in and return the card below to receive a free subscription to the Wrox Press Developer's Journal.

Instant PowerBuilder Objects Registration Card

Name _____

Address _____

_____

_____

City_____ State/Region _____

Country_____ Postcode/Zip _____

E-mail _____

Occupation _____

How did you hear about this book?_____

☐ Book review (name) _____

☐ Advertisement (name) _____

☐ Recommendation _____

☐ Catalog _____

☐ Other _____

Where did you buy this book?_____

☐ Bookstore (name)_____ City _____

☐ Computer Store (name)_____

☐ Mail Order_____

☐ Other_____

What influenced you in the purchase of this book?

☐ Cover Design

☐ Contents

☐ Other (please specify) _____

How did you rate the overall contents of this book?

☐ Excellent ☐ Good

☐ Average ☐ Poor

What did you find most useful about this book? _____

What did you find least useful about this book? _____

Please add any additional comments. _____

What other subjects will you buy a computer book on soon? _____

What is the best computer book you have used this year?

_____

Note: This information will only be used to keep you updated about new Wrox Press titles and will not be used for any other purpose or passed to any other third party.

WROX

WROX PRESS INC.

Wrox writes books for you. Any suggestions, or
ideas about how you want information given in
your ideal book will be studied by our team.
Your comments are always valued at Wrox.

Free phone in USA 800-USE-WROX
Fax (312) 465 4063

Compuserve 100063,2152.
UK Tel. (44121) 706 6826   Fax   (44121) 706 2967

Computer Book Publishers

NB. If you post the bounce back card below in the UK, please send it to:
Wrox Press Ltd. 30 Lincoln Road, Birmingham, B27 6PA

NO POSTAGE
NECESSARY
IF MAILED
IN THE
UNITED STATES

BUSINESS REPLY MAIL
FIRST CLASS MAIL   PERMIT#64   LA VERGNE, TN

POSTAGE WILL BE PAID BY ADDRESSEE

WROX PRESS
2710 WEST TOUHY AVE
CHICAGO IL 60645-9911